Magdalen College Library

KV-371-975

PERFORMING AUTHORSHIP IN THE NINETEENTH-CENTURY TRANSATLANTIC LECTURE TOUR

Ashgate Series in Nineteenth-Century Transatlantic Studies

Series Editors: Kevin Hutchings and Julia M. Wright

Focusing on the long nineteenth century (ca. 1750–1900), this series offers a forum for the publication of scholarly work investigating the literary, historical, artistic, and philosophical foundations of transatlantic culture. A new and burgeoning field of interdisciplinary investigation, transatlantic scholarship contextualizes its objects of study in relation to exchanges, interactions, and negotiations that occurred between and among authors and other artists hailing from both sides of the Atlantic. As a result, transatlantic research calls into question established disciplinary boundaries that have long functioned to segregate various national or cultural literatures and art forms, challenging as well the traditional academic emphasis upon periodization and canonization. By examining representations dealing with such topics as travel and exploration, migration and diaspora, slavery, aboriginal culture, revolution, colonialism and anti-colonial resistance, the series will offer new insights into the hybrid or intercultural basis of transatlantic identity, politics, and aesthetics.

The editors invite English language studies focusing on any area of the long nineteenth century, including (but not limited to) innovative works spanning transatlantic Romantic and Victorian contexts. Manuscripts focusing on European, African, US American, Canadian, Caribbean, Central and South American, and Indigenous literature, art, and culture are welcome. We will consider proposals for monographs, collaborative books, and edited collections.

Performing Authorship in the Nineteenth-Century Transatlantic Lecture Tour

AMANDA ADAMS
Muskingum University, USA

ASHGATE

MAGDALEN COLLEGE LIBRARY

© Amanda Adams 2014

All rights reserved. No part of this publication may be reproduced, stored in a retrieval system or transmitted in any form or by any means, electronic, mechanical, photocopying, recording or otherwise without the prior permission of the publisher.

Amanda Adams has asserted her right under the Copyright, Designs and Patents Act, 1988, to be identified as the author of this work.

Published by
Ashgate Publishing Limited
Wey Court East
Union Road
Farnham
Surrey, GU9 7PT
England

Ashgate Publishing Company
110 Cherry Street
Suite 3-1
Burlington, VT 05401-3818
USA

www.ashgate.com

British Library Cataloguing in Publication Data
A catalogue record for this book is available from the British Library

The Library of Congress has cataloged the printed edition as follows:
Adams, Amanda, 1977–
  Performing Authorship in the Nineteenth-Century Transatlantic Lecture Tour / by
    Amanda Adams.
  pages cm. — (Ashgate Series in Nineteenth-Century Transatlantic Studies)
  Includes bibliographical references and index.
  ISBN 978-1-4724-1664-3 (hardcover: alk. paper) — ISBN 978-1-4724-1665-0 (ebook) — ISBN 978-1-4724-1666-7 (epub)
  1. Authors, American—19th century--Travel--England. 2. Authors, English—19th century—Travel--United States. 3. American literature—19th century—Appreciation—England. 4. English literature—19th century—Appreciation—United States. 5. Lectures and lecturing—United States. 6. Lectures and lecturing--England. 7. Authorship—Marketing. I. Title.
  PS159.E5A34 2014
  810.9'003—dc23
                                                                          2013047659

ISBN: 9781472416643 (hbk)
ISBN: 9781472416650 (ebk – PDF)
ISBN: 9781472416667 (ebk – ePub)

131623

Printed in the United Kingdom by Henry Ling Limited, at the Dorset Press, Dorchester, DT1 1HD

For my parents, Vicki Millard and David Adams

Contents

List of Figures

Acknowledgments

This book was years in the making, and during that time, many people and institutions contributed to the formation of the project and its author. The earliest readers of this project, including Linda Kintz and John Schmor, helped shape and clarify its goals. In particular, Richard Stein and Henry Wonham gave my work close readings and offered perspective, encouragement, and instrumental critique. They have generously continued to advise me as the project has evolved.

As an alumna and former Visiting Assistant Professor at Miami University, my interests and my work have been deeply shaped by that institution's faculty, especially William Hardesty, who years ago enthralled me with classes on nineteenth-century literature, and Lana Kay Rosenberg, who has nurtured my interest in performance for many years. More recently, the English Department at Muskingum University has been a wonderfully welcoming place to find an academic home. I thank Jane Varley, Donna Edsall and Jane Wells, especially, for their professional guidance.

This manuscript received institutional and professional support at all stages. Early on, an Ernst Fellowship from the English Department at the University of Oregon gave me the time to write, while a University of Oregon Humanities Center Fellowship provided me a place in which to do it. Portions of this book have been previously published in journals. I thank the University of Illinois Press, who allowed the reprinting of sections of the articles "Performing Ownership: Dickens, Twain, and Copyright on the Transatlantic Stage" and "The Uses of Distinction: Matthew Arnold and American Literary Realism," both from *American Literary Realism*, as well as the editors of *Symbiosis: A Journal of Anglo-American Literary Relations* for permission to reprint sections of "'Recognized by My Trumpet': Celebrity and/as Disability in Harriet Martineau's Transatlantic Tour." The Library of Congress and the New York Public Library have been extremely helpful in obtaining images for use in this book. Ashgate Press and its editors have been supportive at all stages. I thank Ann Donahue, as well as Kevin Hutchings and Julia M. Wright, the editors of the Nineteenth-Century Transatlantic Studies Series, and the anonymous reviewer for their constructive insights and professionalism.

My personal debts are numerous. Many friends and members of my family have provided support for this project, whether they know it or not, through their perspective, loyalty, and good humor. Elizabeth Tatko and Nicole Casal Moore are always making my world a better place to be. Ryan Hediger, with whom I built a home despite years of constantly moving, has been my best reader. Jason Adams and Nathaniel Adams beautifully perform their roles as older brothers, offering support and provocation by turns and in just the right measure. Finally, I thank my parents, Vicki Millard and David Adams, who are my models of scholars, teachers, parents, and human beings. It is to them I dedicate this book.

Introduction:
The Nineteenth-Century
Transatlantic Lecture Tour and
the Case of Frederick Douglass

In June of 2006, the now-late author John Updike published an essay in the *New York Times* in which he worried that books would become obsolete. Responding to a recently published article about the digitization of libraries and books, Updike saw this future as a "pretty grisly scenario." The article to which he responded claims that books will be broken up, sampled, combined into literary play lists, and, most importantly, free. According to this vision, it is readers' desire to have access to the author, not the book, that will generate economic value. Updike resisted this possible change, asking, "Have not writers ... imagined that they already were, in their written and printed texts, giving an 'access to the creator' more pointed, more shapely, more loaded with aesthetic and informational value than an unmediated, unpolished personal conversation?" He lamented the prospect of a world in which "an author's works, be they one volume or 50, serve primarily as his or her ticket to the lecture platform." Updike mourned for a time period when "the written work was supposed to speak for itself" and the author needn't speak at all.

That time is further removed than Updike imagined. While digital texts and the internet in general have changed the character of reading in certain ways in the last 20 or so years, the responsibility of the author to speak for the work through various media, indeed, to *stand in* for the work is nothing new. Nor is the author's discomfort with this scenario, as I argue in this book. *Performing Authorship in the Nineteenth-Century Transatlantic Lecture Tour* is a study of how nineteenth-century authors and audiences in Britain and America struggled with these same issues. Like Updike, authors were suspicious of the need to perform the role of the author, but they also felt a keen desire to remain a cultural force. Otherwise, they risked going unnoticed. Facing an increasingly massive audience, nineteenth-century authors approached this issue in a distinctive way. In addition to giving interviews and sitting for portraits, they also engaged in live performances for audiences, in lecture or reading tours. Many nineteenth-century authors threw themselves into their self-promotion, representing themselves, then, not only through discursive text but also by standing in front of the audience, night after night, in front of footlights, and performing the role of the author. The forces which Updike pointed out in the twenty-first century literary sphere, then, differ in degree rather than kind.

Performing Authorship in the Nineteenth-Century Transatlantic Lecture Tour investigates this previously overlooked phenomenon of nineteenth-century literary culture. I argue that such tours were a central aspect of nineteenth-century authorship, not simply, as they are often treated, the milieu of a few talented performers. Fundamentally, transatlantic lecture tours expand our notion of what it meant to be a nineteenth-century author through an emphasis on authorial embodiment and live performance. The expectation that authors could, or even would, lecture in the transatlantic marketplace in fact demanded that nineteenth-century audiences (and now contemporary critics) take account of the author in person as well as on the page. In addition, such tours reflect the literary culture of the nineteenth century brought to light by recent scholarship that has focused on its transatlantic context, the development of literary hierarchies, the explosion of celebrity, and a wide-ranging performance culture.

The cultural importance of transatlantic lecture tours makes them vital for inclusion in any study of Anglo-American authorship, but this has rarely been done. Studies of lecture tours have been generally biographical and limited to those authors who were particularly successful, such as Mark Twain or Charles Dickens; or they have treated lectures as qualitatively indistinguishable from commercially savvy authors' participation in the marketplace. In fact, literary studies have tended to share Updike's stated bias for the book as the fundamental object of literary culture. This project reverses the archive-oriented approach, focusing instead on the lecture tours themselves. Its coverage selects among the many who lectured transatlantically, a list which includes, on the British side, Charles Dickens, Wilkie Collins, Anthony Trollope, William Makepeace Thackeray, Matthew Arnold, and Oscar Wilde, in addition to several others who traveled to the United States and lectured occasionally, such as Harriet Martineau and Bram Stoker. On the American side, transatlantic lecturers include Washington Irving, Ralph Waldo Emerson, Frederick Douglass, and Mark Twain, in addition to Harriet Beecher Stowe, who, like Martineau, traveled across the Atlantic to be greeted as a celebrity but spoke only once, to a ladies' group. Finally, that self-consciously transatlantic author, Henry James, who concludes this study, traveled to America to lecture after a 20-year absence. The range of authors—from those who were popular successes to those who were not, from those who considered themselves entertainers to those whose mission was social or political improvement—suggests that the lecture tour as a genre serves as a microcosm for nineteenth-century authorship in all its contradictions and complexity.

"The Great Exchange of the World": The Popular Lecture in the Nineteenth Century

This study treats lecturing as an aspect of literary authorship and, in doing so, focuses on the embodied lives of authors. That said, the lecture system, especially in America, developed outside the realm of literary authorship, and lecturing as a vocation or pursuit for many kinds of professionals—not just authors—had its own life in the nineteenth century; it has likewise inspired myriad critical approaches. Unlike the American system, which I'll come to later on, what we might call the "popular lecture" in Britain didn't develop in an organized way. The lecture system in Britain was less of a "system" than a cultural practice drawing from several aspects of nineteenth-century British culture, among them the theater and the Mechanics' Institutes. Perhaps as a result of the disparate roots of such live performances, there has been less critical focus on the British popular lecture as a distinctive genre.

The American lecture system, all the way to the Chautauqua Institutes in the beginning of the twentieth century, drew its inspiration from the many branches of the British Mechanics' Institute. Carl Bode's early and useful history of the American lyceum initiated the critical tradition of tracing the American system to these British popular lectures. Indeed, it is often Americanists who write this history. It goes roughly like this: Beginning in 1800, a scientist working at Andersonian Institute in Glasgow (now the University of Strathclyde), George Birkbeck, offered lectures on scientific principles to a few local workmen. He later participated in the creation of the London Institution for the Diffusion of Science, Literature, and the Arts as well as the formation of a London Mechanics' Institute (Bode 6). From this beginning, the idea of making educational lectures available to working men grew.

Birkbeck was joined by politician Henry Brougham, whose speech "Practical Observations upon the Education of the People," published in 1825, helped galvanize the movement. The speech begins with the notion that "the people themselves must be the great agents in accomplishing the work of their own instruction" (Brougham 1), expressing the idea of self-improvement central to the movement. However, he notes, they "must be essentially aided in their efforts to instruct themselves" (1). Brougham's speech puts lectures into the context of other self-improvement opportunities for the working class, including the increasingly cheap publications of texts, the rise of circulating libraries, and self-run book clubs. However, he argues, "The institution of Lectures is, of all the helps that can be given, the most valuable, where circumstances permit; that is, in towns of a certain size" (11). His argument, like Birkbeck's, is grounded in the sciences, since "chemistry" and "mechanical philosophy" must be accompanied by physical demonstrations to be understood. Beginning with Bode, critics of the British system have noted that this *noblesse oblige* attitude was also rooted in the desire for a more efficient workplace, in its early British iteration as well as the later American lyceum system: "For both countries the main purpose of the movement originally was to provide practical scientific instruction for workmen, and to have as a result a more intelligent worker as well as a better product" (Bode 7). Indeed, Brougham's original vision is clearly pitched at the wealthy patrons of such a movement: "it is absolutely necessary that the expenses should mainly be defrayed by those for whose benefit they are contrived. It is the province of the rich to lay the foundation, by making certain advances which are required in the first instance, and enabling the poor to come forward, both as learners and contributors" (11–12). Historically, that is how the movement proceeded, with wealthy patrons initiating a group that would afterward be sustained by membership dues.

In addition to the Mechanics' Institutes' popular lectures, literary authors who lectured in Britain were also drawing from two aspects of Victorian culture that were often in opposition to one another—the pulpit and the stage—and the interest in elocution that both institutions encouraged. The craze for elocution, which was already dominating the nineteenth century before the Mechanics' Institutes emerged, had evolved in ways that affected stage and pulpit. Actors and clergymen were encouraged to take elocution lessons, and as Annalisa Zanola Marcola has written, this practice developed out of the sixteenth- and seventeenth-century interest in the English language and linguistic trends. By the nineteenth century, elocution was coming to be seen as less of an art and more of science. Learning to use the right muscles in the throat and mouth was a medical question, even for actors (Zanola Marcola 81). Clergymen and actors could take lessons from trained teachers, but they could also draw from the growing number of publications in the area (Zanola Marcola 81).[1]

Work on Victorian oral culture has been slow in materializing compared to work in the field on the American side. There is much coverage of the treatment of orality within the creative written literature of the time, but less on the culture of orality that existed outside of narrative throughout the nineteenth century. But Robert H. Ellison, in his rhetorical study of the Victorian sermon done in the later 1990s, *The Victorian Pulpit*, lays the foundation for another of the sources of the nineteenth-century lecture. Ellison notes the "parallels between Victorian homiletic theory and the classical oral tradition" in that both insist "that the sermon be practical and persuasive, rather than merely abstract and informative" (18). In this way, the sermon stands as the model for one version of the popular lecture, especially those by authors such as Douglass and Martineau, who spoke for a political cause. But as Richard Foulkes points out, no lecture tradition, even the most pious coming from the Church or the Mechanics' Institutes, could ignore the need to entertain the people. Indeed, in Britain as elsewhere, "The tension between improvement and amusement ran through the popular education movements of the nineteenth century" (Foulkes 70). The theater, then, would add its own influence to the lecture, especially as the century moved on.

The American popular lecture has received much more attention than lectures in Britain as its own genre, partly because it was institutionalized—through the lyceum system and then the Chautauqua movement—lending itself to more focused study. The resurgence in recent years of studies of the American lyceum has yielded impressively nuanced results. After Bode's foundational *American Lyceum: Town*

---

[1]   A key transition figure in American elocution was the American James Rush, whose book *The Philosophy of the Human Voice* in 1893 helped initiate the turn from linguistics to physiology. Rush's work inspired many other American textbooks on elocution, including Alexander Melville Bell's textbook *Visible Speech in Twelve Lessons*, which claims to offer "unquestionable advantages to the young, in laying a foundation for excellence both in native speaking and in the utterance of foreign tongues" (9). Such approaches turned away from the early British tradition which had emphasized rhetoric and theatrical training rather than science.

Meeting of the Mind in the 1950s and shorter works by historian Donald Scott in the 1980s, Angela Ray most persuasively presents the American lyceum as a key element of cultural nation building. In other words, the popular lecture has been seen as centrally American. To begin with, orality in American culture is well-covered territory. Works such as Sandra M. Gustafson's *Eloquence is Power* and James Perrin Warren's *Culture of Eloquence* have focused much-needed attention on the continuing oral culture of America, a necessary intervention in a field that consistently prioritizes the written word. Thomas Augst goes so far as to claim that "Oratory was perhaps the most popular and venerated literary form of nineteenth-century America … However, it was a contested form, subject to competing claims about the source and nature of truth in civic discourse" (Introduction 60). Gustafson sees orality as central to the early American colonies and Republic, shifting her critical focus to argue that its source was not only the desire to create an American national character but also a combination of cultural traditions, including native ones, and "in the American crucible of cultures, these oratorical traditions collided, merged, and polarized to create vibrant traditions of verbal art" (xiv).

For literary authors, of course, oratory was one of two major undertakings. Those lecturers who were primarily authors—or who have come to be identified primarily as authors—formed a key subset of this culture. Thomas Wentworth Higginson tells us in the 1860s that "Oratory and literature still remain two distinct methods of utterance, as distinct as sculpture and painting, and as difficult to unite" (56). However, historians disagree. Scott argues that

> The society as a whole, as well as most groups within it, participated fully in both oral and printed modes of cultural expression, and there appears to have been considerable similarity in much of the content expressed in the two modes. In addition, most Americans of the mid-nineteenth century were both hearers and readers, and what they read influenced how they listened as well as what they heard, and vice versa. ("Print and the Public Lecture System, 1840–60" 280)

Thus, oral culture has remained an acknowledged force in American culture. For some authors it was a mere side gig; for others, it came to dominate their careers. But either way, as one contemporary reviewer reminds us, "A lecture is the most profitable form of literary labor" (Lectures and Lecturers" 317).

The lyceum system began in America as a local endeavor. Scholars or experts of a community would lecture for their neighbors. These lectures were first modeled on the British Mechanics' Institutes, and were usually on "applied sciences" (Warren 11). By the 1840s, 4,000 communities had a lyceum or something like it for sponsoring visiting lecturers, including lecturers who had attained a level of celebrity.[2] As Ray points out in her comprehensive study, growing technological

---

[2]   Lawrence Buell, in his study of Emerson, makes the point that traveling clerical lecturers were common, but that "Local clergy sometimes even looked on clerical lecturers as threats to their authority" (24).

capabilities meant lecturers began to be invited from farther and farther away: In the 1850s, "The expanding railroads brought an expansion of the traveling lecture system," and lyceum invitations were issued not in person but over the telegraph (35). By the 1860s, the "lecturer" had become a profession, not something done on the side of one's "real" profession (Ray 37). Higginson, writing in *Macmillan's Magazine*, notes this shift with some wistfulness: "With the name 'Lyceum,' is also passing away the 'Lyceum lecture.' The scholar recedes from sight, and the impassioned orator takes his place" (53). In other words, oratory as profession meant that no longer were true experts speaking on topics about which they knew. The performance was everything. Higginson calls this the "American Lecture-System" rather than the "Lyceum." By the 1870s, the Chautauqua system would replace the lecture system, becoming even more mobile and temporary. Now it was the venue, rather than the speaker, that would be mobile in the form of removable tents.

It is in the 1860s that Ray sees a shift to a market-focused lecture culture, with the founding of a few organizations that helped organize and commercialize the system, to the benefit of the now-professional lecturer (39). These included the Associated Western Literary Societies (AWLS), merging in 1870 with the American Literary Bureau and Redpath's Boston Lyceum Bureau, founded by James Redpath and George L. Fall in 1868.[3] Redpath changed the system by working directly for the lecturers themselves rather than the inviting organizations. This resulted in the fees for paid lecturing rising from around $15 per lecture in the 1850s to $300 per lecture in the 1870s. As Ray writes, "The establishment of for-profit lecture bureaus was not solely responsible for the spiraling of lecture fees, but the systematization of the lecture system contributed to the creation of a celebrity culture and the concomitant bestowal of exorbitant wealth on individual celebrities" (40). By the late nineteenth century, then, the lecture system was functionally quite different from its early nineteenth-century incarnation.

The cultural meaning of the lyceum has been understood as a central part of the American cultural project, a cultural practice that both signaled a distinct American undertaking in itself and forwarded distinct American values in the lectures themselves.[4] The lyceum and lecture system were certainly recognized as an American phenomenon during the period. While the British may have laid the foundation for the useful, public lecture, Americans largely saw it as a native-grown, distinctly American endeavor. Indeed, as one writer put it in *Putnam's Monthly* in 1857, "The lyceum is the American theatre. It is the one

---

[3]   See Chapter 3 for further discussion of Redpath and his British counterpart, George Dolby.

[4]   This is not to say that the lecture system has been treated in isolation. Indeed, it has often been seen as part of the larger American cultural project of the diffusion of knowledge, including through membership libraries, then commercial libraries, in the eighteenth century, as Thomas Augst has shown in his introduction to *Institutions of Reading: The Social Life of Libraries in the United States.*

institution in which we take our noses out of the hands of our English prototypes … and go alone" ("Lectures and Lecturers" 317). This same anonymous writer likewise casts it as the best of uniquely American institutions, saying that "it is the American amusement which is most congenial to our habits and tastes. The opera is always an exotic with us; the theatre is a reproduction of the English, in which the actors, the plays, and the local humor are British … The negro minstrelsy, which is partly indigenous, has degenerated in coarse burlesque and sentimental buffoonery" ("Lectures and Lecturers" 317). Higginson claims it as a part of the American frontier myth, calling up the image of the empty American frontier, the railroad slowly covering the vastness, bringing with it "all the signs and appliances of American social order: the farm, the workshop, the village, the church, the schoolhouse, the *New York Tribune*, the *Atlantic Monthly*, and—the popular Lecture-system" (48).

Both he and Margaret Fuller, writing about the topic in 1842, saw it as a natural evolution from colonial outpost to civilized nation. Connecting it to the intellectual culture of the time, Fuller writes, "Intellectual curiosity and sharpness are the natural traits of a colony overrun with things to be done, to be seen, to be known from a parent country" (49). Higginson, writing later, notes that earlier civilizations, for their necessary "social recreation" turn to "a juggler—a traveling 'circus,' a band of 'Ethiopian Minstrels' … But that is not enough" (49). The lecture system would bring a much-needed intellectual development to the nation, as another writer pointed out: "We believe … that no institution has done more in humanizing and refining us than the lecture" ("Lectures and Lecturers" 317).

Such claims of national meaning were tempered by a keen awareness of the regional differences in the burgeoning United States. Some saw it as a New England export that had flowered in the West, an historical fact that both Bode and Ray confirm. Fuller makes the exclusive claim that it is "the only entertainment we have truly expressive of New England *as it is* in its transition state" (50), but seems to mean by this that it is also an "entertainment truly national" (50). Higginson splits the difference, arguing that the lecture system can flourish most in the "Western States, because it is there the most thoroughly organized, and takes its most characteristic form. In the mature civilization of the Eastern States it is more mingled with other intellectual influences, and it also needs less of centralized organization" (52). But he earlier warns that Western lectures can only flourish if the residents are "of New England birth; for the popular lecture cannot exist below a certain parallel of latitude, while foreign immigrants are apt to avoid it" (Higginson 49). A national institution it might be, but New England was still representative of the best version of the national character for some critics.

The politics of the American system of lectures causes some debate among historians. Ray argues that "the value of educational associations to a democratic society quickly became part of the rhetoric of lyceum advocates" (17). Writing in the 1860s, Josiah Holland noted that the lecture system encouraged democratic discourse: "thanks to the influence of the popular lecture mainly, men have made, and are rapidly making room for each other. A man may be in the minority now without consequently being in personal disgrace" (369). Not only do the lecture subjects encourage a tolerant society for Holland but also the system of lectures itself reflects a democratic system. "The popular lecture is the most purely democratic of all our democratic institutions," he writes, rooting the argument in a capitalist meritocratic ideology: "The people hear a second time only those who interest them. If a lecturer cannot engage the interest of his audience, his fame or greatness or learning will pass for nothing" (363).

But Ray and others have pointed out the complexity involved in such contemporary claims. Indeed, while the ideal lyceum represented a democratic, educational accessibility, the reality was often less than ideal. Despite the claim that the lyceum and lecture system offered an avenue for self-improvement for the public, the prices for the lyceum lecturers, and even more for the later professionalized lecturers, could be prohibitive. Certainly middle-class attendees were common, even sought, but the poor could rarely afford such lectures.[5] As Ray points out, not many immigrant names appear on the lists of attendees. Warren has argued there was a central tension involved in the lyceum between such democratic impulses as the lyceum's "open" doors and the fact that it was seen, not without cause, as a way for the educated elite to control the ideas and behavior of everyone else: "The lecture platform, in this way, becomes a theater of competing—often conflicting—interests and ideas" (13).

Scott, writing in the 1980s, makes the argument that along with the claims of democratic mission attached to the lecture system came the audience's certainty that speakers were "free" to speak as themselves. In other words, they represented the individual, not group, viewpoint: "Useful to all and offensive to none, the lecture was an oratorical form deliberately and carefully separated from all partisan and sectarian discourse" ("The Popular Lecture" 793). Thus, lectures were imagined as apolitical, even though they very clearly grew up alongside the anti-slavery movement. Despite that chronology, Ray argues that early lyceum speakers, "In keeping with promoters' rhetorical suppression of partisan and sectarian topics … actively sought to keep current controversies out of sponsored public lectures" (29).

Contemporary critics from the 1840s and on celebrated this aspect of the lecture system. There was a widely held view that individuals should express views free from party loyalty. Holland writes that among the best lecturers,

> it will be found that there are no slaves among them. The people will not accept those who are creed-bound, or those who bow to any authority but God and themselves. They insist that those who address them shall be absolutely free, and that they shall speak only for themselves. Party and sectarian spokesmen find no permanent place upon the platform. (365)

Higginson concurs, idealizing the popular lecturer as someone who represents "the antidote to the caucus. On its free platform, the statesman speaks for himself alone,

---

[5]   See Ray on the lyceum for a precise discussion of prices and wages of the period (24).

and commits nobody" (52). Yet, some of these same idealizations link the popular lecturer clearly to the anti-slavery movement of New England, such as when Holland fondly remembers "the confluent outpouring of living, Christian speech, from ten thousand lecture platforms, on which free men stood and vindicated the right of men to freedom" (371). In this construction, it seems almost natural that those speakers who were "free" themselves (from group identification) would promote the freedom of others. But, like the "freedom" ex-slaves would enjoy, claims of "freedom" for the speaker were also overstated. In fact, "The early lyceum, then, was promoted simultaneously as a means of controlling the potential of mob rule and as a means of expanding individual opportunity. Freedom, that is, as ideally enacted within a preexisting framework" (Ray 18).

Americans may have seen their popular lecture system as unique to themselves and did, indeed, obsess over its meaning for American culture. However, Thomas Wright has recently warned that "seeing the lyceum as a vessel of American exceptionalism stands in the way of an appreciation of how its contradictory engagement with the globe played on the interaction between cosmopolitan and nationalist impulses" (7). Wright undertakes to illuminate the international aspect of the American lyceum system, showing that, in fact, it looked outward as much as inward. Likewise, Andrew Taylor's work on the professionalization of the American intellectual reinforces the idea that even Ralph Waldo Emerson, an important early lecturer so often held up as an icon of American identity, engaged with a global culture. Taylor argues, "Emerson constructs a textual and transatlantic encounter resistant to the kind of consumption that locates him securely as a variation of the familiar nationalist tropes associated with American exceptionalism, manifest destiny, of the American Adam" (41). This was also true in terms of the general vision of the lecture system and in its practicalities. First and foremost, many speakers were foreign. As this book will show, in the literary world, it was nearly obligatory for literary authors to engage in transatlantic trips or lectures on some scale.

Even when it featured domestic speakers, the lecture system was deeply engaged with the world. As one contemporary critic put it, all who know the "magic of speech" should encourage its production and "keep it turning and accumulating in the great exchange of the world" ("Lectures and Lecturers" 317). That "great exchange" would take many forms; lecturing authors weren't always part of the official lyceum system. Yet, their performances depended on a culture—in both Britain and America—that saw the popular lecture as a central part of the international literary world.

Performance and Literary Authorship

Transatlantic lecture tours dramatize what is a central goal of this project: to expand critical concepts of the literary by focusing on embodied performance. Performance studies as a field has worked to revivify work in otherwise ignored areas such as those cultures or subcultures that have produced performed, rather than written, texts. As Diana Taylor has pointed out, it is written texts or the "archive" that has received critical attention, and that attention has not been politically neutral.[6] In fact, it has often been politically disempowered peoples who have produced "repertoire" texts—performance works that are not archived and consequently have been deemed less worthy of study. The result of growing interest in performance has been work that has recovered and taken seriously what were blind spots in critical history. Though the authors in this study have rarely been ignored because of their vast contribution to the archive of nineteenth-century literature, portraits of their careers and of nineteenth-century authorship have remained incomplete, and *Performing Authorship in the Nineteenth-Century Transatlantic Lecture Tour* works to remedy that. Thus, in the case of lecture tours, I assume what work in performance studies has striven to show: that performed texts are worthy of study and that written text, though an important part of the entire performance "scenario" (another term I borrow from Taylor), should not be the sole point of focus. For Taylor, "The *scenario* includes features well theorized in literary analysis, such as narrative and plot, but demands we also pay attention to milieux and corporeal behaviors such as gestures, attitudes, and tones not reducible to language" (28).

Still, in a fact that reiterates many of the difficulties of studying performance, my own portrait of lecture tours is reliant almost entirely on others' written texts, though some images enrich that portrait. But the newspaper accounts, personal narratives of audience members, author accounts, and lecture texts (when available) from which I have drawn are at times preoccupied with *nondiscursive* elements of performance and the context around performance. I use the term "performance," then, to refer to the lectures themselves, but also to the entire tour experience, borrowing Richard Schechner's concept of a "broad spectrum approach." In 1988, Schechner expanded performance studies by moving the focus away from stage performance to include everything from "the performing arts, rituals, healing, sports, popular entertainments, and performance in everyday life" (7).[7] My analysis, then, treats the following lecture tours as performances in the broadest sense—on and off the stage—and delineates how these performances were understood by authors and audiences.

Performance is in part a narrowly individual undertaking. The body of the lecturer—his or her voice, body movements, tone, timing, etc.—is the central tool and prop in the performance. This act can be deeply empowering to individuals who may be disempowered, say, in a publishing culture in which power is limited to a few. Nonetheless, performance, by its very nature, is creative, suggesting a distance between the individual and the performed self. If we consider the

---

6   Taylor asks, "Whose memories, traditions, and claims to history disappear if performance practices lack the staying power to transmit vital knowledge?" (5).

7   Likewise, in 1992, Richard Poirier imagined the "performing self" with regard to writers, including Henry James, "who treat any occasion as a 'scene' or a stage for dramatizing the self as a performer" (86).

theoretical uses of the term "performative," then performance allows identity to be realized—as an action, not a state of being. In other words, it contains potential for artificiality or, put more positively, creativity and invention.

The experience of Frederick Douglass, whom I discuss as a case study later in the chapter, emphasizes the very high human stakes of this paradox of performance in the pre-Civil War transatlantic sphere. In later years, the relationship between embodied self and performed self played out not in a context of slavery but in the transatlantic literary marketplace. In one sense, these touring authors are responding to the crisis Walter Benjamin identifies in "The Work of Art in the Age of Mechanical Reproduction." It is not just the work of art that "mechanical reproduction" puts at risk. International mass circulation increases authorial distance and decreases the sense of a living presence behind the work. To lecture is to attempt to bridge that gap. What is also at stake for many of these lecturing authors is both "authenticity" and "authority." With books being reproduced at an accelerated rate and photographs of authors being sold and printed, the lecturing author became an event, offering audiences a chance to see the "real thing," "the genuine article," the original, authentic source of the reproduced art object that they had in their homes. The lecture tour, then, offered a way for authors to take a more active role in the creation of their personae—to counterbalance the reproduction of their print identities with live, in-person performances.

Performance also produced a paradoxical effect with regard to the market. Even as authors stood on stage authoring their own selves, lecture tours fed the celebrity culture that was, more and more, replacing the published work with the author; this meant that in the public marketplace, an author's persona was beginning to be consumed as a commodity. In other words, performance clouded the notion of a stable limited self in the marketplace. Almost all the authors in this study were concerned, in one way or another, with the excesses of the marketplace. To find themselves (or a public version of their selves) thrust into that marketplace was deeply disturbing to most. In fact, while performance was a site of agency, the effect of it—the commodification of the author's persona—was disempowering, placing them in a passive relationship to a public on which they were trying to assert themselves. This phenomenon reached a fever pitch in the 1880s with the arrival of Oscar Wilde and, surprisingly, Matthew Arnold, both of whom found themselves represented, reproduced, and impersonated far beyond their lecture tours. Authors' individual performances served as only one part of their tour history, as we will see in these chapters.

Lecture tours highlight the difference between published work and the embodied person, with important consequences for marginal authors. Indeed, one of the constant themes in these lecture tours has to do with representation; that is, who gets to represent themselves in the flesh (and who doesn't) and, also, what is it, exactly, that they are representing: Themselves? Their work? The larger culture? A hegemonic identity? For authors who fought to be heard at all, performance had its benefits, in part because of a changing culture of oratory. As Terry Baxter points out, the movement toward public acceptance of speakers of "questionable" character opened up the public oratorical sphere to those who didn't come, as Emerson did, for example, with pedigree and community respect. In other words, African-American men and women, as well as white women, might be listened to if their individual "personalities" made it possible. Ideally, oratorical culture moved toward something like a meritocracy of "personality."

But if socially marginal authors had trouble being acknowledged in print culture, where the title page alone unequivocally communicated identity, how were they accepted in a performance sphere, where identity was signaled by much more than a name? Long before Charlotte Brontë still felt the need to publish under the name Currer Bell, for example, Harriet Martineau was appearing in person in front of an American anti-slavery group—as a female writer of political economy, no less. It didn't always go well. For all the growing admiration for "personality," Martineau, Harriet Beecher Stowe, and Douglass had a difficult task presenting themselves in person, as authors, to the public. Indeed, oral slave testimonials *and* female performances of any kind were occasions for objectification of the speaker.[8] These speakers stood in complex relation to their audiences.

To put this another way, before the lecture tour, authors were disembodied to their public—a name on the frontispiece, a target in reviews, an imagined concept sometimes an ocean away. But transatlantic lecturing was inescapably embodied: an author stood on the stage, rather than the page, displaying much of his or her physical self through voice, accent, hand gestures, and stature. The most successful lecturers—including Frederick Douglass, Mark Twain, and Charles Dickens— understood this and used their bodies to great effect. But Douglass's case presents us with an important consequence of the lecture tour for authorship. Indeed, for some authors, lecture tours force us to recognize the way in which performance is gendered and political; after all, for authors who challenged, in their person, the idea of who an author was (i.e., women, those with disabilities, and African Americans), embodied performance forced the issue in that they stood in front of audiences, not disembodied words but marginal bodies for all to see. Douglass would navigate the challenge well, but for women, this fact presented an almost unconscionable barrier to the form in an era when a woman's physical presence in a public space was already problematic. A lecturing female body was a vulnerable body, a fact which Harriet Martineau's brief career as a lecturer shows. For most of the authors in this study, however, lecturing, which emphasized the connection between an author and his work, was understood as a stave against the overflow of mass reproduction of work, celebrity culture, and, especially clear in the case of Frederick Douglass, a chance to author one's own public selfhood. In other words, performance could be a site of authorial agency. Certainly, though, the dialectic between performance as empowering and disempowering for the authors who undertook it plays out with even greater starkness for those authors who did not fit the public's understanding of an "author."

---

[8]   This topic has been well mined in works by Terry Baxter, writing on Frederick Douglass, and Susan F. Bohrer, writing on Harriet Martineau, for example.

Literary Celebrity in the Marketplace

In order to function, lecture tours depend on an audience with interest in a visiting author. The lecture tour as a genre, then, came of age at the same time as literary celebrity was booming, in no small part because of a growing mass literary market and commercialization of literary authorship. Critically, the past 20 years mark an important move in literary scholarship to reinsert the author—often against his or her apparent will—into the marketplace of professional authorship. Rather than imagining a separate sphere where canonical authors hover above economy in artistic isolation, critics have uncovered how deeply affected by, and engaged with, authors were in the business of publishing. In modernist studies, it has taken a Herculean effort to challenge modernist authors' claims of disengagement with popular culture. The nineteenth century has lent itself more readily to criticism of this kind, since authors more explicitly tended to comment on their relationship to the market, even if it was to disavow one at all.

The resulting criticism has sometimes identified those who came to be canonical authors as defining themselves against popular literature of the market. In American literature, this turn in criticism has yielded such work as Amy Kaplan's foundational *The Social Construction of American Realism*, in which Kaplan argues that realist authors such as William Dean Howells defined "realism" against the concurrent mass publications of popular novels and periodicals rather than according to some autonomous aesthetic standard. Such critical interventions have identified the nineteenth-century literary market as expanding, with periodicals exploding in number and scope. Loren Glass further specifies the later nineteenth century as being the real beginning of "mass publication," a term he rightfully warns us against using imprecisely; early nineteenth-century periodicals were, by contrast, really a minor extension of the genteel book publishing market (22).

The emergence of this nebulously termed "mass market" offered new possibilities of professional authorship. William Dean Howells, for example, exalted the professional writer as a masculine ideal in opposition to the gentlemen poet he saw abound in English literary culture.[9] Indeed, Charles Dickens and Mark Twain made fortunes by publishing their novels. But the expanding market led to other anxieties. As publishing grew easier, the definition of authorship became blurred; virtually anyone, it seemed, could produce books. Nathaniel Hawthorne's famous indictment of the "scribbling women" with whom he must compete suggests (as many, including Bell and Glass, have discussed) that male writers identified the mass market as a feminine monster against which they must assert their masculine literary power.

Concerns over publication and market should, but often don't, point critics toward studies of transatlantic literary culture. Harriet Beecher Stowe's *Uncle Tom's Cabin* was a bestseller in England, while Dickens's novels and his person excited as much interest in America as in England. The idea of a "mass market,"

---

[9]   See Michael Davitt Bell, 17–39.

then, meant more than simply an expansion of media or readers in one's own country. America represented a valuable market for English writers, while the nineteenth century was the beginning of American writers being read in England on a significant scale. The transatlantic market served authors struggling to capture an audience. The lecture tour provided one way in which authors reestablished connections with readers they no longer knew and could barely imagine. Traveling across the Atlantic to face audiences was one way to alleviate the sense of distance that mass readership produces.

The result was, of course, to encourage the burgeoning culture of celebrity. Literary celebrity, of which Glass's work *Authors Inc.* provides the first book-length study, thus becomes a key element in my discussion.[10] Glass's account is useful in emphasizing how literary celebrity differs from general cultural celebrity: authors participate creatively in producing their public selves. Additionally, he uses literary celebrity as a way of complicating the claims made by both Foucault's "What is an Author?" and Roland Barthes's "The Death of the Author," two works that celebrated the liberation of the text from an imagined author even as they helped establish Foucault and Barthes as cult celebrity figures themselves. When Foucault asked "what is an author?" he argued that the author was "dead," that "using all the contrivances that he sets up between himself and what he writes, the writing subject cancels out the signs of his particular individuality" (Foucault 102–3). Many nineteenth-century authors were aware of similar tensions in different forms, reacting not only to the distancing of the author as Foucault describes it but also to changes in reading culture and celebrity: Was the author "Dickens" the name on the title page of *Bleak House*, the face on the marquee for his pirated play, or the man on the stage?

Glass dates the beginning of literary celebrity in the last decade of the nineteenth century. He is able to do this first by focusing on American culture and second by identifying celebrity as occurring only when writers began officially responding to and shaping it through, in his account, the genre of the autobiography. Twain figures into Glass's study as "protomodernist" because of his use of the autobiography as a way of negotiating his public and private selves, but Twain's use of the lecture tour was equally an attempt at doing so, and it was hardly exceptional in the nineteenth century. Richard Salmon points out that the concept of the "literary lion" is a nineteenth-century phenomenon, in fact "coterminous with the century itself" ("The Physiognomy of the Lion" 60). The transatlantic literary lecture tour

---

[10]   Glass provides the first book-length analysis of literary celebrity, though certainly not of celebrity culture in general. Two classics are Leo Braudy's *The Frenzy of Renown: Fame and Its History*, which offers a thorough and inclusive history, and P. David Marshall's *Celebrity and Power: Fame in Contemporary Culture*, which offers a critical apparatus for examining celebrity's blending of a public and private self. Brenda R. Weber's *Women and Literary Celebrity in the Nineteenth Century: The Transatlantic Production of Fame and Gender*, provides a more specific account of women's celebrity.

started in the early nineteenth century and runs parallel to this lionizing celebrity culture. Indeed, it is a central part of it.

Contemporary critics of the lecture were well aware that it was not always the desire for self-improvement or even entertainment that was the driving force behind attending a lecture. Instead, it was the celebrity him or herself. Holland suggests, "The popular desire is strong to come in some way into personal contact with those who do remarkable things. They cannot be chased in the street; they can be seen only to a limited extent in the drawing room; but it is easy to pay twenty-five cents to hear them lecture, with the privilege of looking at them for an hour and criticizing them for a week" (364). There was a certain relish to this fact, as Higginson shows, writing in the 1860s. It is a good thing, he writes, that "[speakers] must, at least face the people eye to eye. This ordeal of the gaslight displays to all beholders the face, the form, the bearing of the speaker" (53). The vulnerability of the celebrity is made even clearer in another contemporary account discussing how lecturers must be effective to maintain an audience. This one claims, while "it was the roar of the animal which attracted the hunters ... it was his strength or his beauty which enchanted their eyes and hearts" ("Lectures and Lecturers" 317). The idea of good lecturing pausing the hunt of the audience may not have been comforting to nervous lecturers, but it does capture the ambivalent position of the object of all this celebratory attention.

Literary Lecturers in a Hierarchy of Culture

In addition to the performance and celebrity at the heart of the story, these performances reflect the nineteenth-century obsession with artistic and literary hierarchies. As Lawrence Levine shows in *Highbrow/Lowbrow*, the nineteenth century was the era in which cultural hierarchies were uneasily put into place. In fact, notions of "high" versus "low" culture are relatively new; a study of the nineteenth century, according to Levine, calls our attention to the fact that "the primary categories of culture have been products of ideologies which were always subject to modifications and transformations [and] the perimeters of our cultural divisions have been permeable and shifting rather than fixed and immutable" (Levine 8). As these categories shifted in the nineteenth century, authors reacted in surprising ways. Nancy Bentley describes the nineteenth-century emerging mass culture as an abrupt shift from preceding public culture, one that unnerved the highbrow establishment: "It is true—and highly consequential—that the advent of mass culture created starkly different aesthetic forms and styles ... But it is a mistake to assume that artists at the highest levels were unmoved by the novel sensory experiences and iconic events that drew mass audiences" (4). Indeed, lecture tours were one meeting point between spectacle and art.

It is no surprise, then, that the lecture tour, with its elements of highbrow culture and lowbrow entertainment, was a site of anxiety. Lecture tours raised the question of where an author belonged in the growing hierarchy of arts and entertainment. Was the author an entertainer, a moral leader, a steward of intellectual life? What we now deem "highbrow" and "lowbrow" were comingled, and the literary arts were struggling to establish a respectable place in that hierarchy without losing all popular appeal. The upside to this was that early nineteenth-century audiences "shared a public culture less hierarchically organized, less fragmented into relatively rigid adjectival boxes than their descendents were to experience a century later" (Levine 9). Thus, an author like Matthew Arnold would take the same stages and charge admission in the same way as P.T. Barnum did for a look at Tom Thumb and the Bearded Lady. Still, Arnold, like most authors in this study, expressed discomfort with this fact. Indeed, it was the uneasiness with this shared, commingled culture which led some to attempt to establish clear divisions. The lecture tour is part of that story.

Part of this project's mission, then, is to examine the uncertainty with which authors approached lecturing in the context of literature's liminal position during the century. The lectures of the authors in this study vary tremendously in terms of twenty-first-century categories. Some lecturers look and sound a lot like preachers or politicians. Those speaking on abolition drew inspiration from this tradition. The first chapter approaches abolitionist speech as a kind of precursor to the literary lecture, since Stowe and Martineau were also literary authors at the time they spoke for abolition. It was, in part, Emerson's domination of the American lecture scene that initiated it as a kind of moral undertaking, as Thomas Augst has shown.[11] Indeed, Emerson said, "I look upon the Lecture room as the true church of today" (qtd. in Gibian 16). Later lecturers, such as Dickens and Twain, look and sound like theater performers, even though both authors took pains to avoid being identified with theater.[12] Some, like Henry James, are academic in tone and subject. Most lecturers incorporate several aspects into their performances— Wilde, for example, is part actor, part "apostle," and part academic; yet all considered themselves, and are considered, "authors." These experiences suggest confusion and discomfort as authors tried to separate themselves from what were becoming less respectable kinds of cultural performance, especially in the later nineteenth century.

As the list above suggests, it was not just, then, "high" and "low" which mingled in the lecture tour of the nineteenth-century. In fact, tours also exposed the fault lines between various versions of authorship available at the time—the man

---

[11]   Thomas Augst includes the lecture tour in his study of young men's "moral life," writing that "Many people continued to find consolation and guidance in the traditional sermons they heard at church, as they had for centuries. But increasingly, the search for wisdom and happiness encompassed a secular appetite for 'rational amusement' and 'useful knowledge'" (*The Clerk's Tale* 118).

[12]   Indeed, these entertainers were probably well aware that they couldn't just be entertainers. As one contemporary writer put it, "if the lecture be only ludicrous or amusing, if the object of the lecturer be plainly only to make himself a buffoon, and to make his audience laugh—they do laugh, but they do not forgive him" ("Lectures and Lecturers" 317). Holland wrote that "Another requisite to popularity upon the platform is earnestness" (366).

of letters, the specialist, the academic, the political activist. As we see in the case of Emerson, for example, whose public identity combined the roles of minister, scientist, model citizen, poet, and philosopher, the early nineteenth century was not the province of the professional literary author. Gregory Clark and S. Michael Halloran have shown that the literary field didn't exist outside the oratorical field in the beginning of the century, so that the nature of literature was primarily epideictic. This would change later in the century as authorship began to be seen as professional, narrowing Emerson's own vision of the expansive, multitalented man of letters. Those whom we call "authors" might be poets, they might be scientist/philosophers like Emerson, they might be part of the growing number of novelists, including "scribbling women," and they might be political orators. A century in which a scientist could also be a poet clearly played host to an expansive concept of the author. In Antebellum United States culture, Harriet Martineau, known for her writings on political economy, could visit a few years earlier than the young novelist Charles Dickens and be received similarly as a celebrity "author."

A clear shift takes place, however, over the course of the century. The tense political atmosphere preceding the Civil War in America and occasioned by the Reform Bill and Abolition debates in England meant that authors who wrote and spoke on political topics faced hostility and controversy much more than later authors, who identified themselves more and more with a literary, apolitical sphere. Speaking in person on controversial topics during this period could be dangerous, as Douglass, as well as Martineau and Stowe, found. Unlike later authors, whose venues and performance styles often signaled the distance between "themselves" and their lecture personae, speakers on abolition were speaking earnestly, morally, as "themselves." The intimate link, especially in the northern United States, between religion and abolition aided the conflation of the speaker's true feelings and his or her words. While this pulpit tradition lent political power to speeches, it also meant that the private person—in name and in body—had to take more personal responsibility for what was said, a fact learned by the three representative abolitionist speakers I include. For later authors, the political lecture would give way to other forms.

Angela Ray notes this trajectory in her study of the American lyceum system. She writes that it "illustrates a process of expansion, diffusion, and eventual commercialization" from an early version which stressed "education and moral uplift" in the 1820s to the late 1860s, by which time, "lyceum lecturers had become a lucrative commercial enterprise, and the most highly sought platform celebrities … earned large incomes from lecturing" (2–3). And this flexibility with regard to authorial identity was reflected in the venues of lecturers. In the second half of the nineteenth century, authors such as Dickens and Twain would find themselves giving "entertainments" in theaters, halls, and the occasional church. Arnold, Wilde, and James drew audiences who identified with the growing sense of "high culture" in America, often speaking to private clubs or universities and earning vastly greater fees than Douglass could. By the end of the nineteenth century, for better or worse, a clearer line between high and low culture and between the literary and other cultural milieus could be drawn.

MAGDALEN COLLEGE LIBRARY

The Lecture Tour as a Transatlantic Phenomenon

Conceptions of the American lecture system, most notably Ray's *The Lyceum and Public Culture in the Nineteenth-Century United States* and Charlotte Canning's *The Most American Thing in America: Circuit Chautauqua as Performance*, often focus on the lyceum or the Chautauqua movement's connection to forming American identity. Ray notes that such performance venues developed alongside cultural nativism, for example, and cites the lyceum as a "location in which people explicitly called selfhood or nationhood into being" and "where group identifications could becoming meaningful through behavioral patterns, through recurring rhetorical acts" (7). Lectures did indeed encourage and generate group identity, but not always of a nativist kind. Rather, the fact that there were so many international speakers and audiences joined together in various performance scenarios provides yet another example of the intricacy of the transatlantic cultural sphere. Indeed, the commonality of such tours points rather to an explicit transatlantic community. Thus, in addition to issues of performance, celebrity, and authorship, this study is in dialogue with the now-established field of transatlantic studies. No one now doubts the interrelatedness of the national cultures or the limitations of a nation-oriented perspective, especially in terms of the literary sphere.[13] Anglo-American literary culture was an imagined and experienced community of its own, sharing culture, ideas, and commerce. In fact, *Performing Authorship in the Nineteenth-Century Transatlantic Lecture Tour* takes for granted that nineteenth-century authorship was transatlantic. It builds on work that insists on the material connections across national boundaries, such as Paul Gilroy's foundational *The Black Atlantic* and, more recently, Amanda Claybaugh's concept of a "new transatlanticism" (in "Toward a New Transatlanticism"). In stressing the movements of writer's bodies across boundaries, the work takes heed of this emphasis on material but also intellectual exchange, a realm explored in depth by Paul Giles in *Virtual Americas* with his "transatlantic imaginary" and Robert Weisbuch in his psychoanalytic treatment of the uneasy relationship between the intertwined intellectual spheres. In fact, the theories of transatlanticism that have emerged in the last 20 years or so are simply acknowledging what nineteenth-century authors already assumed in their rich engagement with literature across the pond, as Claybaugh has pointed out.[14] It may well be that the transatlantic perspective is essential to understanding nineteenth-century authorship.

While this portrait takes the crisscross of authors as its subject—and conceives of that transatlantic sphere as its point of focus—it is essential to note that the motivations and experiences of traveling British and American authors were often

---

[13]   To begin with, as Michael Winship has pointed out, "Books—those international agents of intellectual and cultural exchange—are no respecters of national borders" (5).

[14]   As Claybaugh argues, "The nineteenth-century literary field took for granted the existence of what I will call 'literature in English.' The category is never fully articulated or defended, but it underwrites most contemporary reviews" (*The Novel of Purpose* 12).

different from one another. For some time, critical emphasis was on the American anxiety over cultural independence. In other words, it was generally believed that Americans thought about British culture much more than British writers thought about American culture. This emphasis is, in many instances, supported by the writers themselves. After all, Henry James famously wrote in his notebooks in 1881 that "[The American writer] *must* deal, more or less, even if only by implication, with Europe; whereas no European is obliged to deal in the least with America." He goes on to write that this may not be true "fifty years hence perhaps" but for now, he argues, the European artist who neglects America is *not* "incomplete" (*The Complete Notebooks* 214). At the time, Henry James's primary dissenters of the period came from Americans arguing that they needn't deal with Europe, that they could have, to use Emerson's phrase in *Nature*, "an original relation to the universe" (27). Critics have continued to promote this uneven relationship between British and American authors and audiences. For example, Lawrence Buell sees American renaissance literature as "post-colonial," arguing that "some of the most provincially embedded American renaissance texts bear at least passing direct witness to anticipating foreign readers" (148); he does not dwell on the possibility of anticipation working the other way as well. Meanwhile, Robert Weisbuch treats the literature of the two sides of the Atlantic in dialogue in *Atlantic Doublecross*, but his book ultimately suggests that American authors tended to feel the presence of British literature more than British authors felt that of American writing.

In terms of the transatlantic lecture tour, this emphasis on the American need to gain the approval of the parent country does resonate, at least in part. American lecturers went for an expanded audience, but especially earlier on in the century, with a sense that to gain the British audience would mean more than simply increased revenue. For some, like Douglass and Stowe, this meant an expanded community of support for abolition. For Twain, it meant the opportunity to prove to a condescending imperialist country that the American act could succeed. American obsession with its patronizing cultural parent was enacted in various forms—to begin with, an increase in travel. On the one hand, Europe was something to be understood and experienced, and the Grand Tour was already well established in the nineteenth century. Malcolm Bradbury, in his book *Dangerous Pilgrimages*, points out that for Americans, travel abroad increased because of growing prosperity and technology, most especially in the form of steamships. As the historian Susan Matt has shown, "In the early nineteenth century, the trip from Western Europe to America took between four and six weeks; by the end of the century, it took only seven days" (141–2).[15] British and American authors—and many others—took advantage of the shrinking journey.

---

[15] Nathaniel Hawthorne, for example, made the passage in the middle of the century in only 14 days. The frequency of American visits to Britain and Europe would only increase through the end of the century. In 1860, for example, there were 1,000 American visitors to Rome; in 1900, there were 30,000 (Bradbury 8). Britain was even more accessible.

Still, American authors heartily resented the cultural domination and condescension Britain continued to apply to its former colony. Hence, American authors seemed interested in serving as ambassadors of American culture. The American authors in this study, with the exception of James, represented Americans in a way that suggests their interest not in imitating British authors but in defining a distinct American character. The primary figure here is, of course, Twain, who engaged in his own form of cultural counter-imperialism with his lectures in England. Those performances seek less to teach British audiences how to be better British citizens than to teach them how to better *see* Americans. Twain's incorporation of the American rustic—at times simple, at times worldly—was a way to show that the American author could outdo the British in parody and insight. Twain later would explicitly denounce imperialism even while he engaged in his own form of it during a world lecture tour. In his first British lecture tour, he rehearses this argument by showing that British attempts to teach Americans were misguided.

But it is the other part of James's formulation—British writers had no obligation or need to "deal" with America—that, in light of transatlantic lecture tours, strikes one as simply untrue, as James himself would demonstrate in 1904 when he began his lecture series in his native country. The lecture tour in general, which grew increasingly one-sided over the course of the century (with more British authors traveling to America than the other way around), shows how central America was to the British literary imagination. Paul Giles, in *Atlantic Republic*, has noted the real and complex way in which American culture influenced British literary texts, and this influence certainly resonates in the lectures as well. Indeed, a list of British authors who lectured in America during the period includes a who's who of prominent British writers of the day: Thackeray, Trollope, Arnold, Wilde, Stevenson, Stoker, and, of course, James himself, after he had happily accepted Britain as his home. They *would* deal with America, sometimes grudgingly, sometimes happily.

For the British traveling to America, a desire to tap the immense American market's hunger for authentic British culture was often a motivator in itself. The British authors in this study depended on America as part of a new concept of international fame and fortune, seeking the revenue from thousands of book-buyers and lecture-goers. However Americans might criticize British elitism, there remained a solid audience interested in gazing at British "lions," who were often more famous in America than American authors. The most popular author to visit was Dickens, but Harriet Martineau, Oscar Wilde, and Matthew Arnold were nearly as feted and sought after. They could all charge prices that benefited themselves as well.

Additionally, British authors had a profound curiosity about the social experiment on the other side of the pond. Those who came toward the first half of the century, notably Martineau and Dickens, on his first trip to the United States during which he did not lecture, were curious to see how American institutions fulfilled the promise of democracy in which they both believed. They were deeply interested in the American experiment in democratic institutions and were impressed by prisons, hospitals, and public services. They were disappointed, not surprisingly, in the continued existence and effects of slavery. They were horrified by the messiness of the American population and drawn to the scale on which all things—messy and otherwise—were conducted. Matthew Arnold, whose strained relationship with American culture has been much discussed, would equate American culture with the British middle class he spent his later life obsessed with analyzing and critiquing. The American behemoth, both as idea of democracy and as very real networks of economy and politics, was central to Victorian writers, whether they explicitly wrote about it or not.

Later visitors such as Arnold, Wilde, and James expressed this same curiosity tinged with a more paternalistic sense of mission. They saw themselves acting as cultural stewards to the people of America, who, they agreed, were in serious need. Lecture tours served this purpose admirably. These tours were secular missionary work, culminating in sermons for cultural salvation. The lectures themselves and those who delivered them served as models of thought, culture, art, and manners. The fact that Wilde, Arnold, and James came late in the century suggests that, as far as the British were concerned, America's adolescent period was still going on.

American prominence is especially clear when one considers the subjects of the lectures detailed in this study. The content of the lectures, whether they were delivered by American authors to British audiences or by British authors to American audiences, covered *American* subjects. The one exception to this is Dickens, who performed his fictional works for American audiences. Douglass, Stowe, and Twain, speaking in Britain, discussed American slavery, American cultural independence, and the American character and geography. Martineau, Arnold, Wilde, and James lectured to American audiences on, again, American slavery, American authors, and American aesthetic or popular culture. Thus, both British authors and British audiences were deeply attuned to and interested in the issues on the American side of the Atlantic, and, previewing twentieth-century American self-centeredness, so were Americans. So, while both sides might acknowledge a paternalistic relationship, no one could ignore the growing child.

A Transatlantic Lecture Tour Case Study: Frederick Douglass

When Frederick Douglass began his lecture tour in Britain and Ireland, he was a slave. When he finished and returned to the United States, he was free. Thus in a very real way, transatlantic performance was freeing for Douglass. Despite his extraordinary circumstances, his lecture tour in Great Britain and Ireland exemplifies the central themes of this transatlantic phenomenon. In fact, it is precisely because of his particular identity that his experience highlights—dramatically—the transatlantic nature of nineteenth-century authorship, the shifts in cultural hierarchies, and the growing world of celebrity. Most important, Douglass's case allows an exploration of how embodied performance worked for lecturing authors, even though, as a slave, his own relationship with public embodiment was necessarily distinct from other authors. Such a case demonstrates even more forcefully something true of all the authors in this study—that their relationships with their texts were complicated by performance. Lecturing endangered the special status of the book, the written artifact, but it could also potentially boost the book's—and author's— value. In all cases, focusing on transatlantic lecturing authors reminds us that the book is never free from a worldly, embodied, performative culture and reality.

In 1845, Douglass had been publicly appearing for almost five years, mostly with the support of William Lloyd Garrison and the Boston Anti-Slavery Society. Not yet an author, Douglass had been lecturing in the United States, giving testimony from the perspective of a runaway slave. Interestingly, he was safe as a speaker— going by the anonymous "Douglass" (an invented name). His "usefulness," as Garrison and other white members of society often put it, was threatened when audience members, in response to his eloquence, began to question his claim to have been a slave.[16] As Dwight McBride writes, slave testimonies relied on the fact that the speakers would "bear witness" to slavery. The oral claim of experience was not enough, however, for skeptical white listeners, and he published his *Narrative of the Life of Frederick Douglass* in 1845 to silence doubt. In doing so, he gained what Augst calls "The literary license of public speech" ("Frederick Douglass" 55). But he also put himself in legal danger. When he admitted in his published work to being Frederick Bailey, the binding formality of published written work meant Douglass the speaker could not escape responsibility for Bailey's illegal act of running away from slavery. It was the combination of the two which proved dangerous to his person. In other words, it was a good time to go abroad. And so he agreed to go as part of the Boston Anti-Slavery Society's lecture tour in Ireland and Great Britain. Unlike the millions of slaves who had crossed in the opposite direction in the preceding centuries, then, Douglass's transatlantic voyage was his salvation.

His speeches were recounted in the third person by listening journalists. The portrait of his tour, then, is filtered through the once-removed language of British journalists, a point that reminds us how mediated all access to performed texts remains. In his speeches, which were arranged by various anti-slavery groups for anti-slavery audiences, he generally began with his account of the *Narrative*'s publication, and in these speeches, Douglass describes how he was forced into becoming an author.[17] In Belfast, a reporter transcribed one explanation:

---

[16]   Augst argues that for nineteenth-century whites, "the value of Douglass's words came from their utility for the Abolitionist movement—not from the personal authority of Douglass, speaking for himself, but to the impersonal authority of his example" ("Frederick Douglass: Between Speech and Print" 54). He goes on to show how Douglass would work against that assumption.

[17]   In *The Frederick Douglass Papers*, editors John W. Blassingame et al. have collected various published newspaper accounts of Douglass's speeches, including different transcriptions of the same speech. Though they are transcriptions and Douglass is the "author," they are written in the third person. Speeches will be cited as *Frederick Douglass Papers*.

In [the] course of time, however, a suspicion arose that he had never been a slave. It was said, "He is a man of intelligence and of education! How comes it that he, having been a slave, can yet read? Besides, he does not tell us the place from whence he came." Thus in New England the rumor went abroad that he was a free negro, and he found that his usefulness would be impaired unless this report were silenced. He resolved, therefore, to publish a narrative giving a circumstantial detail of what he had seen and suffered in connexion with slavery, stating the place of his former abode, his master's name, and other particulars ...
(*Frederick Douglass Papers* 89)

In Glasgow, 1846, a journalist reported a similar tale: "The abolitionists had knocked so much of the rust off him, and polished him to such an extent, that the friends of slavery would not believe he had ever been a slave" (*Frederick Douglass Papers* 133). Ironically, those who read Douglass's account but had never seen him speak also questioned his authenticity, in this case, his authorship of the *Narrative*, as they did with several other slave narratives, including Harriet Jacobs's work, claiming that a slave could never write so well. For an at-risk author such as Douglass, going public both in person and in print meant gaining public acknowledgement of his authenticity. But speaking, especially, also allowed him the freedom of space and creative invention he craved. In his own words in the *Narrative*, the first time he spoke to a white audience, he was reluctant, yet "I spoke but a few moments, when I felt a degree of freedom ..." (75). This somewhat paradoxical aspect of performance—it suggested both authenticity of the self and freedom from the limits of the self—would follow Douglass throughout his career as a lecturer, a curious relationship we will witness in many of the cases studied in this book.

Such authenticity rested on his ability to represent the slave. What made this difficult was a contradiction within abolitionist discourse. As Dwight A. McBride argues, "The slave body is both singular and collective ... The slave is a self that is always engaged in a kind of collective corporeal condition that makes it virtually impossible speak of the self solely as an individual" (10). Douglass himself would exploit this contradiction in his speeches, saying, for example, "I am the representative of three millions of bleeding slaves. I have felt the lash myself; my back is scarred with it" (*Frederick Douglass Papers* 36). As William McFeely tells it, Douglass was always torn between accepting the part of the representative slave—and the aura of authenticity that came with it—and being the exceptional, extraordinary slave. His audiences saw him as representative *and* exceptional. One audience member, Elizabeth Pease, called him "a *living* contradiction ... to that base opinion, so abhorrent to every human and Christian feeling, that the blacks are an inferior race" (*Frederick Douglass Papers* lv). Sarah Hilditch similarly called him "a living example of the capabilities of the slave, and though we do not expect *all* to be *equally* gifted, he proves that *they are not* what they have been misrepresented, mere chattels—with bodies formed for Herculean labor, but without minds, without souls" (*Frederick Douglass Papers* lv–lvi).

Before even going abroad, Douglass quickly learned that going public as author and speaker together meant risking bodily harm. It became clear soon after the publication of his *Narrative* that the details Douglass provided about his past meant that, at any time, his former master could come and claim him. He would be easy to find. He was standing in front of crowds in several states almost nightly. He had had a couple of fearful moments since making it to free soil—enough to urge him to flee another time. He had given a speech in Indiana and had been chased, with a white abolitionist, out of town by a mob, having his hand crushed before escaping. Before he announced his real identity, an audience member recognized him, claiming she had met him in Baltimore as a slave under the name "Edward." McFeely, Douglass's biographer, has not been able to identify why she may have known him as Edward, but it was enough to make Douglass wary of meeting other, less kind, people from his past.

As he told audiences in Britain, the Boston anti-slavery society and he decided it would be best to continue his work abroad: "By [publishing his *Narrative*] he silenced doubt; but his danger increased, and on the advice of friends he undertook a mission to Great Britain" (*Frederick Douglass Papers* 38). Since there was, as he often said, no soil in America on which he would be free, he took to the ocean, joining a transatlantic community of abolitionists and fugitive slaves. As McBride explains,

> the abolitionists constituted a new kind of transnational identity, drawing what they needed to support their cause from a variety of sources from around the world. The same, too, can be said of the pro-slavery advocacy. In addition, discussions of narrative authenticity in slave testimony require a kind of hegemony of form and content, also across national boundaries, which also suggests a new kind of transnational identity for the "slave" as well. (25)

As a key figure in abolitionism, a former slave, and a performer, Douglass needs to be viewed in this transatlantic context. Ironically, he is often written about as the penultimate American figure. Augst calls him the image of "the enduring fantasy of America: that an ordinary man might rise to distinction on the strength of his own character rather than the pretensions and artifice of the aristocratic learning" ("Frederick Douglass" 59). But both Paul Giles and Fionnghuala Sweeney argue that Douglass's own thinking and his public persona were cosmopolitan. Giles has revisited Douglass's association with American nationalism—through his embrace of the self-made man—and argues that he was as engaged with British culture. In fact, Giles suggests, "Nationalism for Douglass thus came to involve not so much a positive or universal ideal but, rather, a set of fluctuating contrary terms" (*Virtual Americas* 23). Similarly, according to Sweeney, "transnational encounters were key to Douglass's project of American self-fashioning." His "career represents a tactical synthesis of national and transnational concerns, including slavery, citizenship, manhood, and broader debates concerning the individual within the nation state" (Sweeney 3).

Douglass certainly viewed himself this way, writing in *My Bondage and My Freedom* that "as to nation, I belong to none. I have no protection at home, or resting-place abroad. The land of my birth welcomes me to her shores only as a slave, and spurns with contempt the idea of treating me differently" (220). He argued for transatlantic moral pressure, not military action, from his British and Irish audiences, thus imagining a community of shared values among "civilized" people (which, he believed, Americans could not yet be called), where one group's moral admonition would be felt by another. He urged ladies in Ireland and Britain to contribute needlework or painting to be sold in the Boston Anti-Slavery Bazaar, a formidable annual fundraiser that lasted from 1834 to 1857. To accomplish this, he spoke several times a week, for 90 minutes to two hours, tirelessly canvassing Ireland, then Scotland, and finally England, in small towns and the islands' metropolitan areas, never losing faith that what he did there would aid the work across the Atlantic. Lecturing, for Douglass as for most performing authors, was an international undertaking.

Douglass's success was quickly established in reports of his appearances and in letters written home by those traveling with him. The London *Nonconformist* in September 1846 reported that Douglass's speech was "replete with thrilling statements, fervid denunciations and stirring and eloquent appeals. We have rarely listened to an orator so gifted by nature, and never to a man who more thoroughly threw his whole heart into the work in which he is engaged" (*Frederick Douglass Papers* liv). In Ireland, one reporter condescendingly claimed to have been "far from prepared for such a powerful appeal, couched, as it was, in the most correct language, clearly enunciated and eloquently reinforced" (*Frederick Douglass Papers* liv). William Garrison, his companion on the trip, wrote home that "I made a long speech which elicited the strongest marks of approbation. Douglass was received in a similar manner, and made one of his very best efforts. I never saw an audience more delighted" (377). Later he remarked that Douglass was "rapturously received" (379).

These superlative assessments of Douglass's success must be weighed against the disturbing growth of racist ideas in Britain at the time. As Sarah Meer points out, racist visions of the African were circulating in London during Douglass's visit, thanks in part to a group called the Ethiopian Singers, white singers who performed in black face: "the Serenaders' success suggests how poignantly limited Douglass's impact in Britain as antislavery orator and exemplary black man may have been" (Meer 161–2). Still, she admits, "the Ethiopian Serenaders were never allowed to represent American blacks alone in Britain, for they had to contend with Douglass's living example" (Meer 162). Douglass's audiences were fascinated; whether this fascination translated into political or moral persuasion is another issue.

Douglass's account of his imminent and physical danger at home formed part of his stage power. Almost every speech began with the tale of why he came to Ireland and Britain, a narrative that combined a titillating story of escape and still-imminent danger with a flattering tribute to British progressivism. The irony of the democratic United States being less free than the monarchical Britain was a favorite theme. In *My Bondage and My Freedom*, written after his return, he restated what he generally said in speeches, "The writing of my pamphlet, in the spring of 1845, endangered my liberty, and led me to seek a refuge from republican slavery in monarchical England. A rude, uncultivated fugitive slave was driven, by stern necessity, to that country to which young American gentlemen go to increase their stock of knowledge" (218). In a speech in Scotland, he made a similar claim, complimenting his audiences while criticizing his homeland: "And now, since I am in the free hills of old Scotland, treading upon British soil, I can appreciate and perceive the grandeur of the noble, the patriotic sentiments, uttered by Curran on universal emancipation. Liberty is commensurate with and inseparable from British soil" (*Frederick Douglass Papers* 185). In a letter he'd written to Garrison (and intended for publication), he stated that "Instead of a democratic government, I am under a monarchical government. Instead of the bright, blue sky of America, I am covered with the soft, grey fog of the Emerald Isle. I breathe, and lo! the chattel becomes a man" (*My Bondage and My Freedom* 222). The journey from America to Ireland here figures as a journey away from existing merely as a material thing, owned and sold at the whim of others.

Accounts of his speeches are full of references to being hunted by American "bloodhounds," reminding us of the potential risk—and dramatic opportunity—of lecturing publicly. Again and again he asked audiences to imagine bloodhounds on his track, bloodhounds he had escaped by crossing the Atlantic: "There was not a spot in all America in which he could stand securely free" (*Frederick Douglass Papers* 89), or, "He was glad to be here, where no blood-hound could be set upon his track" (133). In Dublin, a reporter stated that Douglass was "Recently a slave himself, and still liable, by the laws of his country, to be seized and carried back into bondage" (*Frederick Douglass Papers* 35). Another Irish reporter transcribed that "One of the reasons why he was there to-night was that he was not secure in his own country; he was a fugitive, and it was no disgrace to be a fugitive from a nation of men-stealers" (*Frederick Douglass Papers* 81). As his tour wore on and more information was obtained, a Birmingham, England, paper reported that "The last American papers contained a declaration from his former master and other friends of slavery, that, if he ever set his foot in the country, he should be reduced to slavery again … he was liable, if ever returned to it, to be hunted down with bloodhounds." The author records the audience's reaction to this news as "Cries of 'shame'" (*Frederick Douglass Papers* 310).

While most of Douglass's anti-slavery audience was horrified to think of him being recaptured, there were still threats to his person. One of Douglass's primary missions abroad was to convince the Free Church of Scotland to return the support money it had received from slave-holding Southern Presbyterians. His speeches focused on this issue, urging the audience to join him in shouting "Send Back the Money." Once, with the help of two British women, he carved the mantra into the sod at a city park. But the slogan was picked up by pro-slavery advocates, or, at least, anti-abolitionists in Belfast, where notices posted around the city read "Send Back the Nigger" (McFeely 133). Even in "free" Ireland, then, Douglass was not out of danger until his freedom was purchased with the help of British supporters during his visit. Quietly and without fanfare, Douglass gained his freedom; interestingly, he did not discuss this in his public performances. The drama of the bloodhounds may have been too rhetorically effective to give up.

In addition to generating drama, Douglass's eloquence on the lecture platform is evidence of his faith in the centrality of performance to the ideal of the "self-made man." It was a faith that all lecturing authors share—the ability of performance to allow a space of creative identity fashioning. While he needed to establish his authenticity as a slave, he also performed a different identity. In his written work,

> Slave is a category that Douglass the narrator seems to want to claim firsthand knowledge of but does not want always to claim for himself. This speaks to the tension of presenting oneself ... as both the authentic eyewitness to slavery ... and as the cultivated man of letters who produces the narrative and advances the argument for black humanity. (McBride 164)

What McBride doesn't note is the fact that both of these identities are located, for Douglass, in the body: the source of his claim to have been a slave (the scars on his back) and the tool he uses to perform a denunciation of slavery from the position of an extraordinary speaker outside of it. His lectures negotiated between biographical experience and performance—by which Douglass could move beyond biography to become a self-made man.

Accounts of his speeches almost always focus on his physical appearance. Douglass was known for being extremely handsome, and reviewers emphasize the number of ladies in the audience night after night. One can detect an early sense of the threat surrounding the black man too closely associated with white women which would follow Douglass throughout his life (as he fought against gossip concerning him and his close, white, female friends). Douglass, safe on the stage away from the audience, was partly admired for his sexual appeal, or his "manly speech" (*Frederick Douglass Papers* 36).

While his appearance pleased audiences, it also left them wondering about his heritage, suggesting how the live performance created a different set of issues from mere written publication. Douglass dwells on this issue in his own writing. The second paragraph of his *Narrative* explains that "My father was a white man. He was admitted to be such by all I ever heard speak of my parentage" (Douglass 12). He further notes that relatives on his mother's side were all "quite dark" (12), as if to prove that he must have some other heritage. Irish and British accounts struggled to determine his racial identity. A report from the Cork, Ireland, *Examiner* gave a disturbing description before moving on to his speech. This reporter claims that Douglass was

> a gentlemen of nature and society. Evidently, from his colour and conformation, descended from parents of different race[s], his appearance is singularly pleasing and agreeable. The hue of his face and hands is rather a yellow brown or bronze, while there is little, if anything, in his features of that peculiar prominence of lower face, thickness of lips, and flatness of nose, which peculiarly characterize the true negro type. His voice is well toned and musical, his selection of language most happy, and his manner easy and graceful. (*Frederick Douglass Papers* 37)

The reporter makes no distinction between basing his judgment of Douglass's mixed identity on his appearance and on his eloquence. Douglass noted how at times he seemed not black enough. He wrote home that "It is quite an advantage to be a 'nigger' here ... I am hardly black enough for the British taste, but by keeping my hair as wooly as possible—I make out to pass for at least a half a negro at any rate" (qtd. in McFeely 131). He appears amused in this account that he should have to "play" the part which he was most anxious to escape—the British conception of the African-American slave. Here again, he was doing what all authors in this study do, only with so much more at stake. Each author, when performing, had to "play" his or her self much as Douglass does. He was quite comfortable with such identity performance as an element of his life on the lecture circuit, as long as it didn't interfere with his "authenticity" as a slave.

Douglass actually encouraged interest in his physical appearance. Though he is often read as performing the bourgeois gentlemen in an attempt to gain equal treatment, his manipulation of audience expectations of slave bodies shows he could, at times, exploit his past. He often complained in his speeches that slaves were not men because they were merely "bodies," or chattel. But in his public appearances, Douglass did not try to escape the body. As Baxter has shown in his study of Douglass's rhetorical style, "He was, in so many words, allowing himself to be objectified as a sexual object all the while decrying the objectifying effects of slavery to his audiences" (134). Additionally, lecture after lecture focused on the physical brutality of slavery, grounding its rhetoric in the body. As any good speaker does, Douglass asked audiences to visualize the accounts he gave—of the beating of his aunt Harriet, for example. He did this with the help of visual aids. First, he carried the tools of slavery—the chains used for torture, the restraining devices. In an account of a Dublin speech, the reporter describes Douglass's use of such props: the churches of America "were all implicated more or less in the sin of maintaining the infernal slave system—of placing their brethren in chains like this—(holding up to the audience some of the horrible instruments of torture used by the slaveholders)" (*Frederick Douglass Papers* 35). In Limerick, Douglass showed several instruments of torture: an iron collar taken from around a young woman's neck with blood and flesh on it, fetters for chaining the feet of a slave, hand cuffs from a fugitive slave, and a whip with blood on it, which he showed while narrating the story of a slave girl being whipped while her master quoted the Bible (*Frederick Douglass Papers* 85).

Douglass explicitly connected the tools of torture with his own physical experience: "I was subject to all the evils and horrors of slavery—to the lash, the chain, the thumb-screw; and even as I stand here before you I bear on my back the marks of the lash (sensation)" (*Frederick Douglass Papers* 37). Douglass told an Irish audience that "I stand before you with the marks of the slave-driver's whip, that will go down with me to my grave" (*Frederick Douglass Papers* 41). Again, in such moments, Douglass performs his identity yet he also insists on authenticity, on a truth beyond performance. He referred to his scars in an argument against those who claimed that slavery existed in England in the form of extreme poverty. A journalist's version of his speech reads, "While he admitted that they had severe want, poverty, wretchedness, and misery here, he denied that they had slavery. What was slavery? Let the slave answer the question to them. Let one who had felt in his own person the evils of slavery—let the mark of the slave-driver's lash on his own back tell them what it was (applause)" (*Frederick Douglass Papers* 134). With such remarks, he made the link between these props and his own body, using it as another prop in his performance. A prop can be taken up and put aside by the performer. Douglass represented his body similarly, pointing to it as physical evidence yet ready to render it figurative if necessary.

As a lecturer, then, Douglass presented a knowledge born of bodily experience, displaying an authenticity that even his statement of names and places in his *Narrative* did not evoke. Apparently, this impressed his audiences. A British abolitionist, Lucy Browne, reported to the American Maria Chapman that his claims carry "double weight, since drawn from his own painful experiences: no Englishman however gifted could call forth the same kind of enthusiasm" (*Frederick Douglass Papers* lv). An Irish abolitionist, Isabel Jennings, reported that

> we think we have got contributions from persons belonging to the Church (of England) who never could have been influenced except by a person who had himself suffered ... They have got our old anti-slavery papers and are determined to understand the subject ... they say, "Mr. Douglass said so and so—his authority is given—and who can know better than he?" (*Frederick Douglass Papers* lv)

Douglass made these claims of authenticity during a transitional period in public understandings of identity and performance. Baxter argues that what it meant to be "authentic" at this period in Anglo-American culture was shifting toward a more performance-based model. Whereas traditional rhetorical effectiveness was established in part through a speaker's social position, the nineteenth century was prepared to imagine that speakers could be "authentic" even if they had no such social position—so long, that is, as they were speaking "from the heart," even if that heart seemed to shift from moment to moment, speech to speech. Baxter points to Douglass's occasional losses of temper, denunciations of Christianity, and confessions of his own cowardice or bad judgment as evidence for this shift in audience acceptance. Ultimately,

> Douglass earns the modern critic's trust in roughly the same way he established ethos with any audience. He always seems ready to be merely speaking from his heart, detesting slavery in no small part because of his own hurtful experiences. He gives his immediate audience and us, as an extended audience, the strong impression that he is being entirely transparent. (Baxter 23)

Likewise, Clark and Halloran have shown a parallel shift in rhetorical culture, away from a time when a speaker's position was grounded in culture and community consensus. Rather, the source of authority became focused in the individual speaker. Clark and Halloran argue that "oratorical culture ... was transformed by an emerging individualistic spirit that, in diverse social and institutional forms, challenged the traditional principle of collective moral authority by establishing as a new principle the moral authority of the individual" (3). It is a shift, in other words, away from the importance of the "character" of the speaker, authorized by the community and based on a stable characterization of the speaker, to the importance of the "personality" of the speaker. Baxter, whose *Frederick Douglass's Curious Audiences* treats Douglass himself as the transitional figure in this shift, argues that "personality" was based on an individual's appeal, even if he lacked appropriate background: "When Enlightenment ideals met Jacksonian politics, audiences were willing to listen to speakers of questionable character who had powerful personality" (123).

Part of this authenticity of personality was derived, for Douglass, from the oft-mentioned scars on his back. Unlike representation in a printed text, this speaker himself was the evidence of his claims, human evidence—living, changeable. Within this context, Douglass didn't use his scars as a stamp of finality on how the audience must regard him, despite their being "stamped" on his body. He never did, as far as the record shows, exhibit the scars. Why not? Perhaps they emphasized his authenticity too well. In performance, he could make reference to the scars, claiming authenticity without opening himself up to an objectification which would suggest a more essential identity—a slave, and only a slave. Indeed, Douglass's body has duel signification. He presents it as both visually present and elusive; the unexhibited marks on his back become symbolic and textual even though they are also real reminders of the body of the slave.

For Douglass, now safely out of the United States, the body contained a double meaning: the inescapable record of his prior experience *and* proof that a former slave could be "self-made" into whatever he wanted. In *My Bondage and My Freedom*, he describes the beginning of his lecturing career with emphasis on its simultaneously prospective and retrospective character: "Here opened upon me a new life—a life for which I had had no preparation. I was a 'graduate from the peculiar institution,' Mr. Collins used to say, when introducing me, '*with my diploma written on my back!*'" (214). The academic metaphor is telling. Douglass's claim to have scars on his back, made again and again on the platform in England, accomplished several things: On the one hand, the emphasis on the body was his expression of the imminent danger in which he found himself—he thematized it, exploited it, made it a reality for audiences. On the other, the fact that he never showed his back with scars on it—only offered to—suggests that Douglass didn't limit himself to this "inscribed" proof of his hard-won authenticity but, rather, used it as a tool of performative identity. Douglass's scars were, then, at least in part, a trope for escaping mere biography, not just authenticating it. He wasn't the only author to see the potential of embodied performance in this way.

Indeed, Douglass thematized performance in his lectures, showing a faith in the invention of identity, the self-made man. Performance was a site of agency, as it could be for many authors, in the face of a history that scarred the body. Douglass performed a shifting identity, suggesting that the same body that bore the marks of slavery was also capable of telling that story on the lecture platform or telling other stories, enacting other identities. His standard speech included his famous material self-presentation: "I stand before you with the marks of the slave-driver's whip, that will go down with me to my grave" (*Frederick Douglass*

Papers 41). The same speech goes on to show he can play many roles by imitating a "slave" voice: "And such is the ignorance in which the slaves are held that some of them go home and say, 'Me hear good sermon to day, de Minister make ebery thing so clear, white man above a Nigger any day' (roars of laughter)" (*Frederick Douglass Papers* 43). Douglass claimed both his identification with slaves and his separateness from them here, touting his scars but showing he must "play" a slave and certainly calling attention to the difference between his own speaking style and the one he imitates. Imitation is another performance of the malleability of identity—to us, as critics familiar with the concept, and to an audience that was beginning to accept inconsistencies on the platform.

Perhaps the most poignant analysis of Douglass's liberating performance comes from the author himself in *My Bondage and My Freedom*. When he writes about his beginnings as a speaker leading up to his trip abroad, he discusses his employers' advice in the Anti-Slavery Society:

> "Give us the facts," said Collins, "we will take care of the philosophy" …. I could not always obey, for I was now reading and thinking. New views of the subject were presented to my mind. It did not entirely satisfy me to *narrate* wrongs; I felt like *denouncing* them … "People won't believe you ever were a slave, Frederick, if you keep on this way," said Friend Foster. "Be yourself," said Collins, "and tell your story." It was said to me, "Better have a *little* of the plantation manner of speech than not; 'tis not best that you seem too learned." These excellent friends were actuated by the best of motives, and were not altogether wrong in their advice; and still I must speak just the word that seemed to *me* the word to be spoken by *me*. (215–6)

Douglass is protesting objectification at the hands of his allies here, and not without cause. As McBride has pointed out, "the slave serves as a kind of fulfillment of the prophecy of abolitionist discourse. The slave is the 'real' body, the 'real' evidence, the 'real' fulfillment of what has been told before" (5). But Douglass would not simply be that evidence, fill that defined role. He used the body and laid claim to a freedom of expression (including "theorizing" on slavery), figuring public speaking as an embodied *and* intellectual endeavor. Douglass also stated a faith in the immediacy and changeability of identity on the speaker's platform. He would say what, at the moment, seemed to represent his identity.

Douglass's embrace of performance as an avenue to "freedom," as he put it, was accompanied by suspicion, then, of how audiences might read such performances, what preconceptions they already possessed, what expectations they held. Like all authors who lectured transatlantically, he had, ultimately, mixed feelings about such performances. So while Douglass's experience was unique compared to many of the other authors in the project, his story serves as an introductory case study, dramatizing commonalities for all lecturing performers. And in this sense he is "representative," not just of "three million slaves" as he said, but of authors who undertook similar tours. In fact, he encapsulates the paradox of the performing author, which is to say the lecture is both an embodied endeavor that should focus our attention on the individual author and an artificial gesture outward, in which the author performs a public, reproducible, sometimes representative version of him or herself. This basic paradox remained true for any author who chose to not just write, but speak, for his or her public.

The following chapters explore this paradox, and others, proceeding through the experiences of several British and American authors. These chapters are not meant to be an exhaustive study of each author's biography during his or her stay in the visited country. Instead, I have chosen to pair authors with a fellow country person or with a mirroring foreign author (with the exception of Henry James, whose iconoclastic national affiliation deserves its own chapter) in order to examine some issue or aspect of the lecture tour experience. This selection of authors is necessarily exclusionary. Not all the authors who lectured transatlantically make their way into this study. I have instead chosen authors—both British and American—whose experiences highlight a particular issue within the lecture tour experience. Two early American authors who traveled to lecture transatlantically are not included: Washington Irving and Artemus Ward were successful American humorists traveling in England in the first half of the century; I included Mark Twain, who was heavily influenced by both, instead. Ralph Waldo Emerson was an early, important transatlantic lecturer, and yet other early lecturers such as Frederick Douglass and Harriet Martineau seem to me to offer more compelling narratives for the issues of performance and embodiment in early nineteenth-century culture that are at the center of the study. Trollope's and Thackeray's experiences were similar enough to and less compelling than that of Charles Dickens.

I have moved roughly in chronological order, tracking nineteenth-century authorship from its broadly defined, often political, early incarnation in the early-to-mid part of the century to the full-scale celebratory, commercial, and more strictly literary form found later in the century. The result is that the first part of the study focuses more tightly on the political nature of authorial identity, while the majority deals more fully with the marketplace of celebrity culture and mass production. Chapter 1 looks at two women traveling abroad in the context of abolitionist discourse in the 1830s and 1850s—Harriet Martineau and Harriet Beecher Stowe—both of whom negotiated the tension between celebrity authorship and the cultural repugnance at women speaking publicly in very different ways. From there, I turn in two chapters to the relationship between transatlantic lecture tours and the literary marketplace: first, I look at the wildly successful lecture tours of Charles Dickens and Mark Twain in relation to their mutual fight to control their work from unauthorized publishing abroad; next, I examine the uses and abuses of British celebrity identity in the American marketplace, using the tours of Oscar Wilde and Matthew Arnold as case studies. I finish with James's skeptical authorial performance at the beginning of the twentieth century, a mournful and exclusionary account of public authorship as it looked to him at the dawn of modernism. James would evince a concern over the nature of celebrity authorship in 1904, 100 years before John Updike would do the same. The intervening century, it seems, did little to settle the questions about authorship and performance that the transatlantic lecture tour had raised.

Chapter 1
Seen and Not Heard:
The Transatlantic Tours of Harriet Martineau and Harriet Beecher Stowe

On May 7, 1853, Harriet Beecher Stowe, in the midst of her European tour, addressed a group of ladies at Stafford House, the London home of the Duchess of Sutherland. It was one of the few times she would speak (semi-) publicly about slavery, a subject to which her name was so publicly bound. As various papers reprinted parts of her address, they also signaled ambiguity, if not outright hostility, toward anti-slavery meetings run by women. But an anonymous writer for the *London Daily News* expressed support for the Stafford House meeting, writing, "Slavery is a subject about which women may and should speak and act as freely as men, and if men do not speak and act as freely as they ought, women are quite right to choose their own method of expressing their own protest, individual or collective." We know now that the anonymous writer was in fact Harriet Martineau, 51 years old and a veteran of both the political scene and the cultural hostility toward women who ventured to be a part of it.

Public speech was a right Martineau was at special pains to point out. But in her article she emphasizes two other elements about Stowe's tour of England that are worth noting. Martineau distinguishes Stowe from other "celebrities," a category Martineau herself detested and with which she resisted identification. Unlike celebrities, who selfishly encourage idol worship, "[Mrs. Stowe] is no wonderful new novelist, whose pictures of the sufferings of the heart provoke and tempt an inquisition in the personal experience of the idol of the season" (Martineau, "London"). Instead, Stowe is selflessly devoted to the cause—a martyr, a role Martineau consistently saw as the very opposite of a celebrity. Finally, according to Martineau, while Stowe is no idol, she (and her reception) is something of a symbol of England's role in the anti-slavery movement. Martineau calls Stowe, who had been harshly ridiculed at home, "the embodied rebuke of the lovers of freedom and the advocates of popular government, addressed to the brethren of whom they have hoped, and still hope, so much." For Martineau, then, Stowe is a kind of icon, representing transatlantic involvement in abolitionism.

Martineau's article in the *London Daily News* brings together several key historical realities of which Stowe's trip to England and her single address were a part. First, that political and literary culture by the mid-nineteenth century was at least in part transatlantic. After all, Martineau's *Illustrations of Political Economy* had been widely read in America, and Stowe's *Uncle Tom's Cabin* broke records in England. This international fame meant not only the movement of texts across the ocean but also, because of the extended reach of fame, the movement of bodies in the form of visiting literary celebrities. Second, women writers entertained a strained relationship with the role of "literary lion," or celebrity, no matter how many books they sold nationally or internationally, largely because of the conflicting expectations of respectable women and public personalities. Finally, this transatlantic celebrity culture was more and more dependent on authors not only visiting their international audiences but also appearing in public and, often, speaking. Thus Martineau's primary claim about Stowe—that women should speak out—was the most necessary and controversial to make. It was also, perhaps, the one which evoked the most visceral memories in its author.

Resistance to women's right to speak publicly was something with which Martineau was painfully familiar. Nearly 20 years before Stowe's address at Stafford House, Martineau had had a similar experience abroad, in Boston, speaking to the local ladies' anti-slavery group. The resistance and threats of violence that followed her transatlantic address would reach dangerous extremes for three reasons: the hyper-sensitivity of Americans to the issue, her status as a deaf author, and the fact that Martineau negotiated her status as a public woman and literary celebrity in less acceptable ways than did Stowe.

Indeed, while the two women had very similar lecture experiences, each speaking once to a ladies' anti-slavery group, their handling—or performance—of the contradictory roles of transatlantic celebrity and respectable woman writer differed greatly. It is helpful here to consider Richard Schechner's foundational definition of performance as "a broad spectrum of activities" outside traditional performance, such as a public speech (7). Taking this "broad spectrum approach," the experience of these two women highlights how authorial performance wasn't limited to the stage. While the two women's formal public speeches formed a key moment in their transatlantic experience, this kind of performance was so minimal that it is the other kind of performance—the performance of everyday life, of gender, of authorship, of celebrity and, especially, of silence—that actually shapes their lectures' meaning.

Their speeches, taking place in 1835 and 1853, were only part of the story. While this is true of all authors who performed, because these two were women and because a woman performing was already a contested act, Stowe and Martineau's experiences highlight authorial speech and authorial identity as a site of anxiety. As Frederick Douglass demonstrated, performance could avail a talented and savvy performer the chance to subvert or exploit social prejudices against a speaker, and Stowe, in her way, found ways to balance her one formal performance with an informal (or broad-spectrum) performance style that generally set public minds at rest. In fact, she performed public "silence" brilliantly. Martineau, ever the idealist, did not balance her lecture with culturally appropriate behavior, and she suffered a scathing public reaction as a result. Neither author conducted, in the strict sense, lecture tours, but they help clarify the limits of the availability of such tours. It remains clear that British and American women writers would be asked, as part of the transatlantic celebrity culture, to travel abroad and appear in public. They could not, as Martineau found, speak in public the same things they had written. In a century that saw male authors as varied as Frederick Douglass and Matthew Arnold, Washington Irving and Oscar Wilde engage in just such performances, we can see that nineteenth-century's women's authorship, already a site of deep anxiety, was further complicated by the need to negotiate speaking in person as well as in print.

Literary Lionesses

Both Martineau and Stowe conducted their careers during a period when the woman writer's role was being redefined against a host of social changes. Their literary careers surrounding the specific incidents of speech (or lack of) are, then, performances in themselves; they are shows that were acted out in publication of books, in periodical writing, in writing about them, in travels, in caricatures in the *London Times*, and in the much-fabled comment from President Lincoln blaming (or crediting) Stowe for the Civil War. Before getting to the formal speeches themselves, I want to look at a few elements of these complicated career performances.

Celebrity status for women challenged two nineteenth-century norms: because celebrity status turned the eyes of the culture onto the author, instead of the other way around, it challenged such an author's claim to objective observation, a nineteenth-century prerequisite to all good authorship, but especially to the author of political writing and travel writing. Second, celebrity status assumed a public persona, and for women who were encouraged to exist in a "private" sphere, this posed a problem. For Martineau, whose work sometimes protested against the simple binary of objective, rational male thinking and subjective, emotional female thinking, being a "literary lioness" meant losing her objective "observer status," in fact pushing her toward embodying the derided stereotype of women. For Stowe, being a public celebrity risked exposing the inherent contradiction in her own career, one built on the publication of a political book she worked hard to cast as the emotional outburst of a Christian woman, mother, and wife, happy to exist in the private sphere.

Both women would confront these two issues throughout their career, but the highlight of their international celebrity status—their trips abroad—would bring these conflicts to a head, in part because it engendered a third challenge to the norm, as women left their "domestic" nations to become foreigners in a more "public" international scene. In fact, the Victorian interest in women's proper spheres can be mapped onto the national and international arena. As Janet C. Myers shows in her study of "portable domesticity," for example, women travelers were using the language of home even as they left it. In other words, the public/private or domestic/foreign spheres were concepts applicable to an individual's home and her country. The transatlantic travel of women, then, seems to have been an affront to a nationalized domesticity. While host countries, especially the

United States, would often tell a presumptuously vocal foreigner to "go home," the gusto and malevolence with which Americans told Martineau to leave suggests a gendered subtext. For both women, celebrity authorship, and especially that which required the public presence of their private persons, put pressure on the delicate performance of both respectable womanhood and public authorship in which they were engaging. In terms of their careers, their performance of a woman's public authorship differed significantly. While Martineau would be more explicit in her challenge of accepted ideas about gender, Stowe would generally exploit those ideas by seeming to adhere to them. The stress surrounding their celebrity as well as their individual speeches, then, was distinct.

Critics have long been interested in Martineau's construction of her public image; she is often understood as adopting a male perspective in her writing, especially with regard to an uncomplicated faith in the promise of objectivity.[1] While most admit Martineau's formidable intellectual presence, some critics have read this faith as submissive to patriarchal ideas, with devastating consequences to her health and mental balance.[2] The removal of the personal, of the egotistical, is something Martineau at times explicitly condoned, no doubt encouraged by the fact that women writers were generally understood to write with inferior "objectivity," fit for the emotionality of domestic fiction but not for "objective" sociological or political writing. Martineau's extensive anonymous periodical writing was one way to avoid such censure. Alexis Easley points out that because "famous women authors were often held accountable to confining definitions of 'female authorship,' which constrained their choice of subject matter and exposed their personal lives to public scrutiny," some of them turned to the tradition of periodical anonymity ("Victorian Women Writers" 1). Writing for magazines or newspapers provided a way to subvert the prejudice against women writing on certain subjects and to protect their personal, respectable, identities. Anonymity enabled Martineau to write with the tone of objectivity. In fact, it was this commitment to "objectivity" that would sour her on celebrity, a status which challenged an author's ability to remain an objective observer.

More recently, Susan F. Bohrer has warned against reproducing such nineteenth-century binaries as objective/subjective, public/private, or agent/victim, challenging readings that locate Martineau on one side or the other of such equations in her rhetorical self-identification. Bohrer argues that Martineau subtly refused to accept the critical designation of the "masculinity" of her mind, instead seeing her deafness and femininity as creating a unique position of authority. Martineau's claim in *Society in America*, for example, is that femininity allows her access to places in the domestic sphere where men couldn't go. As

---

[1]   Portions of this chapter were earlier published as "'Recognized by My Trumpet': Celebrity and/as Disability in Harriet Martineau's Transatlantic Tour in *Symbiosis: A Journal of Anglo-American Literary Relations.*

[2]   See Smith, *A Poetics of Women's Autobiography*, and David, *Intellectual Women and Victorian Patriarchy: Harriet Martineau, Elizabeth Barrett Browning, George Eliot.*

Martineau argues in her introduction to that work, "I am sure, I have seen much more of domestic life than could possibly have been exhibited to any gentleman travelling through the country. The nursery, the boudoir, the kitchen, are all excellent schools in which to learn the morals and manners of a people: and, as for public and professional affairs,—those may always gain full information upon such matters, who really feel an interest in them,—be they men or women" (53). Bohrer argues that this "pattern of discerning truths through scenes of domestic life ... [of finding] the embodiment of truth within the example ... pervades Martineau's work and reshapes the meaning of her autobiographical texts as well as her political and social commentaries" (23). Indeed, Martineau appears, in this account, to argue not for her exceptionality in possessing a "masculine" mind capable of sociological writing but to destabilize the binary by arriving at objective political or sociological truth through personal, subjective experience.

Martineau's delicate negotiation of gender would be the focus of much of the criticism surrounding her work; she also negotiated a similar and related authorial identity as a deaf author, another point of focus for her critics. Indeed, most of Martineau's career is punctuated by attacks that center around her gender and deafness. It was easy for nineteenth-century critics to conflate the two, as Bohrer points out, because derisive stereotypes of both groups share similarities. Like women, the deaf were seen as incapable of abstract thought due to a dependency on sign language. To some nineteenth-century critics, every concrete sign had direct correlation to an object—making the deaf, in this view, unable to capture an abstraction. Rosemarie Garland Thomson has likewise noted that "Femininity and disability are inextricably entangled in patriarchal culture," evidenced, in part, by a common "equation of women with disabled men" (27). "The little deaf woman from Norwich," as Martineau was called, who carried a trumpet into which others could speak, had, in the eyes of her contemporaries, two visible disqualifications from authorship on "objective" political economy.

A sampling of contemporary criticism of Martineau reveals this bias. The redoubtable John Wilson Croker from the *Quarterly Review* wrote a now-notorious review of Martineau's *Illustrations of Political Economy*. After announcing his intention to "tomahawk Miss Martineau" (qtd. in Logan 16), Croker proceeded to criticize her principles of political economy and population control by attacking her inexperience, meaning in part her transgression of gender norms, which were exacerbated by the fact that she was a single woman writing about reproduction. He writes, "it is quite impossible not to be shocked, nay disgusted, with many of the unfeminine and mischievous doctrines ... of which these tales are made the vehicle" (Review of *Illustrations* 136). Another review mocked Martineau's gender as well: "Still the wonder grew/How one small head could carry all *she* knew" (qtd. in Logan 91). Not unusually, Martineau's head, her body, becomes an object of dissection as well as hostile criticism: "The exceptional woman, she figures forth an outrageous body, her abilities disproportionate to the brain she's allocated" (Bohrer 24).

In response to *Society in America*, published after her return from her American voyage, a defender of slavery wrote an essay faulting her inability to "hear" the truth about the society she claimed to observe: "she gets nothing from her hearer, for she does not hear him … That she has never listened while in America, is evident from these volumes; though I doubt not that a great many words have gone through her trumpet" (qtd. in Logan 95). Croker, in a later review of *How to Observe Morals and Manners*, wonders how she could argue that deaf and blind travelers have superior powers of observation, noting that she is "stone *deaf* [and] we cannot but wonder where Miss Martineau has collected all this valuable information" ("Miss Martineau's *Morals and Manners*" 65). Martineau herself recalled that after the publication of *Society in America*, she received "envelopes, made heavy by all manner of devices, with a slip of newspaper in the middle, containing prose paragraphs, or copies of verses, full of insults, and particularly of taunts about my deafness" (*Autobiography* 2:57). She was not exaggerating, as a review in *The Southern Literary Journal and Magazine of Arts* exhibits: "Miss Martineau is a lady of great observation. 'She is all eyes,' and we are sorry to say, that she is not 'all ears,' too. But unfortunately, Miss Martineau is troubled with deafness, and this deafness is the source of many errors" (Review of *Society in America* 568).

Despite these myriad criticisms of a deaf woman entering into the field of political economy or "objective" travel writing, Martineau had written about one of the most controversial political subjects—slavery—even before she spoke about it in the United States. In "Demerara" (1832), one of the *Illustrations*, her abolitionist sentiments are clear. As she states in recollection, "Every body who knew any thing about me at all, at home or in America, knew that from the spring of 1832 I was completely committed against slavery" (*Autobiography* 2:9). She adds, "I was a well-known anti-slavery writer before I thought of going to America; and my desire to see the operation of the system of Slavery should hardly be wrongly interpreted by anyone who took an interest in my proceedings" (*Autobiography* 2:17). Still, while Martineau did state in recollection an acknowledgment that she was already opposed to slavery, she was not yet an "abolitionist" when she came to America. In fact, she wished to see the institutions of America for herself — putting her faith in empiricism and fairness to the test. Apparently her American hosts held the same faith in empirical observation. Southerners eagerly offered to host the published anti-slavery advocate, hoping to change her mind.

Martineau's belief in her own ability to faithfully observe the visited country, as well as the customs of her own country, was challenged, however, as she dealt with her celebrity status. In fact, the visiting, in-person Martineau would deal with different expectations than her books had. While she was greatly admired as an author, her arrival in America in 1834 betrayed a more conflicted public acceptance of her authorship. On the ship carrying her to America, she learned that the captain of the ship took an interest in her expressed—not published—opinions. He questioned one of Martineau's fellow passengers about her statements on board. The informant reported that "I was opposed to slavery; but that I had been more than once heard to say on board, when questioned about my opinion of American institutions, that I went to learn, and not to teach … [The captain] avowed that if he had been less well satisfied, he should not have ventured to put me ashore" (*Autobiography* 2:11). Similarly, Martineau's openness to interracial relationships in "Demerara" caused less of a stir than her stating them orally to a hostess: "I was specifically informed of imprisonments for opinions the same as are found in 'Demerara'; which indeed might well be under the laws of South Carolina, as I found them in full operation. Hints were offered of strangers with my views not being allowed to come out alive." After hearing this, Martineau wrote to a friend and "requested that my letter might be kept in evidence of my never returning" (*Autobiography* 2:19).

Southern hosts who wished to have a favorable account of slavery written by the famed authoress had much at stake, but so did Martineau. In the face of so much encoded resistance to a deaf woman's involvement in political and travel writing, and considering her long, fraught negotiation of ideas of objectivity and authority, it is no wonder that she eyed celebrity and the public performance that celebrity entailed with deep suspicion. For Martineau, who was part literary lion and part transgressor at home, was highly anticipated as a strange spectacle upon her arrival. American curiosity was captured by one writer in a poem for the *Southern Literary Messenger*. How would it be, this author wonders, to meet this authorial rarity in the flesh?

> When Martineau came, I was curious to see
> What sort of body the damsel might be:
> A writer of sensible stories, I knew,
> On labor and wages; but was she a *blue*?
> Was she grave as a judge? Did she talk like a book?
> (A sort of man-woman), and how did she look?
> So I waited upon her, and, venturing near,
> I whispered some words in her ivory ear;
> When she broke forth at once in her voluble chat,
> And talked away freely of this and of that,
> With such feminine ease, and such masculine sense,
> Without any portion of pride or pretense;
> (*Illustrating* all that she said with a smile,
> That showed she could charm if she thought it worthwhile);
> That I dub her, you see, 'an agreeable dame,
> And worthy of Hymen, as well as of Fame.' ("Lines: On Miss Martineau" 319)

The "man-woman" with her "ivory ear" (ivory being one material used for an ear trumpet), appears in these lines as benevolently monstrous on three levels: her gender, her deafness, and her fame all figure her as extraordinary, though in this case, acceptable. While jabs at being a spinster, a bluestocking, and a masculine woman raise the question of her fitness for womanhood and celebrity authorship, her "charm" renders her "worthy." Despite this author's highly problematic characterization, his noting of her fame as partly monstrous does accord with Martineau's own sense of it; she would often write about it as far more disabling than her deafness.

Thomson's work in Disability Studies can help explain why celebrity might be so uncomfortable to Martineau and other nineteenth-century authors. Thomson has noted that in his hailing of individualism, Ralph Waldo Emerson used contrasting images of otherness, including the "invalid" to make his point: "[Those extraordinary bodies] Emerson enlists to define the liberal individual by opposition are, above all else, icons of bodily vulnerability. The invalid body is impotence made manifest" (42). This impotence would be felt by most nineteenth-century celebrities who no doubt embraced Emerson's ideal, not just those whose bodies formed a challenge to it. Celebrity would come to mean, for some, a loss of agency and a sense of public vulnerability.

Martineau's personal relationship with celebrity was even more complicated. One characteristic she associated with celebrity was vanity—a characteristic long associated with women and the deaf as well. A lifelong opponent of the literary lionism she saw around her, Martineau urged authors, especially women, to escape the personal. As Easley puts it, "rather than viewing authorship as an egotistical process of asserting her own individuality, she saw herself as an instrument of social progress" ("Victorian Women Writers" 36). Martineau was frustrated when her lion-status disabled her ability to observe and interact with people in private homes to which she was invited. She later wrote that "The prominent features [of such visits] are the sufferings" of the celebrity, and "the selfishness of all the rest. They are too much engrossed with excitement of their own vanity and curiosity to heed the pain they are inflicting on one who ... can hardly enjoy being told that children cannot be interesting to her, and that young people do not wish to speak to her" (*Autobiography* 1:277–8).

What is fascinating is that Martineau sees celebrity as a far greater hurdle to good authorship than that which others claimed was her greatest liability— her deafness. In *Society in America*, recounting her trip, she acknowledges that "there is no estimating the loss, in a foreign country, from not hearing the casual conversation of all kinds of people, in the streets, stages, hotels, &c." and yet she argues that

> This does not endanger the accuracy of my information, I believe, as far as it goes; because I carry a trumpet of remarkable fidelity; an instrument, moreover, which seems to exert some winning power, by which I gain more in *tête-à-têtes* than is given to people who hear general conversation. Probably its charm consists in the new feeling which it imparts of ease and privacy in conversing with a deaf person. However this may be, I can hardly imagine fuller revelations to be made in household intercourse than my trumpet brought to me. (54)

For Martineau, celebrity, which made people afraid to speak to her and reduced her to her trumpet (a device she saw as indispensably practical and helpful, not reductionistic), was the only aspect of her person which fundamentally limited her access and her observation.

Her one public speech, given in Boston, which I'll come to later, was a moment of crisis for her conception of the public author: in addition to placing her in the middle of an already heated debate, public embodiment and public exposure crystallized the tension between the involved, subjective author who spoke and a removed, objective observer who had the authority to write. For Martineau, the stakes were even higher than was the case for other lecturers since subjective, personal authorship was derisively associated with female authorship. Up until the speech to the Boston Female Anti-slavery society, Martineau had maintained a neutral authorial position as an objective observer. The invitation to speak in Boston, she recalls, signaled a distinct change: "The moment of reading this note was one of the most painful in my life. I felt I could never be happy again if I refused what was asked of me: but, to comply was probably to shut against me every door but those of the abolitionists. I should no more see persons and things as they ordinarily were" (*Autobiography* 2:30). To Martineau, then, no publicly recognized figure could be a wholly objective observer. The speaker she was forced to become compromised her outsider vantage point; in her discussion of these events, she saw these roles as mutually exclusive. One was either an observer, an objective collector of impressions and judgments, or, one was an actor being observed. She felt that the speech was essential to the abolitionist cause; still, it meant the sacrifice of objective authorship. Speech, then, led to an intensification of Martineau's celebrity status. Celebrity meant both that her person rather than her work would become the focus of attention and that her public persona was less and less under her control as it was constructed in media accounts. Both of these results—objectification and mass reproduction—placed her in a passive role. And both made her uncomfortable.[3]

Indeed, her criticism of Boston society after her public speech contains a critique of public adoration and rejection of the celebrity figure she had become:

> I saw nothing of Boston society ... I am told that many people who were panic-stricken during that reign of terror are heartily ashamed now of their treatment of me. I should be glad if they were yet more ashamed of the flatteries and worship with which the Americans received and entertained me, till I went to that meeting. The "enthusiasm" of which they boasted, and which, I hereby declare, and my companion can testify, was always distasteful to me, collapsed instantly when I differed publicly from them on a sore point: and their homage was proved to be, like all such idolatries, a worship of the ideal, and no more related to myself, in fact, than to the heroine of a dream. (*Autobiography* 2:37)

---

[3] Martineau's complicated relationship with celebrity continues to be examined. Alexis Easley has read Martineau's *Autobiography* in conjunction with her other 1850s work, *The History of England during the Thirty Years' Peace*. Easley argues that "in the *Autobiography*, she reinserted her own life history into the broader narrative of national progress," thus balancing "her claim to historical objectivity with an assertion of her own historical significance as a literary celebrity and social reformer" (*Literary Celebrity* 96–7). Such a reading bears on Martineau's lifelong negotiation of the expectation of objectivity and reminds us that Martineau's *Autobiography*, like all texts, constructs as much as it reveals.

Martineau communicates a frustration many authors shared—a sense that public adoration was fickle and, worse, that it encouraged vanity rather than personal responsibility. But like it or not, the role of celebrity was one Martineau had to play.

And it was one that Harriet Beecher Stowe, arriving in person on the British public scene in 1853, played very differently. Stowe's discursive framing of her authorship and her womanhood has fascinated scholars for some time. Joan Hedrick's exhaustive biography suggests that in writing *Uncle Tom's Cabin*, "[Stowe's] very conventionality, her insistence on the forms of 'true womanhood,' was her armor in the battle to transform the meaning of the term ... [her wife and mother status] gave her some latitude in following out the implications of unconventional ideas ..." (232). She goes on to credit Stowe with fundamentally changing the way public and private issues were framed so that by the time she was finished, "true womanhood and social revolution now marched hand in hand" (232). Indeed, Stowe would differ from Martineau in her performance of female authorship: while the unmarried Martineau equivocated on what it meant to be female and an author, shuttling between claiming an exceptional "masculine" mind and claiming a different, superior authority through her feminine insight, Stowe unequivocally claimed her authority through her position as a traditional mother, wife, and Christian—all acceptable, and private, roles for a woman to play. At the time of Stowe's visit to England, Martineau played up this aspect of Stowe's persona in her article written for the *London Daily Times* and referenced at the beginning of this chapter. Ted Hovet, Jr., writes that Martineau does this by arguing "that Stowe's position as an author was 'involuntary' and that her novel tells the truth" (Hovet 69). The two women were defining female authorship in a political context during a period of debate "over the public involvement of women in the cause" of abolitionism (Hovet 69). Still, as Caroline Field Levander shows, while "Women began attempting to intervene in this historically male arena of US politics in the 1830s ... women's political activism relied on the power accruing to domesticity and so failed to challenge overtly the masculinity of the nineteenth-century political arena" (Levander 13). In this context, Stowe's approach caused comparatively less backlash.

Her framing of the issue of slavery in moral terms in *Uncle Tom's Cabin* was perhaps her most important contribution, and it also set the debate over slavery on ground shared by women and men, in that she constructed the issue as not political (a province of masculinity) but moral. Indeed, in her direct addresses to the reader, Stowe appeals to the sentiments of mothers and Christians more often than she appeals to abstract concepts of freedom. For example, the early scene in which Eliza runs with her son away from the slave catchers, she asks the reader, "If it were *your* Harry, mother, or your Willie, that were going to be torn from you by a brutal trader ... how fast could *you* walk?" (50). Similarly, during a debate over the Fugitive Slave Law between the Senator and Mrs. Bird, Senator Bird makes a point about political compromise, to which his wife replies, "I don't know anything about politics, but I can read my Bible; and there I see that I must feed the hungry and clothe the naked, and comfort the desolate" (79). The radical result, as Amanda Claybaugh has recently written, is that in her novel, Stowe "does not dispute the presumption that the public sphere is properly masculine. Instead, she redefines public questions as domestic ones and thereby claims them as her own" (Claybaugh, Introduction xx). This strategy would play out again in her public performance as a celebrity author.

After publication, as she dealt with the celebrity her book brought, she continued to obscure the political nature of her novel. In a much-quoted letter to Lord Denman just before her visit abroad, Stowe writes that she is "incredulous" over the flattery for her novel. She figures herself as a non-agent in the writing of the book, saying "I can only see that when a Higher Being has purposes to be accomplished, he can make even 'a grain of mustard seed' the means." She goes on to explicitly stake her authorship in the realm of acceptable women's work: "I wrote what I did because as a woman, as a mother I was oppressed & broken-hearted, with the sorrows & injustice I saw, because as a Christian I felt the dishonor to Christianity—because as a lover of my country I trembled at the coming day of wrath." She ends by again denying credit for her work: "It is no merit in the sorrowful that they weep, or to the oppressed & smothering that they gasp & struggle, nor to me, that I *must* speak for the oppressed—who cannot speak for themselves" (qtd. in Hedrick 237). In this, and in other writing, Stowe simultaneously respected traditional gender boundaries and challenged them, even if "unwittingly," as Margaret McFadden has suggested about women's transatlantic work in general. Decidedly apolitical, Stowe entered into two political arenas—race and gender.

As the Stowes traveled to Europe following *Uncle Tom's Cabin*'s publication, her husband's account of the book furthered the image of Harriet having little agency in the production of *Uncle Tom's Cabin*, thus furthering the idea that Stowe's authorship had been "involuntary." During a speech in Glasgow, Stowe, as reported by a journalist, claimed "He could not imagine any book capable of exciting such expressions of attachment; indeed, he was inclined to believe it had not been written at all—he 'spected it grew' [tremendous cheers]. Under the oppression of the fugitive slave law the book had sprung from the soil ready made" (qtd. in Beecher, Introduction xxiv). Calvin Stowe, in the journalist's account, downplays Harriet's authorship, instead figuring the book as a supernatural Athena springing from the head of a Zeus-like political context. Only recently has this account been contradicted. Hedrick's biography and others have rightly recognized the performative nature of both her and her husband's rhetoric on this issue. Rhetorically concealing Stowe's role as author made the book and her public persona easier to accept in both England and America.

If the Stowes' rhetoric about the writing of *Uncle Tom's Cabin* successfully cast Harriet as maintaining her femininity through a miraculous passive creation, there was still the problem of Stowe's public performance as a celebrity, heightened during her trip abroad, where her comings and goings were reported daily and people came to stare at her as she made her way through public locations. Interestingly, while Martineau faced a barrage of criticism, Stowe found the transition much easier, in part because her own rhetoric in and out of the novel had so successfully managed to create a *private* public persona, avoiding the hostility that faced more baldly public women writers like Martineau.

When she arrived in England, Stowe later recalled, she found "quite a crowd on the wharf, and we walked up to our carriage through a long lane of people, bowing, and looking very glad to see us ... They stood very quietly, and looked very kindly, though evidently very much determined to look" (Stowe, *Sunny Memories* 18–19). Proclaiming a modest reservation about the "looking," Stowe would handle the limelight well. An account from the *Manchester Times* gives a similar view, noting that a large group that had gathered to "catch a glimpse of the celebrated novelist was manifested in the jostling and excitement to secure commanding positions on the platform." Despite Stowe's own reservations, the journalist records that she "appeared highly gratified with the warmth of her reception" ("Mrs. Beecher Stowe in Glasgow").

Another journalistic account pits the enthusiasm of the crowd against the modesty of the authoress:

> A rush was then made to the place of landing, and the greatest anxiety was evinced by the dense crowd to catch a glimpse of the popular writer ... Mrs. Stowe, then, closely veiled, walked ashore, leaning on the arm of her husband ... The people, up to this time, managed to suppress their enthusiasm, but when a large portmanteau with the letters "H.B.S." was lifted on top of the car, all doubts as to the identity of the lady were dispelled and loud cheers were given ... Dr. Stowe appeared to be much pleased with the reception given to them, and his wife bowed her acknowledgements at the windows of the car. ("Mrs. Harriet Beecher Stowe in Liverpool")

Banked by her husband, the "veiled" author acknowledges the crowd only through the windows of the car—acting as a kind of second veil—a depiction in keeping with the modesty required of women, even very famous ones.

We see this same balancing of a public author with a private woman again in an account of the author's portraits for sale. Portraits were a fairly common commodity at the time and key to celebrity culture. In her introduction to the collection *Women Writers and the Artifacts of Celebrity in the Long Nineteenth Century*, Maura Ives shows that such celebrity "involved the cultivation of visual images made increasingly ubiquitous through the commercialization of photography and the emergence of the celebrity as icon" (9). Portraits of the famous made the private person a public commodity, precisely the aspect of celebrity culture that could be challenging to a woman writer. However, the account in one Liverpool paper, like the description of Stowe's arrival, manages to counter this threatening publicity: "All of the portraits of Mrs. Stowe that are exhibited in the shop windows are little better than caricatures. Instead of the hard, frigid look which they bear, her countenance wears a soft and gentle expression, quite in accordance with her affable and pleasing manners." In this account, the writer counters the public version of Stowe—and the masculine adjectives that go along with it—with a private "true" version of her, one that highlights traditionally feminine qualities of "softness." This author claims that the "real" Stowe is nothing like this public, celebrity monster. Instead, "No consciousness of her fame ever, by any chance, obtrudes itself … the same simple, genuine naturalness that gave such power to her book belongs in an eminent degree to the character of the author" ("Harriet Beecher Stowe"). The British public readily accepted Harriet Beecher Stowe's (often sincere) public performance of a reluctant celebrity, a public woman who wishes she were not public and whose true character goes against all that this public role calls for.

Still, Charles Beecher's letters home from the trip he took with his sister (gathered later under the title *Harriet Beecher Stowe in Europe*) suggest a more vibrant—and funny—Harriet, even as he continues to construct an image of modesty. He writes, "You would be amused to see how demure Hatty looks when these great folks get to saying their fine things to her. There isn't a grain of art or affection or of anything but just genuine, quiet simplicity with just a dash of fun and a tinge of puzzled feeling in her eye" (*Harriet Beecher Stowe in Europe* 27). Despite this association with the "simple" —one that will be made again and again—Harriet herself, according to Charles, didn't mind the public running to look at her, saying, "I declare, if the people want to look at me, I don't see why they shouldn't" (*Harriet Beecher Stowe in Europe* 27). She was happy to be seen, according to Charles, even as she maintained the "modesty" and femininity that wasn't normally associated with fame.

Stowe's own account of fame in England in her *Sunny Memories in Foreign Lands* likewise gives little account of the public fame she enjoyed—for that we must rely on her brother's account and journalistic accounts. But there are two exceptions: in framing the narrative of her trip, she did include two "fan" scenes in which she was asked for an autograph or asked to "be seen." One was during a visit to Speke Hall in the North, during which time the housekeeper, who was showing them around, "produced her copy of Uncle Tom, and begged the favor of my autograph, which I gave, thinking it quite a happy thing to be able to do a favor at so cheap a rate" (*Sunny Memories of Foreign Travel* 36). Soon after this, at the home of some antislavery sympathizers, "the lady of the house said that the servants were anxious to see me; so I came into the dressing room to give them the opportunity" (Stowe, *Sunny Memories of Foreign Travel* 37). It is notable that both of these incidents, unlike the scene on the wharf during her arrival, take place in domestic settings. Indeed, Stowe's belated construction of what it means to be a famous woman often sounds like something that takes place privately, in the home of friends. She would be similarly careful in her comments on her speaking role.

Speaking Women

This was the context surrounding the speeches the women gave in their visited countries. The speech and, just as important, silence in which both women engaged highlight for the authors, and for us, the difficult part celebrity women writers who were asked to appear publicly would play. Indeed, the very tools of public performance were not available to women.[4] That said, recent critical work has striven to complicate a too-easy dichotomy between the public and private lives of women. The long-held critical acceptance of the nineteenth-century's rhetoric of separate spheres has been called into question, as critics look at the lives of real women and the ways they blurred those boundaries. Simon Morgan, writing on women in the public sphere, argues that ultimately "there can be no simple identification of the ideology of 'separate spheres' with a clear-cut division between 'public' and 'private.' In the face of mounting empirical evidence of women's activities beyond the home, and indeed of the often 'public' functions of the family unit itself, such arbitrary and ill-defined distinctions become increasingly difficult to sustain" (3).

Such attention to the reality of women's speaking lives has led to more complex studies of the way women functioned in the public sphere, especially with regard to their speech. Sandra M. Gustafson's work on oratorical culture points out that women's speech and silence in America was also well established by the time Martineau arrived. Gustafson contends that during Jonathan Edwards's revivals, women were both important conversion narrators and were often "silenced" by the loss of consciousness which became a convention in these oral narratives.[5] But while there was certainly a tradition of silencing women, there was also one of women speaking, particularly in American culture. The reform movements of the early nineteenth century opened up spaces for women's speech. Elizabeth Peabody, a well known reformist, for example, contributed to more than the causes in which she was interested. According to James Perrin Warren, she also created a "gendered theory of language" by identifying "a specific cultural space for its application" (114). Warren also points out that the style of speech differed for those women who would speak. Comparing Margaret Fuller to Ralph Waldo Emerson, James Perrin Warren makes the case that eloquence—the nineteenth-century concept on which his work focuses—took different forms for men and women:

> For both [Emerson and Fuller], eloquence functions as a means of effecting institutional and individual reform, and the reform of culture acts reciprocally upon language ... [However] For Emerson, eloquence takes the form of the secularized sermon—the lecture or address—in which the poet is equally the orator. But for Fuller, as for most women in nineteenth-century America, eloquence develops from the give and take of conversation, not from oracular utterances of a divinely inspired speaker." (Warren 102)

---

[4]   For example, Helen Rogers tells us that male speakers regularly adopted the style of speech and even the dress of other public heroes, but that these "theatrical conventions could not be adopted with ease by the woman reformer, for the female politician and the actress were both associated closely with that other 'public woman,' the prostitute" (10).

[5]   The fact that women like Abigail Hutchinson and Sarah Edwards and others fainted during such speaking opportunities, Gustafson argues, "reflects their internalization of the prohibitions against women's speaking publicly" (58).

If the form of women's speech differed from men, so did the scientific study of it. As Levander has argued, the patriarchal separation of women and men's spheres related to the science of speaking as well, in the form of expert work linguistics:

> [By] highlighting the tone of the female voice, as opposed to its content, and [by] linking that tone to the female body, linguists tried to place women's speech firmly in the private arena. Claiming to have discovered a "natural," socially unconstructed link between the female voice and body, linguists strategically policed women's vocal intervention in political power. (14)

Such thinking offered scientific cover for the traditional identification of women with the body (rather than the mind) and helped to neutralize the potential power of women's speech. Such nuanced readings are key to a complete historical understanding of the context of women's speech. In fact, women could and did speak publicly, at times, yet there is no doubt that they had to operate differently than their male counterparts in the public sphere.

A fictional version of this concern over the growing number of women speaking appeared in the intervening years between Martineau's and Stowe's experiences in 1839, with the publication of Sarah Hale's *The Lecturess; Or, Woman's Sphere*, a book worth briefly examining. The fictional story of Marion Gayland, "one of the handsomest women in the city," follows a young woman's fluctuations between lecturing or political work and marriage (Hale 5). While the narrative articulates all sides of the debate around women's presence in the public and political world, it ultimately teaches the lesson, in as didactic a way as Martineau and Stowe could have done, should they have chosen to, that a woman lecturing is incompatible with the private sphere of wifedom and motherhood, and may even lead to death.[6] The book begins with a debate between the hero, William Forster, and his cousin, Edward Greene, about the propriety of a woman lecturing and, by extension, of the propriety of Edward wanting to marry a woman, Sophia, who befriends a lecturess. William's opposition is broadly painted in reactionary terms. He tells Edward,

> I would sooner listen to a maniac's ravings, for there is some *method* even in a *man's* madness; but when a woman steps from the sphere allotted her by God, and enters upon an office for which she has neither physical nor moral strength, and exposes herself to the gaze and observation of a gaping crowd, we must in charity suppose her laboring under a delusion which it must be painful to a refined mind to witness. (Hale 5–6)

While William will fall in love with Marion, the lecturess, he, and the story itself, will never get over her original vocation or allow her to take it up again. Most of this is founded on the clarity of gendered spheres the subtitle promises. William can't "bear to see a woman unsex herself, and barter the admiration and love

---

[6]   The association of death as a consequence of a woman speaking may seem to be part of Hale's histrionic approach, but as Martineau's experience will show, it actually expressed a potential reality.

which man willingly renders, for a noisy popularity, which degrades when most it seems to exalt her" (Hale 8). In concert with the main male character's disdain for a woman's public speech, the story never does allow us to read the words of Marion when she is actually speaking. Forster asks Marion to marry him with the condition that she will "Lecture no more" (Hale 36). She gives it up, that is, after she has one failed lecture that shakes her confidence. After marriage, she agrees not to even attend lectures given by women.

But Marion is seduced, in a manner, back into political life. While she begs her husband to accompany her, he replies in a way that forcefully reifies the private sphere for women: "I had much rather hear you talk, my love, at our own fireside" (Hale 62). The story ends in their separation and decline in health. Marion, on her deathbed, tells us that "I have been very, very wicked, but ... I repent" (Hale 116). Hale adds that the purpose of telling Marion's story was "to hold up, as a warning to every woman, the folly, the wickedness of a stubborn, unyielding disposition; to show the beauty of a mild and gentle forbearance" (Hale 92). Of course what Marion has been stubborn about is her right to partake in the public sphere, especially to speak there. While Henry James would treat the subject of women lecturers almost 50 years later in *The Bostonians*, this story treats the subject without any of the ambivalence and irony of that later text. It is an unequivocal statement for the times, one which both acknowledges the various opinions on the subject of the period and earnestly retreats from the then-radical notions which were brewing.

The Lecturess demonstrates the stakes for women writers, like Martineau and Stowe, who would be speakers. Their extraordinary experiences likewise demonstrate the tense negotiations required of women lecturers. After all, if women writers' public personas were already tensely performed in print (as evidenced by the anonymity or pen names they frequently adopted), what would it mean to present one's person to the public and even to speak? These speeches would be performances in a strict, semi-formal sense, but they would be accompanied by other performances and rituals, with Martineau and Stowe, their companions, their audiences, both present and virtual, all taking part. The final lesson from both experiences would be that women, however famous and beloved, could be seen but not heard. Any other course of action would be swiftly discouraged.

"Cut My Tongue Out, and So Forth"

Martineau was feted in America under an unspoken condition she didn't speak some of the things she had written. However, in direct response to the request for her to do so, Martineau felt compelled. At a meeting of the Boston Female Anti-Slavery Society in the politically charged Fall of 1835, Martineau received a handwritten note from one of the men guarding the door against a small mob asking if she would address the group. Rising, this is what she said:

> I have been requested by a friend present to say something—if only a word—to express my sympathy in the objects of this meeting. I had supposed that my

presence here would be understood as showing my sympathy with you. But as I am requested to speak, I will say what I have said through the whole South, in every family where I have been; that I consider Slavery as inconsistent with the law of God, and as incompatible with the course of his Providence. I should certainly say no less at the North than at the South concerning this utter abomination—and I now declare that in your *principles* I fully agree. (*Autobiography* 2:31)

With this short declaration, reprinted in newspapers at the time and later in her *Autobiography*, Martineau earned a place in the history not only of abolitionist testimonies but also of British intellectuals who spoke publicly to American audiences. She had stated her opinions in the most modest and qualified way possible—much more so than she did in her published writing, both signed and anonymous. She had, of course, already published materials which betrayed her abolitionist leanings. That said, she also had been suspicious of abolitionists because of the horror stories she had heard about their methods. Though she later fully endorsed Garrisonian methods, in this speech she emphasized her reconciliation with the group's "principles" only. The reaction, once her speech was published and widely circulated, was far from modest or qualified, nor was this a surprise. Her friend and fellow abolitionist, Maria Weston Chapman, said of her speech: "A sublimer act of self-renunciation for the sake of right it had never been my happiness to witness," because Chapman knew it would mean the sacrifice of the country's good will (Chapman). This is largely due to the fact that public response to all women's speech "depend[ed] less on the speakers' specific politics than on the political implications of their physical intrusion into a supposedly male arena" (Levander 14). Claire Kahane agrees: "the figure of the speaking woman had a profoundly unsettling effect on nineteenth-century cultural discourse. By claiming discursive authority and the legitimacy of a public as well as a private voice and performing that claim, the figure of the speaking woman disturbed ... the patriarchal structure of social relations" (ix).

Martineau realized the gravity of her speech act on the ride home, recalling that "On our road home, [Dr Ware, her host] questioned me about the meeting. 'What have you been doing?' he asked. 'Why,' said I, 'I have been speaking.' –'No! you have not!' he exclaimed in alarm" (*Autobiography* 2:32). After a transcript of her statement was leaked to the papers, including the *Liberator*, the broader public read her speech and was outraged.

Some publications' editors condemned Martineau's act as foreign effrontery and dangerous radicalism. An item in the *New York Courier and Enquirer*, reprinted by *The Liberator*, compares Martineau to a snake, perhaps recalling George Cruikshank's notorious illustration of Martineau, seated within a group of people, her serpent-like ear trumpet winding its way around the gathering, listening in. These writers turn that metaphor on Martineau herself, calling on the readers to "remember the fable—no fable as applied to her—of the serpent, who being warmed into life at the fireside of the peasant, displayed its gratitude by stinging his child to death." The author goes on to lament that "The continued and obstinate interference of females in concerns so out of their sphere, has become the disgrace and curse of our country" ("Miss Martineau" 1). By both animalizing Martineau and aligning her with Christian evil, these authors betray a tendency to see the speaking woman, the speaking deaf, as monstrous and uncontrollable. Thomson touches on this general issue, suggesting why a speech by Martineau might offend so deeply: "On the one hand, the disabled figure is a sign for the body that refuses to be governed and cannot carry out the will to self-determination. On the other hand, the extraordinary body is nonconformity incarnate" (44). Like the slaves with which Martineau sympathized, Martineau's own body—especially her speaking body—represented to those around her a refusal to be controlled; they would rush to silence her.

Indeed, what is interesting about the reaction against Martineau's speech in Boston is the marked preoccupation with her body. Her controversial *writings* were met with hostile writing in return (even if they occasionally used the metaphor of physical violence, such as Croker's claim to "tomahawk" her by means of a nasty review). But Martineau's in-person, public speech played catalyst to a different sort of reaction. No longer only a benign, if annoyingly transgressive, writer, the speaking Martineau initiated a period during which her personal life and her physical well-being, rather than her published work, were the target of threatening response. She recounts the reaction in her *Autobiography*:

> From Boston, the abuse of me ran through almost every paper in the Union. Newspapers came to me from the South, daring me to enter the Slave States again, and offering mock invitations to me to come and see how they would treat foreign incendiaries. They would hang me: they would cut my tongue out, and cast it on a dunghill; and so forth. (2:46)

Anti-abolitionists wanted to silence the author: Martineau herself, not her penned persona or her writing, was the focus of the threat. Both the emphasis on Martineau's physical location and the gruesome mention of cutting out her tongue suggests that, again, her body—especially her voice—was the focus of retaliation against an embodied expression. A less violent, if equally pernicious, response is found in the review of *Society in America*, in which the author, after expounding on how deafness makes Martineau ill-fitted for writing, moves on to the specter of Martineau speaking publicly, clearly referring to her American engagement: "She is fond of moralizing on all occasions, and if her hearing had been a little better, would have made an excellent pulpit orator. Persons so deaf that they cannot hear their own voices, make bad speakers" (Review of *Society in America* 568). Again, deafness precludes an author from expression, especially spoken expression.

Following her speech, as she prepared to navigate down that liminal space of the Ohio River—the dividing line between slave state and free state—she was warned that "I was expected down the Ohio in the spring: that certain parties had sworn vengeance against me; and that they had set a watch upon the steamboats, where I should be recognized by my trumpet" (*Autobiography* 2:48). Again, Martineau's body, in this case her deafness, becomes the focus of retaliation for those offended by her speech. The rumor she hears shows how celebrity could work in dangerous ways, as Martineau's notoriety depended on a public association (or reduction) of her name and reputation with her trumpet. Recognition, in Martineau's case, brought danger rather than celebration, as she recalls in her *Autobiography*:

> At Cincinnati, the intention was to prosecute me, if possible; and, at any rate, to prevent my going further. Much worse things were contemplated at the slave-holding city of Louisville ... the people to be feared were not the regular inhabitants of the towns, but the hangers-on at the wharves; and especially the slave-traders ... Mr. Loring said: 'Well, then, I must tell you what they mean to do. They mean to lynch you.' And he proceeded to detail the plan. The intention was to hang me on the wharf before the respectable inhabitants could rescue me. (2:48)

Reacting quickly and decidedly, Martineau began sending back her written work piecemeal to England for protection. She also asked a local clergyman to safeguard her journal. She did not, however, take such care with herself. As she traveled north and months passed, she remained in danger. Martineau maintained that in the South she had been better treated than when she traveled to Boston or in Michigan, betraying surprise that the "free" North should be more vehemently opposed to abolitionist statements. Reporting on her travels in Michigan, she remarks,

> The woods of Michigan were very beautiful; but danger was about us there, as everywhere during those three months of travel. It was out of such glades as those of Michigan that mobs had elsewhere issued to stop the coach, and demand the victim, and inflict the punishment earned by compassion for the negro, and assertion of true republican liberty. I believe there was scarcely a morning during those three months when it was not my first thought on waking whether I should be alive at night." (*Autobiography* 2:55)

The account underscores her position: having spoken publicly, she now traveled as an identifiable figure, objectified as an author and as an "extraordinary body," to use Thomson's phrase. The remarks to the ladies' antislavery group was the only "speech" Martineau gave during her trip, but it was more than enough to bring down a wave of cultural hostility and threatened violence upon her.

"The Still Small Voice"

If Martineau's experiences with public speech were a warning to women writers who might attempt it, Stowe's experience with speech, as well as silence, was a model. Like Martineau, she gave one public address, but rather than define her transatlantic identity, it was eclipsed by other, more acceptable performances. In the private home of the Duchess of Sutherland, Stowe did address some women in a room, separate from the men, including her own husband and brother. Some report of it did leak out, and what we have is, like reports on Martineau's speech, rather conventional and unsurprising. Even more, it was barely considered a "speech" in a formal sense. The *London Daily News* refers to Stowe entering "freely into conversation with her numerous visitors" and speaking about the transatlantic relationship of British and American women. Apparently under the impression— due to published reports—that most American women supported slavery, Stowe, according to this brief report, claimed that "the ladies of England were not at all aware of the real state of feeling of the ladies of America on the subject of slavery." In fact, she maintains, "there was no bitter feeling between the ladies of the two countries but the ladies of America cannot, because of their husbands' personal and political feelings, stand forth and say what they feel on the subject" ("Mrs. H.B. Stowe at Stafford House"). *Reynold's Newspaper*, who critiqued the gathering of women abolitionists on the grounds that it showed hypocritical ignorance of the plight of free but impoverished British laborers (a common complaint), records her remarks as a speech, reporting that "Mrs. Stowe made a speech, —in the course of which she said, 'I have not exaggerated the horrors of slavery: I could not exaggerate them. You in England happily do not know the horrors of slavery'" ("Black Slavery Abroad and White Slavery at Home"). While the paper goes on to cry foul at what they saw as her overstatement, this account does recognize the speech as political.

However, most of the accounts of the speech (and seemingly the speech itself) were designed to deflect away from its political, public nature. Stowe evidently dwelled on the issue of what British ladies thought of American ladies, and, as always, located her critique of slavery and political awareness in personal feeling as in the following section, reported by *Reynolds*: "I could not tell you what I have seen, the sufferings I have witnessed, and what I felt in witnessing them. Your address has shown your sympathy and sympathy is very sweet" ("Black Slavery Abroad and White Slavery at Home"). Like her novel's rhetorical strategy, Stowe cites her overwhelming empathy with suffering as her dominant approach to slavery and decidedly apolitical (but in this case, international) sympathy as the cure. The *Daily News* reports a similar concern with sympathy, emphasizing that "She looked first to God, but man also could do something. Sympathy must continue to be expressed," along with some practical (and impractical) prescriptions: "British subjects in Canada must be educated. The use of free grown cotton must be encouraged, and there were other ways in this great work may be aided by the people of England, remembering, that after all, the issue is in the hands of Him that ordereth all things" ("Mrs. H.B. Stowe at Stafford House"). These uncontroversial ideas, as uncontroversial as Martineau's, did little to change the political scene. They do, however, give a sense of how conventionally Stowe proceeded in her public performance.

Even more interesting than what she said is how she and those present frame the address. Charles Beecher records that after the luncheon at Stafford House, "the ladies drew together into a small apartment, the gentlemen were requested to withdraw, and Hatty addressed the ladies." Of her attitude during this part of the evening, he claims that "She was just as simple, natural, and self-possessed as ever, and tomorrow I am going to make her tell me what she said. Afterwards, [one of our party] heard the duchess say, 'What a good thing she is so simple'" (*Harriet Beecher Stowe in Europe* 85). Beecher does not record "what she said," if indeed she did tell him, but his emphasis as well as the back-handed compliment from the Duchess about Harriet being "simple" has the effect of minimizing the political nature of her speech while playing up her traditional femininity.

For Stowe's part, she oddly doesn't record the event at all. While her letter home (gathered in *Sunny Memories of Foreign Travels*) details the meeting at Stafford House in a lengthy description, she never mentions that she slipped away to speak, however informally, with the ladies. Martineau, of course, rather proudly documented her own speech in her autobiography. In contrast, Stowe recalls how, intimidated at meeting powerful members of British society and government as grandiose as Macauley, Gladstone, and Whately, she shrank from the gathering. As she recalls it, "I sought a little private conversation with the duchess in her boudoir, in which I frankly confessed a little anxiety respecting the arrangements of the day: having lived all my life in such a shady and sequestered way, and being entirely ignorant of life as it exists in the sphere in which she moves, such apprehensions were rather natural" (*Sunny Memories* 287).[7] While she emphasizes that she moves in a different sphere of class, there is also the sense of fear of public exposure. Like those around her, she naturalizes a woman's shrinking from the limelight and her reference to the "shady and sequestered" way in which she has lived emphasizes, again, her private version of celebrity. That her brother describes her as perfectly at ease before and after her speech suggests that Stowe chose to highlight one side and downplay the other in this public letter.

Stowe's speech was, then, a formal performance of sorts, but one that was not fully recorded. In fact, what is better documented, in the press, in Charles Beecher's journal, and in Stowe's own letters home, is her avoidance of public speaking generally, or, her public performance of silence. Most of Stowe's public appearances involved her husband speaking for her: directly, often reading her own words, and indirectly, using a conventional "we." In her biography of Stowe, Hedrick notes this "singular contradiction: although hers was the most powerful voice on behalf of the slave, by the canons of nineteenth-century womanhood, she could not speak in public" (235). Stowe's reticence is based on the British convention, more conservative than American conventions. Her one semi-public performance of speech needs to be considered in light of these other "silent performances," which were much more acceptable and common.

A usual public address would, then, begin, as it did in Liverpool, with Calvin Stowe speaking. He usually began with his wife's "speech," before beginning his: "On behalf of Mrs. Stowe, I will read from her pen the response to your generous

---

[7]   Beth L. Lueck has further researched this "private conversation" and concluded that the Duchess attempted to put Stowe more at ease by helping with her "toilet," making her able to "return to the public event confident that her ensemble was now more appropriate for the occasion" (99).

offering: 'It is impossible for me to express the feelings of my heart at the kind and generous manner in which I have been received upon English land'" (qtd. in Beecher, Introduction xviii). As the speech continues, it remains fairly consistent with much of the uncontroversial statements she made in person and in print. But in this particular rendering, we have a figure of speech grounded in political reality; indeed, given conventions, it is indeed "impossible" for her to "express" herself. Instead, with unintentional irony, her husband Calvin Stowe will do it. After reading his wife's speech, Mr. Stowe adds, "These are the words, my friends, which Mrs. Stowe has written, and I cannot forbear to add a few words of my own …" (qtd. in Beecher, Introduction xix).

Similarly, in Edinburgh, it was reported that "Professor Stowe then rose, and was greeted with loud cheers. He begged to read the following note from Mrs. Stowe, in acknowledgment of the honor: 'I accept these congratulations and honors, and this offering, which it has pleased Scotland to bestow on me, not for anything which I have said or done, not as in any sense acknowledging that they are or can be deserved, but with heartfelt, humble gratitude to God, as tokens of mercy to a cause most sacred and most oppressed'" (qtd. in Beecher, Introduction xxix). The author's humility, which she always maintained, is supported here by her lack of voice.

Harriet Beecher Stowe, as author, receded at such times into the background. Her words, spoken in a man's voice, become not her own.[8] It is no leap, then, when Calvin speaks of the two of them as one. At a breakfast party for them, he thanks his hosts by saying, "'If we are silent, it is not because we do not feel, but because we feel more than we can express. When the book was written, we had no hope except in God" (qtd. in Beecher, Introduction xiv). Casting the book as a joint venture, Calvin Stowe offers a cover for his wife that was unavailable to the unmarried Martineau.

The convention barring women from speech was, of course, not limited to Stowe. In fact, there were several incidents during which Stowe met other women at public gatherings but would have their messages and addresses read to her by other men. In Liverpool, for example, a local leader took the opportunity of passing along a message from the local women, who were also present, to emphasize the silent role of the respectable woman. He justifies his own performance by describing the "modesty of our English ladies, which, like your own, shrinks instinctively from unnecessary publicity." He goes on to outline a prescriptive account of public women: "the path most grateful and most congenial to female exertion, even in its widest and most elevated range, is still a retired and a shady path." He implicates Stowe in this prescription by claiming that "you have taught us that the voice which most effectually kindles enthusiasm in millions is the still small voice which comes forth from the sanctuary of a woman's breast, and from the retirement of a woman's closet—the simple but unequivocal expression of her unfaltering faith, and the evidence of her generous and unshrinking self devotion."

---

[8]   Shirley Foster aptly calls this version of Stowe's voice "ventriloquized" (151).

Finally, he excuses the once-removed public address which the ladies are making by claiming that despite women's shrinking nature, the Liverpool ladies

> have still felt it entirely consistent with the most sensitive delicacy to make a public response to your appeal ... They engage in no political discussion, they embark in no public controversy; but when an intrepid sister appeals to the instincts of women of every color and of every clime against [this] system ... it is surely as feminine as it is Christian to sympathize with her in her perilous task." (qtd. in Beecher, Introduction xvii)

Like Stowe herself, this local leader safely encodes the public (though silent) meeting of Stowe and the local anti-slavery ladies within the realm of Christian womanhood, locating their wish to do the extraordinary in their emotional sympathy, and intervening between women's communication and political alliance in the meantime.

Even these indirect communications—her husband speaking for her, local men speaking for local women—were less common than Stowe simply appearing to be looked at. These public meetings were well documented by the local papers and her brother, who in many ways gives the most sensitive accounts. For example, at a meeting in Edinburgh that lasted "seven mortal hours," Charles Beecher notes that "As Hatty went in, a loud shout arose. They made way, and we went up. We heard the house uproaring as we went up. Took our seats in the gallery" (*Harriet Beecher Stowe in Europe* 36). Beecher is amazed at the celebrated reception his sister receives, partly because, as he puts it,

> I saw the New Orleans reception of the Great Danseuse. I saw the reception of Jenny Lind and of Kossuth, but nowhere did I see an enthusiasm so genuine, so high, so spiritual as this. When they welcomed her, they first clapped and stomped, then shouted, then waved their hands and handkerchiefs, then stood up—and to look down from above, it looked like waves rising and the foam dashing up in spray. It seemed as though the next moment they would rise bodily and fly up. And the best of it is—Hatty is worthy of it all, through the grace of that Savior who lives in her and in whom she lives. And more, the enthusiasm was true, based on principle and on deep eternal realities, not on mere art or frivolity. (*Harriet Beecher Stowe in Europe* 36–7)

In this account, Beecher places Harriet in a line of performative successes, acknowledging that the reception she receives is less literary, more popular. Even as he does this, however, he is sure to situate her in a proper sphere, away from, for example, the actress Jenny Lind, to whom he has just compared her. That her fame comes from her religious faith and not from "mere art or frivolity" saves her from being the worst kind of celebrity, especially for a woman. Jenny Lind, after all, might have been an international superstar, but she wasn't respectable in the same way Stowe was—partly, perhaps, because as an actress, Lind spoke.

In contrast, Stowe sat and was talked about but didn't speak herself. According to Beecher, during the speeches, "Hatty looks exactly right. Still, timid, modest, yet self-possessed and apparently feeling rather funny on the whole. I love to look at her" (*Harriet Beecher Stowe in Europe* 30–31). Many people "loved to look at her," enveloping her in a wave of public adoration that at once exalted and pacified her. In a sense, both Harriet and Calvin had been rhetorically encouraging this blending of identity and ventriloqual speech all along. Her constant downplaying of agency in the creation of the book and his puppet-like speech encouraged a public welding of her identity into his—which was exactly the reason she escaped appearing too "public" a woman.

Martineau and Stowe did not, could not, conduct transatlantic lecture tours in the way that their male counterparts did, and that fact helps shape this history. As women, their formal performances were limited even as their performances of authorship were fraught with tension. Despite their shared experience, the two women had differing fears of celebrity and of appearing in person in front of audiences: the loss of an objective observer position (for Martineau) and the publicizing of a private identity (for Stowe). Interestingly, both of these concerns would be voiced by the male authors that followed them. For example, Charles Dickens complained bitterly of his total loss of privacy (and private property, as he saw it), of the larger-than-life images he saw of himself on Broadway, of the selling of his hair clippings from the floor of his barber in America. Henry James detested the confluence of authors' life stories and their works. Mark Twain complained that it was hard to write a satiric account of a nation who graciously hosted and celebrated you. But a woman writer's position was far more precarious. After all, her hold on the quality of infallible "objectivity" was all but rejected outright and her need to maintain an aura of the private far more essential. So while Dickens might complain about his hair clippings being sold on the open market, he and his audience—both at home and in America—were able to accept him as an embodied performer, a writer of objective realism, and a respectable man. The same cannot be said of Harriet Martineau and Harriet Beecher Stowe, two intrepid travelers, struggling to be heard amid a transatlantic rush to silence them.

Chapter 2
Performing Ownership:
Dickens, Twain, and Copyright
on the Transatlantic Stage

In December of 1867, a public reading of the novel *Martin Chuzzlewit* occurred on the stage of Steinway Hall in New York City. The next day, a reviewer wrote that the novel was "faithfully and delightfully reproduced in the reader's interpretation." That "the reader's interpretation" was "faithful" is hardly remarkable, because the reader that night was none other than the *author*, Charles Dickens. On another night, a reviewer compared Dickens's performance favorably with a recent performance by an actress, saying that while she "did but interpret the inspiration of others, he presents to us, in all their charming freshness, his own."[1] That the audience in New York, which included the author Mark Twain, couldn't decide whether Dickens, at the height of his celebrity, was the embodiment of his literary inspiration or just another interpreter of that inspiration suggests that to nineteenth-century audiences, the nature and extent of an author's authority over his own work was uncertain.

The legal and economic realities of the time period, as well as the transatlantic context, encouraged such ambiguity. In 1890, Samuel Warren and Louis Brandeis penned the still-debated "Right to Privacy" essay for the *Harvard Law Review*. One year later, the US Congress and British Parliament signed the much-anticipated International Copyright Agreement. Their publication within a year of one another was a legal culmination of a century in which ownership of work *and* self were at issue in transatlantic literary culture. Until 1891, there was no Anglo-American agreement on copyright protection, and the transatlantic reprinting of books without the author's approval or benefit—often more cheaply than the authorized edition—was unregulated and rampant. While in England, for example, Harriet Beecher Stowe, in addition to appearing on behalf of abolitionism, was concerned with the way *Uncle Tom's Cabin* was reprinted without any monetary benefit to her. Popular authors like Stowe felt a waning economic and legal connection to their works as their books traveled the Atlantic as cargo by the thousands. Feeling the need to assert control and inspired by a transatlantic world which by mid-century was easier to traverse, authors traveled the same course as their books. These visits also allowed authors to meet with foreign publishers in the hopes of securing compensation. Of course, a smaller number moved from being the observer to the observed and performed lectures or public readings for their

---

[1]   Review excerpts are from "Charles Dickens: His Second Reading" and "Charles Dickens."

transatlantic audiences. As a supplement to their private meetings with foreign publishers, public performances presented the author in person, face-to-face with readers, enacting a symbolically important connection between authors and their peripatetic books.[2]

In the cases of Charles Dickens and Mark Twain, whose performances in 1867–68 and 1873–74 this chapter takes as its subject, public performances played a crucial role in managing each author's conflicted relationship with their transatlantic reading public. The intervening decade since the transatlantic tour of Harriet Beecher Stowe had brought immense changes to literary culture and consequently to the nineteenth-century transatlantic lecture tour. The overt political tenor of the earlier tours was gone, literary writers were more strictly literary, and entertainment had come to rule the public performance sphere. Celebrity culture had taken off, as Stowe's experience had foretold.

Dickens and Twain (though to a lesser degree at this point in his career) were both immensely popular celebrities, and both lost a great deal of potential revenue from reprinted editions of their books. Through their work and especially their performances, Dickens and Twain both fashioned an authorial persona that was decidedly "popular," and most studies of their lecture or reading tours understand the phenomenon of public performances as a means of marketing the authorial persona to an even larger public.[3] Yet, both authors resented the popular appropriation of their works in unauthorized foreign editions, and this chapter treats their performances as, at least in part, tools of resistance to such appropriation. In fact, Dickens and Twain struggled to make up ground in what they saw as the fight for ownership by performing that ownership in their public appearances.

Both Dickens and Twain differed from most touring transatlantic lecturers in that they performed fictional narratives, never speaking as "themselves" but rather through the medium of one or more characters (including the narrator) from their published work. This approach to lecturing—which involved performing or inhabiting the text—worked to close the gap between an author and an author's work, if only for an hour, in a way that paralleled their more explicit fight for intellectual property. In these public performances, Dickens and Twain worked to establish their authority over and, more important, their ownership of the texts they performed by striking an important balance, a balance that reflected the eighteenth-

---

[2]   A theatrical solution to market problems was not new in the nineteenth century, as Jean-Christophe Agnew has argued in *Worlds Apart: The Market and the Theater in Anglo-American Thought, 1550–1750*. Of the early days of market capitalism, Agnew asks, "What rhetorical devices or forms of address could accommodate the new and unsettling confusion over personal distance and intimacy that perplexed those brought together in commodity transaction? … and if such conventions, devices, and imagery were indeed available, where might they develop freely enough to coalesce into an intelligible, formal analogue of the increasingly fugitive and abstract social relations of a burgeoning market society? Where else, we might ask, but the theater?" (10).

[3]   Malcolm Andrews's *Charles Dickens and His Performing Selves* and Robert McParland's *Charles Dickens's American Audiences* are the most recent to do so.

and nineteenth-century debate over intellectual property. On the one hand, they performed an authorial persona that stressed the author-as-source; on the other, they achieved an embodied intimacy with the published work from which the reading came. In other words, the particular nature of these performances allowed them to perform the role of both the protected author and the protected text.[4] And both approaches to ownership emerged in the context of similar questions about the right to privacy, or ownership over one's self.

Ownership in the Transatlantic Marketplace

Most current critical accounts of copyright point to its "invention" in the eighteenth century. Authors moved from being imagined as transmitters of already present great ideas, on the model of Shakespeare or Milton, and less important than publishers, to being the sources and sovereign owners of works that expressed their inner selves rather than borrowed ideas. Historicizing copyright exposes its dependence upon the concept of a stable author, which much of literary criticism has dismissed as a fiction. In the shadow of Foucault's "What is an Author?" the idea of an individual author claiming ownership over his or her text can appear as a cultural anachronism and theoretical impossibility. To accommodate these critical evolutions and to create a fuller genealogy of copyright, recent criticism has taken an interdisciplinary approach. Martha Woodmansee and Peter Jaszi's volume *The Construction of Authorship* made significant progress in connecting legal and literary theories on the subject, and much of what follows here depends on that volume's basic premises. Literary scholars, particularly Mark Rose, have looked at literary copyright culture through an investigation of economic and legal issues. The cultural criticism movement in law has approached copyright by complicating what they see as a certain obtuseness in histories that look at only the written law, ignoring cultural, legal, and economic realities. The "new economic criticism," in contrast, approaches copyright law through the political assumptions which underlie it as well as aesthetic ideas surrounding it. All of these approaches complicate the simple conception that naturalizes one version of authorship—that of the aesthetically isolated author given complete control and ownership over his or her work.

Addressing the nineteenth century more specifically, Paul K. Saint-Amour's *The Copywrights: Intellectual Property and the Literary Imagination* suggests that nineteenth-century authors themselves were uncertain about their own exclusive ownership. This uncertainty emerges in their writing: "To find intellectual property law firmly ensconced in the period's literary imaginary, whether in overt or covert deployments, is to … [find] a place where the aesthetic demonstrably fails to be

---

4   This argument is an expansion of one previously made in "Performing Ownership: Dickens, Twain, and Copyright on the Transatlantic Stage" from *American Literary Realism*. Copyright 2011 by the Board of Trustees of the University of Illinois. Used with permission of the University of Illinois Press.

at one with itself by admitting its contingency on the property and commodity status of the literary artifact" (Saint-Amour 14). He points to figures such as Oscar Wilde, who engaged in what we would now call plagiarism and liberally interpreted ownership. For Saint-Amour, some late nineteenth-century authors recognized copyright not as an inevitable legal reflection of a natural state but as part of a growing mass literary culture. Meredith McGill, who approaches the issue culturally by looking at nineteenth-century America's "culture of reprinting," argues that American reprinting of texts, including Dickens's, paralleled political and economic resistance to centralized power. McGill's *American Literature and the Culture of Reprinting* shows that reprinting (she avoids the word "piracy" because the practice was legal) "operated as a hedge against the concentration of economic and political power" (5). McGill wants to reclaim transatlantic "piracy" from being dismissed as purely mercenary. These studies, among others, make possible a more comprehensive history of copyright in nineteenth-century transatlantic literary culture, opening up that history to alternate or challenging narrative accounts.

Though transatlantic copyright remained legally unstable until 1891, nineteenth-century culture was generally preoccupied with what Brook Thomas has called the "promise of contract." Even in the absence of legal protection, most authors clearly believed in a social contract that bound readers and publishers to compensate the author for his or her works. But, as Thomas argues, "contract" implies an agreement between *individuals*. It may have been difficult to apply contractual thinking to a literary culture focused on "mass readership." Authors, then, may have undertaken transatlantic nineteenth-century lecture tours in part to reestablish a desired contract—and contact. Presenting themselves in person, authors reminded audiences of the authorial role, of the individual. While the reprinting of texts without authorial oversight or acknowledgement may have been legal, the role of the author was even more inescapably clear when the author stood in front of an audience, a text in his or her own right.

Rose's history of copyright offers a comprehensive portrait that I don't wish to reproduce here. There are a few points in his history, however, that are particularly pertinent to these tours, especially as they help to map the cultural framework for ownership of literary work that was in operation when Dickens and Twain took the stage. Rose traces such cultural understandings to the eighteenth-century dichotomy between tradition and originality:

> A work of literature belonged to an individual because it was, finally, an embodiment of that individual. And the product of this imprinting of the author's personality on the common stock of the world was a "work of original authorship." The basis of literary property, in other words, was not just labor but "personality," and this revealed itself in "originality." (114)

Eighteenth-century conceptions of copyright, then, moved away from seeing property as the result of labor and, hence, transferable. Rather, "an individual's 'person' was his own property. From this it could be demonstrated that through labor an individual might convert the raw materials of nature into private property" (Rose 114). While, according to Rose, this concept was generally true in conceptions of property, literary property was especially concerned with the individual's originality and creativity. The product was an expression of that "personality," transmitting some part of the author's self:

> a literary work in the eighteenth century was coming to be seen as something simultaneously objective and subjective. No longer simply a mirror held up to nature, a work was also the objectification of a writer's self, and the commodity that changed hands when a bookseller purchased a manuscript or when a reader purchased a book was as much personality as ink and paper. (Rose 121)

One issue facing literary culture regarding the question of copyright was what constitutes the originality of the work—whether a work's *content* or *form* was the object of protection.[5] As copyright developed, content, as expression of personality, became the site of originality, and, hence, protection. Rose looks to the eighteenth-century writer Francis Hargrave, whose *Argument in Defense of Literary Property* connected written composition to the human face in its distinctness and, more interestingly, its variability. As human faces change, so could the form of texts themselves (Rose 124–9). To see text remaining "private property" even if it changed form is relevant to a literary culture in which Dickens, for example, could publish *A Christmas Carol*, watch it performed by a theatrical troupe in dramatic form, and present a generic hybrid of the two himself for audiences. The nineteenth-century author could be a kind of essential source, presenting various versions of himself in multiple works or varied adaptations of them. The text might change; the source remained the author, his or her "personality," a self.

In the nineteenth century, these changing visions of ownership and work surfaced most prominently in the realm of international authorship, where copyright was still under legal debate. The concept of an unimaginable, unseen author whose works traveled the Atlantic without a person attached inspired liberal interpretations of ownership, especially in the United States, where there was far less interest in working toward an agreement. Ultimately, this would require the physical presence of the authors, working out private deals with foreign publishers, until the 1891 International Copyright Agreement was signed.[6] Before

---

[5]   Sundeep Bisla, in a discussion of nineteenth-century copyright, defines the two opposing views of the "author-as-creator" and the "author-as-disseminator," arguing that both concepts depend on the new form (not content) being original (186).

[6]   While they were sometimes difficult to achieve, there were some ways around the problem for foreign authors: American or British authors could follow the advance sheet system, allowing them to authorize foreign publishers to release their work before the release at home, essentially anticipating the "unauthorized" versions; British authors could also have an American sponsor who would act as a kind of legal co-author, allowing the American to obtain copyright protection for the work. In addition, British law allowed copyright protection for anyone who established residency in Canada. Twain would take advantage of this later in his career in 1881, spending some weeks in Montreal to obtain British copyright protection for *The Prince and the Pauper*.

1891, however, authors like Dickens and Twain remained somewhat powerless to stop their work from being reprinted and sold without their aesthetic control or financial gain. Both traveled the Atlantic in part to address the issue of lost funds and the need for an international copyright law.

The frustration of Dickens and Twain over what they both saw as the theft of their works has been well documented.[7] That frustration falls neatly into the context of copyright history outlined above. By 1842, when Dickens made his first trip to the United States—not as a lecturer but as a visitor—he already considered himself robbed of considerable profits. The visit was controversial, since he continually and publicly made reference to the copyright issue and followed his visit with two scathing accounts of American culture: *American Notes* (a title that puns on the currency he wasn't receiving) and the novel *Martin Chuzzlewit*, both of which emphasize "self, self, self!" as the national mantra (*Martin Chuzzlewit* 42). His arguments had little effect except to earn him the reputation of a mercenary, for-profit author, a reaction which betrays American readers' investment in a Romantic authorial self somehow above or outside of the market. Dickens's varied responses to such criticism offer insight into one author's frame of reference in thinking about authorship and ownership.

During this first visit, Dickens's moral indignation over the "theft" of his work reveals his perception of writing as labor or external product. His attitude came close to that of Thomas Carlyle, who, at Dickens's request, penned a letter to American audiences in 1842 in favor of an international copyright agreement. Carlyle framed his arguments in moral terms, but they relied on the idea of literature as property. He writes, "Congress and Parliament discuss the time and manner of the thing rather than whether the thing should be at all. The Bible tells us 'Thou Shalt not Steal.' That thou belongest to a different 'nation' and canst steal without being certainly hanged for it, gives thee no permission to steal" (qtd. in Dickens, *Letters* 3:623–4). Dickens often made a similar argument. In a February, 1842 speech in Boston, he introduces copyright by saying, "There is one other point connected with the labours (if I may call them so) that you hold in such generous esteem, to which I cannot help adverting" (*Speeches* 20). The apologetic reference to literature as labor suggests Dickens was aware of other models of authorship and that he felt uneasy referring to himself as a laborer. Still, like Carlyle, he chose to appeal to the right of economic reimbursement for labor spent. Dickens explains that it is only fair that he should receive payment for his "work"; American authors should as well. He hopes "the time is not far distant when they, in America, will receive of right some substantial profit and return in England from their labours; and when we, in England, shall receive some substantial profit and return for ours" (*Speeches* 21).

---

[7]   In addition to those mentioned, see the following on Dickens: Jerome Meckier, *Innocent Abroad: Charles Dickens's American Engagements*; Sidney P. Moss, *Charles Dickens' Quarrel with America*, Alexander Welsh, *From Copyright to Copperfield: The Identity of Dickens*; and the following on Twain: Howard Baetzhold, *Mark Twain and John Bull: The British Connection*, and Dennis Welland, *Mark Twain in England*.

Part of Dickens's anger manifested itself in counterattacks on American culture, claiming that it was selfish and economically driven—exactly the claim made about him in American responses to his call for a copyright law. In *Innocent Abroad*, Jerome Meckier argues that Dickens's idealism was seriously challenged as a result of his visit to America, a country he had looked to for answers to some of the social problems he saw in England. Instead, Dickens found that the most pronounced obstacle to copyright he faced was "the national love of 'doing' a man in any bargain or matter of business" (*Letters* 3:231). He also questions whether the men in Washington "care one miserable damn for Mind?" (*Letters* 3:450–51), perhaps hinting that they also don't care one miserable damn for "mine." His disillusionment is clear; he blames the lack of copyright protection on American culture, represented by the individualist selfishness that dominates the American characters in *Martin Chuzzlewit*.[8]

Beyond economic loss, Dickens was perturbed by the presumption of textual, even aesthetic, authority. He saw his work reprinted and altered, or reprinted faithfully, but in publications that placed his work alongside others he deemed unworthy. McGill agrees that "Dickens is appalled at a print culture that fails to enforce reliable genre and class distinctions, and at the collapse of the structures of mediation that hold authors at a safe remove from the distribution and reception of their work" (114). He privately complained that "Directly [a novel] is printed, it is common property; and may be reprinted a thousand times" (*Letters* 3:274). "Common property" takes on dual meaning here, as Dickens steams under the presumption of shared ownership, which, as McGill points out, includes "the American press's insistence that authors are and should be a kind of common property," *and* the level of culture with which he must be associated (McGill 113). He is filled with moral and aesthetic indignation over unauthorized changes to text. He complains in a letter to Forster that a reprinting of one of his speeches in a periodical was incorrect or worse: "by the omission of one or two words, or the substitution of one word or another, it is often materially weakened. Thus I did not say that I 'claimed' my right, but that I 'asserted' it; and I did not say that I had 'some claim,' but that I had 'a most righteous claim,' to speak" (*Letters* 3:84–5). Without his exact wording, he, the author, is not precisely represented—a critique slightly different from that which cites economic loss. And his insistence on the term "righteous" reminds us that the case he makes concerns principles; as Carlyle implied, it is a moral issue.

Thus, Dickens did not regard his works as simply "labors," external to himself and therefore deserving of economic reimbursement. Rather, they are reflections

---

8   Gerard Joseph argues that *Martin Chuzzlewit* contains a self-critique, as well—that "self, self, self!" is a self-accusation. Pecksniff's "theft" of young Martin's grammar school plan could be read as a traditional master-apprentice agreement and Martin's indignation an immature selfishness reflective of Dickens's own angry claims to ownership in America. Still, he was generally adamant about receiving compensation.

of himself—of his self. In an 1842 letter to Henry Austin, he makes this reflection more explicit:

> Is it not a horrible thing ... That every vile blackguard, and detestable newspaper,—so filthy and so bestial that no honest man would admit one into his house, for a water-closet door-mat—should be able to publish those same writings side by side, cheek by jowl, with the coarsest and most obscene companions, with which they *must* become connected in the course of time, in people's minds? Is it tolerable that besides being robbed and rifled, an author should be *forced* to appear in any form—in any vulgar dress—in any atrocious company—that he should have no choice of his audience—no control over his own distorted text—and that he should be compelled to jostle out of the course, the best men in this country who only ask to *live*, by writing? (*Letters* 3:230)

Dickens's personification of his work echoes other accounts: he displays less concern about compensation than about himself as a public figure. For that matter, it is his public image as much as his work on which he is losing money. "Dickens" rather than *Oliver Twist* or *Great Expectations* is the valuable commodity.

By the time Dickens returned to the United States for a lecture tour more than 20 years later, in 1867, he had agreements with American publishers, but he continued to notice the use of his work and name for profit by others even if he kept his criticism to his private correspondence. In a letter home, he writes that "They are pirating the bill as well as the play here, everywhere ... Nothing is being played here scarcely that is not founded on my books—'Cricket,' 'Oliver Twist,' 'Our Mutual Friend,' and I don't know what else, every night" (*Letters* 11:526–7).

The reading tour may have allowed Dickens to fight against this loss of control, as Meredith McGill has previously argued. In her chapter on Dickens and copyright, McGill focuses on his earlier 1842 visit, only briefly mentioning his 1867–68 reading tour. In that section, McGill does suggest my argument here, that the readings made a parallel statement about copyright as he toured the country "performing his authorship" (138). McGill argues that in the readings, "Dickens steers audiences away from a definition of the author as an external guarantor of the nature or quality of a printed book, toward a model of authorship as immanent and evanescent presence" (138–9). Indeed, this model is consistent with Rose's claim that copyright was based on a conceptual intimacy between the author and his or her text; still, it ignores an older conception of authorship as source or outside laborer that still had some resonance. A closer examination of Dickens's performance scenario reveals a complex approach and method to that performance, as Dickens taps into the idea that the work was both expressive of and external to the author.

While Dickens struggled to align his private self with both his public image and his texts, we might see Mark Twain as moving toward an even more modern conception of the relationship between public authorship and intellectual property. A look at his lectures in England, as well as his career in general, shows that he understood "ownership" to be concerned with more than his texts. Rather, if an author wanted control over his or her work, then he or she needed to establish a legally recognized version of the author role—enacting what Loren Glass calls the "incorporation of authorship" (59). The disconnect between a private author and published works diminishes, Twain's career shows, when there is a publicly and legally recognized version of the private author.

While Dickens looked askance at the entire American publishing system, Twain focused his anger on the British publisher James Camden Hotten, who had published both *The Celebrated Jumping Frog of Calaveras County and Other Sketches* (in 1867) and *Innocents Abroad* (in 1870) without Twain's participation. In 1872, the year before his lecture tours in Britain, in a piece written for the London *Spectator*, Twain called Hotten "the missing link between man and the hyena" (qtd. in Baetzhold 8). Because both works sold particularly well, Twain saw himself as the loser, though they were also responsible for his British popularity. Having already secured an agreement with Routledge and Sons about *Roughing It* in February, 1872, he had traveled to England later that year to meet with them about a belated authorized version of *Innocents Abroad*. The *Spectator* essay, published during this time, then, is largely devoted to advertising his relationship with Routledge, notifying the public that they could, if they wished, purchase an authorized version of *Roughing It* as well. But there is also a sense of aesthetic outrage similar to what Dickens expressed when a speech was misprinted. Twain writes that Hotten titled one of his books "with so foul an invention" as "Screamers and Eye Openers" (qtd. in Baetzhold 8). In addition, Hotten had included pieces of his own alongside Twain's, a fact Twain did not relish, just as Dickens had complained about his works' unwanted "companions."

Twain urges readers to avoid the "unrevised, uncorrected, and in some ways spurious" Hotten edition. "If my books are to disseminate either suffering or crime among my readers of our language, I would ever so much rather they did through [Routledge], and then I could contemplate the spectacle calmly as the dividends came in" (qtd. in Baetzhold 8–9). Certainly, Twain is self-interested. But along with openly stating that self-interest, he clearly meant to point the public toward the authorized version he would, in the next year, bring to life for them on the stage.

Twain approached the lecture tour in England as an opportunity for varied cultural work. In part, it was undertaken for advertisement—Twain was encouraging interest in *Roughing It*, which had been published the year before, and for the authorized version of *Innocents Abroad*. But he was also advertising a public image. He came to a striking conclusion: if published works were going to be appropriated by a mass market that dealt in commodities, then he might best exert economic and cultural power by making a commodity of himself, but one that he was sure to own. The private self, the individual author, might not be economically recognized in the transatlantic literary marketplace; a public version—combining work, personality, and public image—might be able to claim ownership.

Twain would eventually find a working solution to this problem by trademarking his pen name and incorporating the Mark Twain Company in 1908, a move that Loren Glass argues signaled "a new model of U.S. authorship—one that legitimates literary property less as a mark of intellectual labor than as an index of cultural recognition" (59). Its establishment suggests that "the name, in the end, must somehow mandate a referential relation between the private consciousness from which writing emerges and the public sphere in which it circulates" (Glass 8). Twain's appropriation of the powerful sphere of public celebrity, spectacle, and mass publishing signals his prescience as well. His success marked a new form of "American" authorship precisely because—as he understood—it operated in a broadening, international public sphere. Twain's incorporation reflected late nineteenth-century thinking. As Thomas has shown, "Corporate forms of organization, in which individual members submit their legal identities to the corporate whole, are quite different from contractual ones, in which people form associations while retaining their legal identities" (4). Twain, incorporating his name, sacrificed his legal, individual identity in a move that put the author on equal footing with readers: Rather than two individuals working out a contract, a "mass readership" was met by a corporate author. Around the same time, the international copyright agreement was signed. Before either the agreement or his incorporation had been established, however, Twain undertook reading tours that attempted to carry out similar cultural work.

The experience of Dickens and Twain with copyright, by now well-covered territory, suggests that the recognition of ownership depended on a publicly accepted authorial image and an intimate association with a work. On the national scale, an author's public performances of his or her own work might be understood in relation to established legal thought, which identified the work with the author's "personality." But in the transatlantic context, where this identification was not legally acknowledged, performances reminded audiences buying pirated editions that the author and his or her books were indistinguishable. If intellectual property depended on this recognition, then the author's presence was essential. While the US Congress was stalling on an international copyright agreement, Dickens and Twain traveled across the Atlantic in the wake of their best-selling books in part to argue for their right to be recognized economically and legally as authors of their works. And that "argument," in fact, was performed. These two authors performed the work in such a way as to strike a balance between presenting the author as a removed creator, whose work was the result of labor, and presenting the author as part of the work, whose personality was expressed through that work. In this way, their performances of texts became performances of ownership.

Martin Chuzzlewit vs. "Mrs. Gamp": Ownership as Original Source

When young Martin Chuzzlewit returns to England after his adventures in America to find that his former master, Pecksniff, has claimed Martin's architectural plan for his own, Martin's response seems to express Dickens's own outrage at the loss of compensation for his works. Martin tells Mark Tapley, "'This is *my* building.' 'Your building, sir!' said Mark. 'My grammar-school. I invented it. I did it all.

He has only put four windows in, the villain, and spoilt it!'" (553). Like the legal literary pirates in America, Pecksniff claims ownership by means of a technicality (the added four windows), while violating what Dickens sees as the essential rights of creative ownership. Mark later tempers Martin's simplistic claim, reminding him that "Some architects are clever at making foundations, and some architects are clever at building on 'em when they're made" (555). By the time Dickens came to America for his reading tour, ultimately reading to more than 100,000 audience members, he seemingly meant to be both kinds of "architects."[9] His readings were adaptations, but they were built on his own foundations. After all, Dickens drastically altered his works—in fact, he presented them as essentially alterable—even as he sought to secure a legal claim to a static written text. His claims of intellectual property rights depended upon an assumption that the ideal or "authentic" version of a work was located *in* the author, not in a reproducible, published text. As a result, Dickens's performances of ownership sought to secure copyright protection for works as stable and separate commodities, paradoxically by emphasizing a work's changeability at the exclusive discretion of the author. The representative performance of "Mrs. Gamp," the reading taken from *Martin Chuzzlewit*—a novel in which these issues are paramount—revised and reimagined characters from the novel to make a new, separate work.

The American performance of "Mrs. Gamp" provides a clear case of Dickens's approach to adaptation. Although this was not one of his more frequently performed readings in America, it is the one to which the American audience was perhaps most attuned, still steaming as it was over *Martin Chuzzlewit*'s attack on American culture. "Mrs. Gamp" developed over a decade, with Dickens producing an approximate final version for the American tour. During that decade, he cut the reading from 10,000 to 6,000 words, excising an entire section and devising an entirely new ending, including some passages that never appeared in the novel. As John D. Jordon tells us, the prompt copy was ultimately a mess of black ink, blue ink, and red watercolor or dye, representing years of changes. He literally cut and pasted sections of the novel together—pasting pages together that he wanted to skip or cutting pages out and placing them elsewhere. In 1861, Dickens wrote that there was no printed version which would approximate his readings "save in my copies: and there it is made, in part physically, and in part mentally, and no human being but myself could hope to follow it" (qtd. in Jordon 15).

Dickens's claim of exclusivity is essentially a claim of ownership. Indeed, the manuscript of the prompt copy of "Mrs. Gamp" (like that of "A Christmas Carol") points to an ongoing process of addition and deletion. Even the markings preserved in these manuscripts don't, as Dickens warns us, actually give any final or reproducible version of the reading text. The "mental" part of the printed version is, of course, not printed at all, inaccessible to anyone save the author. Even if he had published a definitive version, Dickens changed his readings from night to

---

9   McParland gives a clear accounting of audience numbers during Dickens's American tour (175).

night, so that no single printed, authoritative version could ever exist. Only the author could decide, night by night, what the latest authentic version was to be.

Dickens's adaptation of *Martin Chuzzlewit* bears its own history in markings and pasted pages. But the alterations in the story also suggest Dickens's flexible approach to the novel. Mrs. Gamp as a character had already been independent from the novel in Dickens's imagination well before the reading version was developed. He had begun a story known as "Mrs. Gamp with the Strolling Players," in which Mrs. Gamp told tales to "Mrs. 'arris." Dickens only completed 25 words of this story, but the fruit of the idea can be seen in the public reading.

As its title suggests, "Mrs. Gamp" takes as its organizing principle the titular character rather than any faithful relation to the plot of *Martin Chuzzlewit*. It isn't an excerpt from the novel or even an extended reading of a specific scene. Instead, Dickens gathered material from various chapters, placing them all in the Chuzzlewit house, merging Mrs. Gamp's tending of Lewsome, the mysterious patient, and Chuffy, Anthony Chuzzlewit's faithful bookkeeper, and relocating the comic argument between Mrs. Prig and Mrs. Gamp. Gone is the mystery of the nameless man who turns out to be Lewsome. Unimportant is the patient Mrs. Gamp attends or the setting in which she attends him.[10] Instead of using Mrs. Gamp as comic relief within the novel's development, Dickens focuses on her comic personality itself. Recreating her in dramatic, edited form allows him to make the reading expressive at once of his claim as author of the work and of its independence from the textual source. In the transatlantic context, this approach gestures toward the tradition in intellectual copyright in which the author, an external source who labors over their original work, is the focus of protection. However, not all his performances—or elements of his performances—emphasized this version of ownership.

"I," Scrooge: Ownership as Embodied Vision

Like "Mrs. Gamp," "A Christmas Carol" offered audiences a chance to see some of their favorite characters interpreted by their creator. Also like his other popular readings, Dickens's reading of "A Christmas Carol" included changes to the text of the published source.[11] However, the changes to *A Christmas Carol* and Dickens's performance of it represent his most theatrical adaptation of a work.

---

[10]   Reaction to Dickens's changes was mixed. Journalist Kate Field noted that "Mrs. Gamp is seen in sections. Large slices having been taken out of her, she is put together again so deftly as to look like quite a good-sized individual" (78). Meanwhile, Charles Kent liked that a scene with "Betsey Prig and Sairey Gamp, was, by a most ingenious dovetailing together of two disjointed parts, incorporated with the adroitly compacted materials of a Reading that was as brief as the laughter provoked by it was boisterous and inextinguishable" (218).

[11]   In the following discussion, the title of the public reading "A Christmas Carol" appears in quotations while the title of the published work *A Christmas Carol* is italicized.

From the textual changes to the non-discursive performance, both of which push the reading toward dramatic theater, "A Christmas Carol" established ownership by mitigating a sense of authorial remove and emphasizing the author-as-book. To put this another way, while Dickens established himself as final arbiter of the various versions of his works, he simultaneously and somewhat paradoxically disappeared into the characters and stories.[12] This is most evident in his public presentations of "A Christmas Carol" to American audiences.

Textually, the public reading version of "A Christmas Carol" moves toward dramatic theater by minimizing the narrative voice. Indeed, Dickens's most successful public reading is notable for its contradictory concealment of the authorial "I," even as it succeeded in lionizing him in that role. To be sure, Dickens began and ended his readings by calling attention to himself as author. On his first night of reading, Kate Field records him as stating, "Ladies and Gentlemen, I am to have the pleasure of reading to you first, to-night, 'A Christmas Carol' in four staves. Stave One Marley's Ghost …" (17). However, during the reading itself, he refrained from references to a narratorial "I," asking audiences to accept an embodied author who was not outside the text but very much intertwined with it. The textual published version of *A Christmas Carol* contains several direct addresses, forcing self-awareness on the reader and calling attention to the narrative voice. The public reading version discards these.[13]

Two representative examples follow: When the first spirit draws back the curtains in his first appearance in the published text, "Scrooge, starting up into a half-recumbent attitude, found himself face to face with the unearthly visitor who drew them: as close to it as I am now to you, and I am standing in the spirit at your elbow" (*A Christmas Carol* 18). The public reading omits this reference to narrator and reader, using the passive voice to indicate only that "the curtains of his bed were drawn" (11). Dickens, was, of course, not at his audience's elbow but on a stage. More importantly, he played the scene dramatically, enacting the parts of Scrooge and the Spirit. During the second Spirit's visit, when Scrooge is taken to the house of his genial nephew, the narrator of the published version offers a few words of his own: "If you should happen, by any unlikely chance, to know a man more blest in a laugh than Scrooge's nephew, all I can say is, I should like to know

---

[12] Dickens's theatricality has been read as a way to bond with his audience: McParland follows Juliet John in arguing that Dickens wanted to create intimacy with his audience, pointing out that his "melodramatic style actualized this connection, stirring sentiment and laughter in city after city" (McParland 174) and that "The bond between Dickens and his audience was supported by the interactive theatrical nature of the readings" (McParland 174). While certainly this bond was important, another key intimacy was between Dickens and his text.

[13] Susan L. Ferguson has noted this textual change. However, she draws a different conclusion, arguing that Dickens's readings "are enactments of reading" (734). I suggest that the textual change suggests less of a reader identification than a textual identification, or a move toward dramatic theater.

him too. Introduce him to me, and I'll cultivate his acquaintance" (*A Christmas Carol* 43). These, too, were removed from the public reading.

But the end of the story contains a reference to "us" that Dickens kept in the public readings: "and it was always said of him, that he knew how to keep Christmas well, if any man alive possessed the knowledge. May that be truly said of us, and all of us! And so, as Tiny Tim observed, God Bless Us, Every One!" (*A Christmas Carol* 31). In his last performance in New York, he followed the end of the story by closing the book and calling attention to it, saying, "as I closed this book just now ..." before going on to thank the audience for their support (qtd. in "Mr. Dickens's Farewell Reading" 4). That the only reference to first or second person emerges in the last paragraph, just before Dickens offered a goodnight in his own person, suggests that he preferred to keep his reading free from reminders of an outside storyteller. Performances were marked, on each end, by references to himself as author; during the body of the reading, however, he studiously avoided this, maintaining dramatic characterization.

A Christmas Carol is a story about visions, about the perceived embodiment of spectral characters. Scrooge's adventure comes through his acceptance of the physical presence of ghosts and figures, of symbols. In many ways, Dickens's public readings—particularly this one—worked on the same principle. Dickens asked readers to see Scrooge and Fezziwig embodied in himself. In "A Christmas Carol," audience member Field saw the book resting on the desk as conflating, for a moment, the man and his text: "With the book 'Dickens' stranded on the little desk, the comedian Dickens can transform the table into a stage" (12). Dickens is to the stage, then, as his prompt book is to the table. This idea, that authors "are" their works, means for Field, at least, that these performances were "living books." The conflation seems especially important in the transatlantic context, where books were being sold as commodities separated by an ocean from their authors. The performance of ownership was as much about visions, about the visual, as they were about cutting text and changing pronouns. In several moments of his performance of "A Christmas Carol," Dickens performed a different version of ownership based on his intimacy and identification with the text. His performance relied on his very physical embodiment of the story, suggesting that claims of ownership needed to be made not just legally and by an external author figure but also as part of a public demonstration, performed again and again, by the author himself. This he did with gusto. Dickens's own body and its relationship to his set and performance hall all conspired to create a vision of "A Christmas Carol."

Dickens traveled to all his readings with a set. Malcolm Andrews argues that its "evolution ... reflects the attempt to strike a balance between what was traditionally a relatively private, domestic occasion (reading a story to a group of friends and family) and a public performance before audiences of around two thousand" ("The 'Set' for Charles Dickens's Public Readings" 211). By the time Dickens came to America, the set consisted of gaslights that framed him, a burgundy backdrop, and small table and desk holding his prompt book and a carafe of water and glass. Twain remembered the effect of the gaslight and backdrop as being "just such

DICKENS'S LAST READING.

Fig. 2.1   Charles Dickens—Scenes in His Life. Source: Print Collection, Miriam and Ira D. Wallach Division of Art, Prints and Photographs, The New York Public Library, Astor, Lenox, and Tilden Foundations

an arrangement as artists use to concentrate a strong light upon a picture" (qtd. in Lorch, *The Trouble Begins at Eight* 152). Indeed, Twain would not be alone in noting the rich maroon backdrop throwing into relief the black-suited author. The lighting also focused the attention of the audience, who sat in semi-darkness (another theatrical element), completely on the author.

Apparently, there was much to see. Dickens performed with his whole body, in ways similar to actors of the time. Field noted that "What Dickens does is frequently infinitely better than anything he says or the way he says it; yet the doing is as delicate and intangible as the odor of violets, and can be no better indicated" (20). His hands were one focus of attention. The *New York Daily News* noted that "he perfectly personated ... Old Scrooge ... even to so slight a detail as the habit of putting the hand to the mouth when speaking" ("Charles Dickens: His Second Reading" 4). He also enacted Bob Crachet warming his hands over the fire, indicating that Dickens physically acted out his "readings" and that he had both hands free for at least some of the time, leaving his prompt copy on the table. Field notes another imaginative use of his hands elsewhere during the dance scene at Fezziwig's: "his complete rendering of that dance ... is owing to the inimitable action of hands. They actually perform upon the table, as if it were the floor of Fezziwig's room, and every finger were a leg belonging to one of the Fezziwig family" (19). Dickens's fingers, that is, were performing five different characters at once.

While his hands were warming over an imagined fire and dancing on the table, his legs were just as active. Dickens's desk and table were both small and without covering, so that the legs of the author were in full view. As Andrews points out, the open table came after the first few years during which Dickens stood behind a lectern. His legs, which reportedly shook during his first few performances as a reader, were well controlled by the time he came to America. The display of an author's whole body—not just the moving mouth and facial expression—encouraged the audience to focus on the embodied author as much as, if not more than, the material he performed. Field notes that "No drapery conceals the table, whereby it is plain that Dickens believes in expression of figure as well as of face, and does not throw away everything but his head and arms, according to the ordinary habit of ordinary speakers" (12). Another reviewer saw Dickens's use of his legs as a sign of his ingenuity: "Convention be damned: He makes just what gesture he has a mind to. He even defies propriety time and again by making gestures with his legs. Viewed from a conventional stand-point, his reading is quite shocking" ("Mr. Dickens's Third Reading" 4). Dickens was inventing a new genre of performance, which drew on the theatrical tradition by embodying characters.

Though he may have employed his body in "A Christmas Carol," his attire deliberately suggested the author, not the actor. Indeed, Dickens's position as author and owner is underscored by the fact that he appeared in evening dress. This fact, while seemingly customary, should rather point us toward that delicate balance the performances struck between theater and authorial reading. Dickens's predecessor in performance, Charles Mathews, was a popular entertainer who influenced

Dickens's conception of a reading, including his use of the "monopolylogue," or one man performing several characters. Still, Mathews chose to change costumes consistently throughout the performance, while Dickens remained in his evening dress. He did so while moving from character to character, changing his voice and using his body as an expressive instrument. Thus, his performance of "A Christmas Carol" tapped into the cultural approach to intellectual property that imagined the work as expressive of the inner life of the author, rather than as merely the product of the author's labor. And yet while his method of dramatic reading performed a connection to text, it also reminded audiences that the performer was an author and not an actor. He was, always, Dickens, not Scrooge.

From the Silver Frontier to the British Stage: Ownership as "Authenticity"

Twain came to England in 1873 armed with two lectures, both having made their debut in the public imagination in the book *Roughing It*. One was entitled "Roughing It on the Silver Frontier" and related stories from his Nevada and California adventures; the other he called "Our Fellow Savages of the Sandwich Islands," and it adapted those parts of the book that dealt with Hawaii. He began with his "Sandwich Islands" lectures in October of 1873, and when he returned for the second leg of his tour in December, switched to his "Silver Frontier" lecture. Though they weren't technically "public readings," these performances interpreted a source text as Dickens had done.[14] While Twain and Dickens were very different performers, Twain's performance in the same legally ambiguous, transatlantic context as Dickens suggests that he too struck a balance between performing the author as an external laborer and the author-as-book. On the one hand, he claimed to be an outside source of the text, the person whose real experiences overshadowed any fictional account of them, similar to Dickens's claim of being the only true source for "Mrs. Gamp." On the other hand, he nightly disappeared into the bumbling narrator of *Roughing It*, suggesting through dramatic authorship an intimate link between book and author.

Twain's performance was at once more and less dramatic than Dickens's. While he remained in one character throughout, never changing voices or taking on the parts of others, his "character" was not meant to be identified with that of the author. Dickens, while excising the "I" from some of his works, still played the part of the narrator between passages of dialogue. Twain's performance was a monologue; he told his own story in the first person. The degree to which his performance seemed "dramatic," then, depended on the audience's assessment of how authentic he was as a storyteller. Authenticity, however, assumes a complex meaning in reviews of Twain in England. Particularly because these audiences

---

[14] Fred Lorch long ago saw the ambiguity involved in naming Twain's British performances as "lectures" or "readings," asserting that those sections from *Roughing It* on the English tour "were no less readings because they happened to be parts of the lecture than they were when they later became parts of a reading program" (*The Trouble Begins at Eight* 155).

were, as Twain says, "foreign," questions of authenticity took two forms. The first had to do with accuracy, or how fully he had reported his own experience in distant places (e.g., the Sandwich Islands). The second involved his ability to inhabit and present the character he portrayed—what Randall Knoper, after Twain himself, calls—dramatic "absorption," or to completely absorb the character and eliminate the perceived gap between character and person (62). Twain's negotiation of authorship and performance, then, relied on his paradoxical ability to claim actual authentic experience *and* to sustain a fictional persona for his audience. In many ways, this authenticity paradox is another version of the two ways to understand ownership: as labor and as personality.

Critics, beginning with Paul Fatout and Fred Lorch, have traditionally understood this tension as Twain's vacillation between two personas: the world-weary and the innocent. It may make more sense for the purposes of this chapter to think of these as the author and the actor. Twain embodied both while on stage. Indeed, Knoper claims that Twain was always "shrewdly exploring, even destabilizing, the meanings of theatricality and realism" (2). In a similar way, his multiple roles enact two dimensions of authorship: there is an implicit claim of authorship (Twain, the relater of actual events, remains the principle critical subject) and a claim of embodied performance (Twain, in character as the western innocent, is the object of the audience's laughter). Both reveal his "authenticity."

Though Twain would later conduct performances he called "Public Readings," he disdained "reading" as a viable performance technique. If an author reads on stage, he argues, "You are a mimic, and not the person involved; you are an artificiality, not a reality; whereas in telling the tale with the book you absorb the character, just as in the case of an actor" (*Mark Twain in Eruption* 216). Rather than use an open book as Dickens did, Twain used "notes," and these performance prompts suggest this dual approach to authenticity. First, they indicate his skill as a dramatic performer. The "notes" are one page of drawings and symbols, referents to *Roughing It*'s textual events. In a clockwise circle, Twain sketched a series of images that suggest the subjects of his anecdotes. The image format would have allowed him to glance quickly at the page while never seeming to study or rely on them. Many of the reports of his lectures in England describe him as never looking at a note and as carrying himself with a confident "air of improvisation" (qtd. in Fatout 182). In fact, Lorch argues that "it is probable that Twain came to the platform in these early days depending largely upon a clear mental picture of his experience, rather than upon manuscript" (Lorch, "Mark Twain's Lecture from *Roughing It*" 292). Since he gave his notes to his assistant, Charles Warren Stoddard, at the end of the lecture tour, they might be understood less as necessary tools than as audacious symbols of his ability as a performer.[15] Twain, ever proud

---

[15]   They could also be understood, in part, as a sign of affection for Stoddard, whom Twain regarded as having "gentleness and high character" (Powers 339). Twain also later wrote that "Ostensibly, Stoddard was my secretary; in reality he was merely my comrade—I hired him in order to have his company" (*Autobiography* 161).

Fig. 2.2   Notes and Sketches for a Lecture, Holograph. With a Signed Note to Charles [Warren Stoddard] in the Margin Dated Liverpool, Jan. 9, 1874. 10:30 p.m. Source: Henry W. and Albert A. Berg Collection of English and American Literature, The New York Public Library, Astor, Lenox, and Tilden Foundations

of his improvisational skill and performance persona (as the act of giving away the notes itself suggests), seemed all too ready to use stage tricks that suggested his independence from notes and his freedom from exact textual imitation—in short, his authenticity.

At the same time, Twain's notes show how flexible he was with regard to his source material. Even more than Dickens's loose adaptation of "Mrs. Gamp" from *Martin Chuzzlewit*, the pictures merely provide a sketched outline of topics and characters. A stick figure of the "Mexican plug," a sketch of the profile of a "good Indian," and the drawing of stick men fighting a duel, followed by the words "close": each represents an anecdote, though newspaper reports suggest that he changed the order night by night and varied the length of individual anecdotes. These graphic symbols constitute a version of Twain's western adventures as does the book *Roughing It* and the elements of oral performance. All that unifies them and authorizes them is the author. That he should also so vehemently covet sole ownership over these various versions—getting angry when newspapers printed his lecture texts, seeking publishing rights for the book version—suggests an interest in ownership resting in the hands of the author but not invested in the text itself.

Twain had already authorized a "British" version of *Innocents Abroad* in 1872. Howard Baetzhold shows how "in the text itself, he omitted certain exaggerations and a few items of purely frontier humor. Seeking to clarify the material for British readers, he substituted a number of English words for their American equivalents (*draught-board* for *checker-board*, for instance)" (5). He had established a precedent, then, for allowing his text to reflect audience expectation. On the stage, he was able to be even more flexible. Even at a point in his career when he was solidifying authorial control, he entered into a kind of dialogue with audiences. Previously, he had delivered both "Roughing It on the Silver Frontier" and "Our Fellow Savages in the Sandwich Islands" in the United States; for his British lectures he made some changes, particularly to his account of the "Sandwich Islands." The British lectures preserved passages mocking American arrogance while omitting those mocking the British. For example, in response to British national pride and interest in acquiring the Hawaiian Islands for themselves, Twain did not criticize the revered Captain Cook or argue, as he had previously, for American annexation. He limited his cannibalism jokes, as well. Such alterations acknowledged the contextual status of the performance, in which his own work was restaged to meet anticipated audience reaction; simultaneously, his spontaneity in delivering the talk attributed the authenticity of the performance to the man on stage.[16]

---

[16]   Lawrence Buell makes a compelling argument that American nineteenth-century culture enacts many of the literary performances we call postcolonial, in part because such authors seemingly write in anticipation of foreign readers. Indeed, Twain does adapt his performance of *Roughing It* for his audience. Meanwhile, Dickens's ready approach to continuous adaptation may suggest more elements at play in these performances. Indeed, while Dickens made continuous adaptations, it does not appear he did so based on different national audiences. The difference underscores the uneven relationship between British and American authors and audiences.

Authorial authenticity was also evident in Twain's simplicity of appearance. He came out of a middle-class American culture that was growing more and more suspicious of theater, while growing more open to "elocution" and lectures, as the later Chautauqua movement would testify.[17] Charlotte Canning argues that the success of this later movement relied on the organizer's ability to separate out "reputable dramatic literature from the material attributes of theatrical illusion— costumes, scenery, and particularly make-up—which its audiences regarded as signs of corruption and immorality" (304). While Dickens was, by the time of his reading tour, in no danger of being viewed suspiciously in this regard, the same could not be said for Twain, who was still early in his career. Additionally, the avoidance of make-up or costume (Twain chose not to appear in "western" garb for his lectures, as he might have) suggests his interest in appearing as a respectable author. But it also suggests a strategy for enacting the author figure, in a way that dressing as his persona would not. Dress keeps Twain in command of his material and gives him a way to withdraw from it at strategic moments in the performance.

Indeed, while his performances were at their most humorous when he portrayed the "simpleton," he just as often countered that role with the persona of the experienced author. Ads for the lectures emphasized his experience, one stating that, "As Mr. Twain has spent several months in these islands, and is well acquainted with his subject, the Lecture may be expected to furnish matter of interest" (qtd. in Baetzhold 17). He claimed to have seen some "of the world's most celebrated lakes" and that they are inferior to Lake Tahoe, which is "a vast oval mirror framed in a wall of snowclad mountain peaks above the common world" (Twain, "Roughing It" 298). Affecting (or revealing) the observant eye of the critical travel writer, Twain played the author here, as reviewers noted. In the *Spectator*, Twain was "the easy man of the world" as opposed to Artmeus Ward, his predecessor in the transatlantic humorous lecture, who was always "childlike" ("Mark Twain" 1302). He also could adopt the voice of a bitter and weary traveler. The "Roughing It" lecture contains the tale of his attempts at becoming a millionaire: "I had supposed in my innocence that silver mining was nice, easy business, and that of course all you had to do was to pick it up ... Then came my disenchantment" ("Roughing It" 300). Here, then, wisdom, or at least clarity of vision, derives from cultural disillusionment. He can guide the audience through social shams because he has learned to see through them himself.

Twain tempered this critical, authorial presence with dramatic touches identifying him with his text, achieved in part through use of the deadpan style. He played with audience expectations by introducing himself, always forcing the audience to be cognizant of the event as a performance. Walking on stage

---

[17]   Lawrence W. Levine has called this movement the "Sacralization of Culture" in *Highbrow/Lowbrow: The Emergence of Cultural Hierarchy in America*. Twain and Dickens were part of a diminishing number of people who "were able to assume a place in a cultural lexicon that cut through class and income" (108).

as if he weren't the main attraction, he'd introduce Mark Twain as "a gentleman whose great learning, whose historical accuracy, whose devotion to science, and whose veneration for the truth, are only equaled by his high moral character and his majestic presence" (qtd. in Lorch, *The Trouble Begins at Eight* 293). After admitting to the audience he was Mark Twain, he told them that he liked to introduce himself, because that way, "I can get in all the facts" ("Roughing It" 293). One result was to keep audiences wondering if Twain was in on the joke. Of course, they ultimately recognized that, yes, he was, but his first-hand tales of the West and Hawaii and his delivery still suggested authenticity in the form of dramatic absorption. Knoper's account of Twain's deadpan style suggests a tension between the "absorption" of a persona and a sense of "theatricality," or falseness—the very thing that was beginning to be separated out as disreputable (62). By the time of his London lectures, Twain had moved away from the exaggerated theatricality of his burlesque days and had fully established his character as the hapless teller (though certainly tempering the "innocent" with interjections of authorial wisdom). In absorbing himself into this character, he also established his authority as the center of the performance. Ownership, then, came from identification with the content of his narrative. He was the actor in his narrative as much as an external author.

His physicality enhanced this kind of dramatic authenticity. While his use of the body might have been less overt than Dickens's—there are no accounts of him kicking his legs out or enacting a dance with his hands—this has more to do, perhaps, with his laconic style, a tendency to exhibit the least amount of energy possible. Twain moved on stage "with a casualness that barely escaped swagger [;] he shuffled upon the stage" (Fatout 179). A reviewer's account emphasizes the relationship between speaking style and physical performance: "He never … raises his voice or gives himself any trouble to do more than talk, and does nothing for effect except to pause and deliver the real point of his jokes after the audience has stopped laughing at them" (qtd. in Fatout 182). Other accounts notice this physical expression of Twain's ownership, as he absorbs his slow-thinking narrator into his slow-moving body. Part of Twain's physical embodiment came in his vocalizations. In his performances, telling the truth is like "pulling teeth to keep it up"; traders in Hawaii "will sell you a mole hill at the price of a mountain, and will lie it up to an altitude that will make it cheap at the money" (Twain, "Our Fellow Savages" 433). Critics of his performances noted this style in their reviews, emphasizing his ability to portray the character of the narrator convincingly. *The Post* claimed that the sometimes jarring "full-flavoured American dialect" was not "unpleasant to listen to when spoken by Mr. Twain in its integrity" (qtd. in Fatout 180). Twain is authentic, here, because he speaks like a real Westerner. And to speak like a "real" Westerner entailed changes in word choice, but also in accent and cadence and emphasis—changes we must imagine from descriptions. There is no doubt, however, that Twain used his body, including his voice, as an instrument in performing his texts.

As his use of a pen name suggests, Twain perceived the public realm—not just the stage—as an opportunity for performance. While British law didn't recognize

Samuel Clemens as the financially deserving author of the books *Innocents Abroad* or *Roughing It*, Mark Twain emerged onto the stage at Hanover Square seeking public recognition of his authorship, to prove his connection—dramatically and biographically—to his book. He would eventually establish himself legally with the Mark Twain Company, which would remain stable, fixed, and publicly recognized beyond the writer's body.[18] Before this solution was in place, however, Twain's dramatic negotiation of roles—that of the knowing author who freely altered his own texts night by night and of the innocent character who absorbed the stories into his own body and performance—was one way to establish a public identification with his books. The claim of private property, then, required a public performance.

Public Readings, Private Property

Transatlantic public readings both reflected and contributed to the changing culture of the public author. Audience and author recognized their changing relationship to literary work, especially with regard to the authority of the writer. But public performances didn't just complicate the relationship of the work to the embodied author: they enabled the author to *become* the text in ways Dickens especially would come to regret. Public readings encouraged a growing conception of the private person as a public—and marketable—commodity. As Dickens learned on his first trip to America, physically presenting one's self to the public as the author of their favorite works meant a loss of privacy. This issue is not wholly unconnected to the issue of copyright protection, as the 1890 legal essay "The Right to Privacy" indicates. Though certainly not tied directly to Dickens, Twain, or the international copyright agreement, this legal essay's concerns with ownership of self and work, and its suspicions of a "mass" public encroaching on both, make it a useful source for further contextualizing the transatlantic public reading experience of Dickens and Twain that preceded it.

Dickens and Twain were certainly concerned to protect their work as property and capital. But both were also concerned with the other element that figures heavily in the law review: "the right to one's own personality." For Dickens particularly, the desire to be "let alone" was strong. In a much-quoted letter to Forster, Dickens complained of his public life in 1842 during his first visit to America:

> I can do nothing that I want to do, go nowhere where I want to go, and see nothing that I want to see. If I turn into the street, I am followed by a multitude. If I stay

---

[18]   Twain was concerned even with control over his posthumous persona, as Annelise K. Madsen has recently written. Analyzing the "cultural work" of Twain's iconic "white suit" photograph in 1906, taken by Frances Benjamin Johnson, Madsen argues that Twain posed "in order to document the dramatic public debut of his (henceforth iconic) white suit. Aiming to craft his posthumous image on his own terms, the celebrated author took particular interest in his photographed self" (56).

at home, the house becomes, with callers, like a fair. If I visit a public institution, with only one friend, the directors come down inconveniently, waylay me in the yard, and address me in a long speech. I go to a party in the evening and am so enclosed and hemmed about by people, stand where I will, that I am exhausted for want of air. I dine out, and have to talk about everything, to everybody. I go to church for quiet, and there is a violent rush to the neighborhood of the pew I sit in, and the clergyman preaches *at* me. I take my seat in a railroad car and the very conductor won't leave me alone. I get out at a station, and can't drink a glass of water, without having a hundred people looking down my throat when I open my mouth to swallow. Conceive what all this is! (*Letters* 3:87)

George Dolby, his companion and manager for most of his later tour in 1867–68, noted that even then, despite a concerted effort to limit his exposure, "[Dickens] had been annoyed at supper by the waiters leaving the door of the sitting-room partially open, that the promenaders in the corridor of the hotel might take a peep at him, through the crack between the door and the doorpost, whilst he was sitting at table" (159). Dickens wanted the public to recognize his sole ownership over his books, but he didn't want them to recognize *him* as he walked down the street. The public readings that tied him to his books but did so in a controlled performance space may have provided him with a workable solution.

Ownership over self and work might be read as contradictory goals, since there is no question that public readings increased public interest in the personal, embodied lives of Dickens and Twain. Indeed, their performance styles tended to dissolve the boundary between author and book, resulting in what we may see as a third category of the literary celebrity: an odd amalgam of fictional text, authorial persona, and public imagination. In the wake of efforts to establish authorial control over texts *and* present a performance of public image, the "right to be let alone" seemed to recede for both authors. Their experience helped define the context in which Samuel D. Warren and Louis D. Brandeis undertook to clarify legal personhood and penned the now famous "Right to Privacy" essay for the *Harvard Law Review* in 1890, a turning point in legal conceptions of privacy and property in America and a culmination of transatlantic nineteenth-century cultural conceptions of these issues.

In addition to its importance in legal and cultural history, "The Right to Privacy" draws together several threads important to this study. Of ultimate interest is the writers' claim to see "the right to privacy, as part of the more general right to the immunity of the person,—the right to one's personality" (Warren and Brandeis 207). The right to privacy (as they define it here) is based not on ownership (of personal documents, for example), but is a preemptory right of sovereignty of the "personality," a term implying personhood or individual subjectivity.[19] The term

---

[19]   Warren and Brandeis use the term "personality" to mean a personhood beyond the body of the person but still essentially individual and subjective. Other writers of the period, as Gregory Clark, S. Michael Halloran, and Terry Baxter have shown, use "personality" in the sense that I have used it elsewhere in this book. "Public personality" is similar in

"personality," then, assists in the legal move from private property to privacy in a more widespread sense. Protection of the things one owns was well established at this point. Not so the right to privacy, or the right to protect one's personal life, one's writings or belongings, from the "gossip mongers" to whom Warren and Brandeis are responding. And in fact their claim that the right to privacy is rooted in the right to one's personality actually engenders a discussion of copyright. Indeed, as they put it, "no basis is discerned upon which the right to restrain publication and reproduction of such so-called literary and artistic works can be rested, except the right to privacy ... the right to one's own personality" (207). Essentially, Warren and Brandeis are relocating the source of intellectual property: it comes, in this essay, not as an extension of the rights of private property or labor, but rather from a more essential right of the "inviolate personality" (Warren and Brandeis 205). Literary productions, then, are protected not as "property" or because they result from labor and therefore are economically transferable. Instead, they become intimately interwoven with the author's person: they are an expression of the self.

This was no new idea in the aesthetic field. After all, the image of the Romantic writer whose poetry is nearly indistinguishable from his person was already well established. Indeed, copyright law had already recognized that a work's originality depended on the author's inner self. In a sense, "The Right to Privacy" is a reaction to the opposite pressure: the inner life of public artists becoming too exposed. The irony of this argument, however, is clear. In moving to conceive of literary work as an expression of the personality rather than as a commodity with market value, "The Right to Privacy"—and its legal and cultural successors—contributes to conceptions of the personality as commodity itself. Warren and Brandeis write in response to what they see as an overreaching, vulgar press that exploits the personal lives of celebrities. But in moving to protect those personal lives as sacred and in some sense nontransferable as sites of value, they verify along the way that writings are a continuation of the person who creates them. The goal of "The Right to Privacy," in part, seems to have been to extricate the public figure from a marketplace of commodities; in fact, it may have suggested the opposite.

Theories of celebrity argue that what appears as the celebrity, in both legal terms and in the cultural imagination, is outside individuals themselves; it is something created and owned by both the individual *and* his or her audience. For Glass, the celebrity is "a new public subject irreducible to either author or audience" (2). David Marshall's *Celebrity and Power* argues that "the celebrity sheds its own subjectivity and individuality and becomes an organizing structure for conventionalized meaning" (56). In a transatlantic context, the author's public, celebrity image was distanced from his or her "private" or individual self even more. Dickens himself recognized this during his second trip to America. He noted

---

meaning to "celebrity image," which may be imagined as constructed variously through the authors themselves and the public; in other words, an invented, constructed image. Warren and Brandeis use the term "personality" here to mean something quite opposed to "celebrity."

that in New York all of his books were being reprinted and produced as plays on Broadway. Not only that, but his own celebrity image haunted him. He writes home that "I can't get down Broadway for my own portrait; and yet I live as quietly in this hotel, as if I were at the office, and go in and out by the side door just as I might there" (*Letters* 11:527.) Dickens the man moves anonymously, at least in this particular memory, feeling alienated from Dickens the celebrity, whose portrait hangs everywhere, authorized and owned by American culture. His feeling of estrangement derives in part from the lack of a legally fixed ownership of that public image. These portraits hang where they do to promote plays which American producers had, in his view, stolen from him. While American culture, then, continued to multiply and manipulate his celebrity image, that image seemed less and less to be his, to be him.

Even aside from the lack of legal protection, Dickens's experience was and is not extraordinary. Indeed, celebrity operates outside the law. Rosemary Coombe points out that while "the law constructs and maintains fixed, stable identities authorized by the celebrity subject ... the celebrity is authored in a multiplicity of sites of interpretive practice" (88–9). Nevertheless, Glass sees authors as contributing more to the substance of their images than most celebrities: "Writers ... have sustained an ethos of creative production over and against the rise of these cultural industries in which they nevertheless have had to participate ... complicating the easy dismissal of the celebrity's subjectivity in so much recent celebrity theory" (4). Although Glass is primarily interested in autobiographies, transatlantic public readings seem to make a similar gesture toward self-authorship. Readings reflect the same anxieties about loss of control over public image while working to establish a publicly (if not legally) acknowledged connection between book and author. Dickens notes in his letters that during his second trip the desire to increase control over his public image *and* protect his private life were one endeavor. He writes that his manager "Dolby has seen reason to make up his mind that the less I am shown—for nothing—the better for the Readings! So I am fended off and kept—so far—unexpectedly quiet. In addition to which I must say that I have experienced—so far—not the slightest intrusiveness, and everywhere the greatest respect and consideration" (*Letters* 11:483). The controlled performance of a foreign author seems to be directed to the same ends that a legal connection between author and work might have secured. Dickens also writes that "The Bostonians have been duly informed that I wish to be quiet, really leave me as much so as I should be in Manchester or Liverpool" (*Letters* 11:488–9). By "leave me," Dickens of course means his private self, because he was simultaneously engaged in a publicity drive to get people to come to see him on stage. His performance, then, is a performance not just of "Mrs. Gamp" or "A Christmas Carol" but of the transatlantic public image he wished to create.

While Twain and Dickens were engaged in the creation of a culturally recognized celebrity image, they were, as I have shown, engaged in a fight for transatlantic legal recognition of the connection between their private property and public image. Hence, in linking private property and copyright as contributing to the protection of the self or personality, the argument made by Warren and Brandeis was not a cultural anomaly. During the years of Dickens's and Twain's lecture tours, ownership over text *and* public image was largely "shared" with an international public these authors at times loved and at times distrusted. The late nineteenth century was, then, heterogeneous in its image of the author as supreme authority and owner. While the international mass market enabled professional authorship, "Celebrity challenged deeply held convictions about authorial inspiration and property in texts by appearing to cede creative agency and control to the mass audience and literary marketplace" (Glass 8). This is the paradox of these particular lectures. The transatlantic reading tours were one answer to these unstable cultural assumptions about authorship and ownership: Dickens and Twain performed ownership of their texts by way of performing their international public image and its inseparability from these internationally successful books; however, that public, celebrity image, by its very nature, was uncontrollable in the public sphere, raising questions about "ownership" of self and work. Ultimately, the reading tours, more than offering a solution, are an expression of the instability and variety with which transatlantic literary culture approached nineteenth-century public authorship and private ownership.

Dickens and Twain were not the only authors to perform for their international readership, but their deft and dramatic use of fictional work in an atmosphere of unregulated textual piracy sheds light on the transatlantic marketplace. Both authors gestured toward conceptions of authorship that imagined the author as removed from the work, as the source and arbiter of the work, whose discretion regarding the work deserved legal protection. Thus, both could alter their work and at the same time argue for protection from alteration by others. Their transatlantic performances blended this implied argument seamlessly with another: their books were an embodiment of themselves. In this way, they challenged the gap between author and text with which nineteenth-century readers (and twentieth-century critics) at times seemed comfortable. This joining of written text and speaking author, in the context of the nineteenth-century unregulated transatlantic market, required the author in person, on the stage, performing the work night after night. In these performances, Dickens's voice became the voice of Scrooge and Mrs. Gamp; Twain's voice took on the cadences and accents of his exotic (to British ears) Western narrator; Dickens's fingers transformed into dancers at a Christmas celebration; and Twain's shuffling feet and slouched back communicated the ethos of *Roughing It*. But when the applause ended, these non-actors, both in the evening dress of the distinguished author, would withdraw, ready to redouble their off-stage roles of author and, they hoped, *owner* of the works they had just brought to life for transatlantic audiences.

Chapter 3
Apostles in the Flesh:
Arnold, Wilde, and the Reproduction
of Personality in America

The lectures of Charles Dickens and Mark Twain functioned as a counter balance to a mass, international market that had distanced the authors from their work—physically, legally, and in the imaginations of their readers. By connecting their performing bodies to their texts, however, they also contributed to a celebrity culture that made the author a commodity. As both Dickens and Twain found, the development of a public "personality" was beginning to be essential to function in the literary marketplace, which now included an expectation for authors to lecture. Ten years later, in the early 1880s, the reign of "personality" was dominating the literary marketplace in America when, first, a young Oscar Wilde lectured in America and, then, an aging Matthew Arnold did the same. Like Dickens and Twain, these authors would experience a sense of distance between themselves and their public image. Their less popular work was less vulnerable to unauthorized printing, but in the celebrity culture that was flowering in the 1880s, their public selves were a thoroughly transatlantic commodity waiting to be sold. It is the gap between private author and public personality—rather than between private author and published work—that this chapter will examine.

One impetus for late nineteenth-century celebrity culture can be traced back to Romantic criticism from the beginning of the century. As Leo Braudy shows in his history of fame, *The Frenzy of Renown*, "Rather than a group of paintings or a collection of books, an artist's life was beginning, with the rise of art and literary criticism, to be considered as a developing organic unity, akin to personal character" (391). It was in this early nineteenth-century context that authors such as Ralph Waldo Emerson and Thomas Carlyle (two formidable lecturers themselves) could propose a theory of "great men" as either "heroes" or "representative men," among whom authors or artists could be counted.

But by the late nineteenth century, a concept of public individual identity would lose out to the disseminating forces of the market: heroes became marketed celebrities, representative men became consumer products. Ultimately, what had been conceived of as the individual subject would become a public self made for sound bites and caricatures. Nineteenth-century authors were well aware of the shift. Everyone from Arnold to his intellectual nemesis Walt Whitman was working to establish how an author could distinguish between the dangerous, superficial commodity culture and a useful and ethical public culture which could, at least for Whitman, embody democratic ideals. Foucault's question, "What is an Author?" was being explored by authors, critics, audiences, and, of course, booking agents for lecture tours.

Such was the celebrity culture in the 1880s when two of Britain's literary stars visited the United States. Neither Matthew Arnold nor Oscar Wilde came to America to lecture in the service of his written work in so direct a way as the popular novelists had. Instead, they came to educate the public—and of course to further their own economic standing. As far as their audiences were concerned, however, each came to promote one idea. The ideology with which each was associated became his identity—it *was* his public personality. Wilde, arriving in America in 1882, was immediately dubbed "The Apostle of Aestheticism," while Arnold, coming one year later, was termed, "The Apostle of Culture." The term "apostle" accurately captured both lecturers' advocacy of ideas. But it also reveals how each was seen as a messenger, coming in from the outside. Although Wilde was not yet as famous as he would be, he was identified almost exclusively with the Aesthetic movement. Arnold, late in his career, was interested primarily in social questions and how "culture" could answer them. Arnold was seen merely as preaching culture; Wilde, Aestheticism. The author-as-apostle is an apt image for this point in each of their lives, and in the history of the nineteenth-century lecture tour. Messengers of ideas, they were also one-note punch lines in newspaper headlines. Personality became caricature. And caricature was easy to commoditize.

For Arnold and Wilde, lecturing was thus an embodied experience that ironically emphasized the distance between the body and the public personality. Lecturing as self-representation, in these examples, gives way to representation in the marketplace; both authors would struggle to retain control over their public personalities in the same way Dickens and Twain struggled to retain control over their work. In other words, lecturing contributed to the emergence of a new phenomenon—the author as transferable commodity. These two authors highlight in dramatic fashion this particular phase of transatlantic lecture tours because both encouraged—whether deliberately or not—a celebrity persona that was easily reproduced, imitated, and "sampled," to use a modern phrase. They did this through their visual self-presentation and through their intellectual discourse. Between Wilde's costumes and epigrams and Arnold's catchphrases and notable muttonchops, both authors created a public person that was easily distanced from their "real" selves.

While the concept of self-promotion and self-performance has almost always been a part of Wilde studies, this has not been the case with Arnold. On the Wilde side, Regina Gagnier's work, especially *Idylls of the Marketplace* in the 1980s, cast Wilde as an apostle of Aestheticism largely constructed in concert with his audience (3). More recently, Michèle Mendelssohn has placed Wilde's willing self-promotion in a transatlantic context, arguing that his Aestheticism must be understood as such (in relation to Henry James's American version) (4). A new edition of Wilde's interviews, the introduction of which argues that Wilde saw interviews as "a collaboration in the creation of his public image" (Hofer and

Scharnhorst 2), has evidenced our continued interest in the self-consciousness of Wilde's public performances.

But the pairing of Wilde with Matthew Arnold, focused on their lecturing in the United States within months of each other, offers additional ways to see Wilde's tours and a much needed consideration of Arnold's relationship to performance culture. Indeed, seeing the two lecturers each in the context of the other emphasizes how ordinary Wilde's experience was, which is not how it is usually cast. After all, Arnold was nowhere nearly as adept at performance as Wilde—he did not think in sophisticated ways about public persona, in-person lecturing, or the celebrity marketplace. And yet, his experience shows that authors of the period, especially those who did engage in transatlantic lecture tours, were a part of a commodified marketplace of celebrity whether they liked it or not.

Their similarity did not end there. Both Wilde and Arnold spoke on behalf of "distance," a concept that explicitly repudiated market forces. In his lectures, Wilde advocated an *aesthetic* distance, an ideal that implied the free play of the mind apart from practical, economic, or ethical pressures. Of course, his experience on the lecture circuit also brought him face to face with market forces and, as I've said, he encouraged the commodification of his image as the spokesperson for Aestheticism. Meanwhile, the "Apostle of Culture" espoused *critical* distance, or "disinterestedness." Arnold conceived of "distance" as the way individuals escaped the sources of intellectual narrowness: the market, the body, the nation, programmatic politics. What he discovered—or at least experienced—as a lecturer was something very different. Lecturing made the body the focus, its national affiliation apparent through manner and accent, revealing a most interested apostle.

Despite their textual arguments in favor of critical or aesthetic distance, in reality both authors experienced another form of distance: between an actual person and his public personality. Wilde's self-representation was well suited to reproduction and representation by others. "The Apostle of Aesthetics" could be drawn, photographed, and captured in an epigram in any of the countless reviews or advertisements for his lectures. Wilde's manipulation of these commodified versions of himself shows his relative comfort with modern celebrity culture, even if it produced multiple, unauthorized images of himself. In Arnold's case, the embodiment required by the lecture tour undercut his explicit arguments for intellectual distance; at the same time, the celebrity borne of the lecture tour created a sense of *dis*embodiment, a detachment from the self in the marketplace. This was made clear in an instance of literary "identity theft" which followed the tour. As we will see, the incident shows that the self, commodified into a public personality (a process encouraged by lecture appearances), could be transferred in the marketplace in ways and forms beyond the author's control. In both cases, however, the apostles would experience a "distance" quite apart from that with which each was associated. Lectures, as embodied as they were, were an essential part of a very disembodied commodity culture.

Institutions of Celebrity: Impresarios, Managers, and Agents

When Wilde and Arnold appeared on the American lecture circuit in the 1880s, the celebrity lecture tour was already regularized and institutionalized. The celebrity interview—a key aspect of the lecture tour—was itself an invention of the 1870s (Hofer and Scharnhorst 1). The scale on which very famous authors were now lecturing meant it was no longer feasible or desirable (from the authors' point of view) to organize logistics, make contacts with potential venues, or handle the publicity. The existence of the "impresario" in one form or another indicated— as much as any author's individual experience—how well developed celebrity lecture tours had become. In fact, one was dependent on the other.

Such broad-scale organization was new. When Frederick Douglass traveled to England, Scotland, and Ireland in the 1840s to lecture to audiences there about the evils of slavery and poverty, he went as part of the Boston Anti-Slavery Society. Douglass's speaking engagements were, then, arranged through the network of political and social organizations already in place during the politically tempestuous first half of the century. That network was decidedly transatlantic and, in Douglass's case, operated mostly outside the marketplace. The price for avoiding such commodification, as Douglass found, however, was subservience to the group's goals. Douglass was at times not at liberty to say what he would (about liberty). Two other abolitionist speakers—Harriet Martineau (in the 1830s) and Harriet Beecher Stowe (in the 1850s)—likewise came to their limited speeches through the networking and connections of politically interested groups. Martineau's ill-fated speech occurred because she attended a meeting of the Ladies Boston Anti-Slavery Society. Stowe spoke at a private home which played host to a gathering of abolitionists. Such experiences were quite distinct from the commercial, apolitical tours that followed. For literary authors, the political speaking tour would give way to the celebrity lecture tour in the second half of the nineteenth century.

When Dickens, the inventor of the late nineteenth-century reading tour, undertook his tours in America in 1867, he was already a practiced hand in England, having given public readings there. He did so, at least after 1866, under the guidance of George Dolby, who came to be called his manager but bears great similarity in his duties to the impresarios and agents who followed him. Dolby came to be well known in his own right, even publishing a work based on his position following Dickens's death: *Charles Dickens as I Knew Him: The Story of the Reading Tours in Great Britain and America (1866–1970)*. After successfully guiding Dickens through domestic reading tours, Dickens trusted him enough to send him in advance to America—twice—in order to arrange his tour. In his book, Dolby details the kind of work he did for Dickens. While Dickens's American publishers, Ticknor and Fields, were handling the bookings for the big eastern city readings, for example, Dolby communicated with smaller cities, sometimes traveling to see them, about the celebrity's schedule, venues, and fees. It was Dolby who, in consultation with Fields and others, decided that Dickens should charge two dollars per person to hear him speak, successfully locating that magic number that would encourage the most number of people to come while being sure to make it worth Dickens's difficult trip (Dolby 142–3). Dolby would later accompany Dickens on his trip to make sure everything went smoothly. He was as much companion as manager.

Dickens lectured more than 75 times, usually selling out and often traveling every other day to a new destination. Such an involved and hectic schedule required a business manager. But even Dolby's machinations couldn't bear all the responsibility. The host country might do something to help ease the process. As Dolby struggled to communicate with disparate organizations, venues, and people in wide-ranging destinations, Dickens noted there might be an easier way. In Boston, Dickens was quoted as saying that "There should be a general headquarters, a bureau for the welcome of literary men and women coming to our country for the purpose of lecturing. They should be made to feel at home among us, and the business of arranging routes of travel and dates for lectures and so forth be in charge of competent workers, and an established fee agreed upon" (qtd. in Wallace 349). Someone was listening.

The great American impresario James Redpath would pick up where Dolby had begun. It was later that year that Redpath founded the Redpath Lyceum Bureau, presiding over it as President until 1875, after which time they kept his name on because of his own celebrity. Redpath's idea was to provide exactly the service of which Dickens had spoken. *He* would contact the various venues, the various lyceum bureaus that had begun springing up around the United States in the late 1860s. The bureau offered security to the traveling author who might be worried about being cheated by independent venues. Unlike that scenario, John McKivigan writes, "Redpath's bureau represented these lecturers, not the lyceums that employed them" (119). He gained a commission from the price paid for the lecturer, so he had an incentive to get the highest price available, watching out for authors so that lyceums would pay the agreed upon amount, not less if poorly attended. Redpath worked with Mark Twain, most famously, but also Henry Ward Beecher, among scores of others.[1] He charged everywhere from 50 dollars to Beecher's record 1,000 dollars a lecture. He also helped create the Chautauqua movement, with its tented, week-long educational and entertaining lectures and performances. Redpath's price of about 25 cents per lecture for the Chautauqua programs helped draw in mostly professional clerks, mechanics, and artisans but rarely laborers or factory operatives (McKivigan 119). Redpath was Twain's agent in lecturing whenever he lectured at home. But it was George Dolby who stepped in when Twain traveled to England. Dolby urged Twain to lecture in England and

---

[1]   Redpath claimed authors and preachers made by far the worst lecturers, since they merely read their essays (McKivigan 131). Twain and Beecher were the exceptions, no doubt.

worked with him to set up his tour and choose the venues and price.[2] The business of managing celebrity lecture tours was thriving.

Ten years later, it was Richard D'Oyly Carte who would manage the lecture tours of Arnold and Wilde. Carte was a vastly successful impresario who would also build the Savoy Opera and nurture the collaboration of Gilbert and Sullivan. Less known for his work with transatlantic lecture tours, he still played a central role in this now very practical business. Carte was producing Gilbert and Sullivan's *Patience*—a play in part about Aestheticism—in New York and wanted Wilde to tour simultaneously to encourage interest in the play. Wilde's schedule, which included more than 150 lecturing engagements and places as geographically distant as Montreal, New Orleans, and San Francisco, was no easy feat to accomplish. He needed an experienced manager and agent, and he had one in Carte.

Carte likewise acted as agent to Matthew Arnold, organizing his only slightly more modest tour the following year. Arnold would speak to more than 40,000 people and travel extensively as well (Honan 408). But like Wilde, Arnold paid a price for having an efficient agent, and not just a monetary one. Both authors' power over when and where they would go was vastly diminished by being, in a sense, produced by someone else. Just as Douglass had come up against the pressures of his white organizers, so Wilde and Arnold complained of feeling powerless over their fates in America—and often exhausted from the nonstop schedule. In addition, Carte's goal was to make as much money as possible—not to safeguard the reputation of his authors. In one such conflict of interest, Carte realized that Arnold was offending the press every time he spoke to them in America. Knowing that notoriety would increase sales, Carte "hoped" Arnold would speak to even more journalists, clearly encouraging him to appear out of touch (Honan 396).

The sheer commodification involved in such an enterprise left the skeptical Arnold feeling powerless and passive. Perhaps it was partly this specter that kept Henry James, whose lectures I treat in the next chapter, from following a similar route. His ambitions were also much diminished in terms of popularity and lecture events. James would speak fewer than 20 times, and generally to smaller audiences. But this fact allowed him to arrange his lectures himself, without working with an impresario.[3] Such stubborn individual bargaining meant James would make less money than most of his fellow commercial lecturers, but it also meant he had some degree of freedom in determining when and where he would lecture. The lecture tour was a thriving business by the last part of the nineteenth century. The business

---

[2]   Fred Lorch, however, argues that it was Twain himself who urged that the lectures be done at the elite Queen's Concert Rooms in Hanover Square, saying "he meant to lecture to the elite of London and charge high prices for admission. If there was reputation to be won in England he wanted to win it from its leading citizens" (*Trouble* 139).

[3]   Michael Anesko points out that James shrewdly employed an agent (James Brand Pinker) in 1898 and beyond, and he did have the help of his Harper's editor, but James himself was often the one doing the bargaining for fees, finding at times he overshot, asking too much (Edel 601).

of being a celebrity—of generating publicity—needed a professional touch, and institutions appeared to manage access to such publicity. Indeed, as Richard Salmon tells us, publicity is "a symptomatic phenomenon of modern culture: one which is linked inextricably to the historical formation of mass culture and mass media ... The modern writer, no less than the modern text, enters into a sphere of public circulation" (*Henry James and the Culture of Publicity* 3). Authors who embraced this fact, like Wilde, hired (or were hired by) a good manager.

Lecturing in Knee-Breeches: Wilde and the Photographic Lecture Tour

The news that Wilde would be lecturing in the United States in 1882 was met with ambivalence. Wilde's Old World heritage made him at once respected and distrusted. Still, the particular movement he embodied, and the way he embodied it, was oddly suited to the culture of celebrity around him and to the lecture tour format.

The lecture tour came early in Wilde's career, when he was experimenting with various public personalities. Gagnier describes two of the options he tried out in his writing:

> Perceiving a fallen art world and an unregenerate public, Wilde had two alternatives and developed two distinct styles to represent them. He displays his cynicism in his technique of ironic reference, his idealism in imaginary dialogues of purple prose between two men. The first technique would lead to his theater and comedies; the second to a select audience of artful young men, romances, and prose poems. The first style was Wildean wit; the second, a prose jeweled and seductive. The doubleness constituted Wilde's response to the modern bourgeois artist's dilemma between private art and the need for a public. (19)

Gagnier focuses here on his textual identity; the lecture tour constitutes a significant point, early in his career, when Wilde would try out both of these alternatives in person, shaping his heterogeneous, American audience's understanding of him. The lectures were performances reminiscent of theater, but Wilde's tone was strikingly earnest in his descriptions of Aestheticism for American audiences, recalling Gagnier's second "alternative." The wit and irony would come out elsewhere— in newspapers quotations, letters, and in his physical performance as a traveling authorial "personality." The result was that Wilde's lecture performances were only one part of a larger tour scenario. He would set up a new standard of "personality" in the marketplace, one that could be easily caricatured and transferred.

Like most lecturers, Wilde combined a healthy interest in receipts with a deeply held belief in his ability to enact the role of the cultural steward. After an attack on his motives by a rival lecturer, the Scottish soldier Archibald Forbes, Wilde wrote privately, "I have something to say to the American people, something that I know will be the beginning of a great movement here, and all foolish ridicule does a great deal of harm to the cause of art and refinement and civilization here" (*Complete*

Letters 129). Indeed, his message to American audiences in "Decorative Art in America," one of three lectures he brought with him, is idealistic about the role of art in culture. Touting art as necessary in education, Wilde sounds far less playful than he would in some of his other work. He claims that students of art

> learn to abhor the liar in art—the man who paints wood to look like iron, or iron to look like stone. It is a practical school of morals. No better way is there to learn to love Nature than to understand Art. It dignifies every flower of the field. And the boy who sees the thing of beauty which a bird on the wing becomes when transformed to wood or canvas, will probably not throw the customary stone. What we want is something spiritual added to life. Nothing is so ignoble that art cannot sanctify it. (15)

This Ruskinian claim of art's moral power is the last point of the lecture. He ended seriously.

While he earnestly undertook his role as the "Apostle of Aestheticism" while in the United States, he later criticized Americans, claiming that their strict morality barred them from the higher plane of the art world. In "The Decay of Lying" (1889), he writes,

> The crude commercialism of America, its materialising spirit, its indifference to the poetical side of things, and its lack of imagination and of high unattainable ideals, are entirely due to that country having adopted for its national hero a man who, according to his own confession, was incapable of telling a lie, and it is not too much to say that the story of George Washington and the cherry-tree has done more harm, and in a shorter space of time, than any other moral tale in the whole of literature. (980)

This much better known paean to artificiality in art stands in contrast to the earnest rhapsodizing in his lectures to Americans. One reason may be, as Gagnier claims, "the contradictions in [Wilde's] work can be understood only by reference to his audiences" (3). In other words, at least in part, Wilde adopted his message for an audience; he was inevitably shaped by them. They welcomed his earnest speeches even as the press and an American mass culture offered a second stage for a different public persona. Indeed, American audiences understood and took part in creating Wilde's public, contradictory personality. Americans might not have had artistic imagination in an aesthetic sense, but neither were they wedded to simple ideas of hero worship.

Unlike Arnold's later lectures, Wilde delivered an aesthetic performance in which text and scenario complimented each other. He spoke about the decorative arts and became an example of them himself through his dress in lectures, appearances, and photographs. Like Arnold, Wilde would have his public personality appropriated by the public in various forms, usually through imitation and mockery; yet in a sense he made this possible—anticipated and even embraced the loss of self entailed in celebrity. While Wilde may have distrusted the marketplace and what it did to the arts, he was engaged in creating a personality that was reproducible. To begin with, Wilde did 98 interviews during his visit to the United States.[4] Additionally, he accomplished this through his "costume" and his visually static presentation of himself during his tour. As Wilde understood, in the booming marketplace, "The only real people are the people who never existed" ("Decay of Lying" 975). Through use of technologies such as photography and audacious self-invention—a most American trait—he became adept at creating a persona that *could* be a reproducible part of the public archive. In fact, Wilde was coming from a British theatrical culture that, like its American counterpart, refused the easy dichotomy of "theatrical" and "authenticity." As many had before him, Wilde drew from a culture in which, as Lynn M. Voskuil has shown, "theatricality and authenticity often functioned dynamically together to construct the symbolic typologies by which the English knew themselves as individuals, as a public, as a nation" (2).

Wilde's public personality had preceded him to the United States in the form of a play about Aestheticism; Wilde was assumed to be the original of at least one of the main characters. Gilbert and Sullivan's *Patience* opened in London in April 1881 and was later produced in America that same year. The two characters— Reginald Bunthorne and Archibald Grosvenor—bore great resemblance in attitude, talk, and look to Wilde, but also to his Aesthetic comrades Whistler, Rossetti, and Swinburne. In his biography of Wilde, Richard Ellmann suggests that the two characters in *Patience* took most of their characteristics from Wilde, the "most articulate standard bearer of aestheticism at the time" (135). In 1881, during the run of the play, Wilde was also being represented as another "type" in England: George du Maurier was publishing caricatures of Wilde as the fictional character Maudle, in dialogue with (probably) Whistler, fictionalized as Jellaby Postlethwaite.[5] In the year before his visit to the United States, then, Wilde was already a type, a caricature, one outside himself.

The producer of *Patience* in New York City was Richard D'Oyly Carte, the prominent impresario who would later bring Matthew Arnold to the States in 1883. He sent Wilde a telegram proposing the tour, expecting "*Patience* to give a fillip to Wilde's lectures, and the lectures to give a fillip to *Patience*" (Ellmann 151). Wilde was coming to explain the growing English movement but also as an advertisement for D'Oyly Carte's production. Americans would laugh more heartily and pay more easily for a play about a type they could picture and understand. Hence, he was advertised to booking agents as the spokesperson of Aestheticism—already a figure of the culture market more than author of his own works. The manager of lecture tours for D'Oyly Carte, W.F Morse, wrote to a booking agent explaining Wilde's appeal this way: "if Mr. Wilde were brought to this country with the view of illustrating in a public way his idea of the aesthetic

---

4   See Hofer and Scharnhorst (2). They also write that Wilde "conducted an interview as if it were a performance" (4).

5   Wilde did nothing to dispel this association; in fact, he embraced it, telling reporters that "I am the original" for Maudle (qtd. in Mendelssohn 22).

... not only would society be glad to hear the man and receive him socially, but also ... the general public would be interested in hearing from him a true and correct definition and explanation of this latest form of fashionable madness" (qtd. in Ellmann 152). Wilde would, indeed, end up explaining the movement in three lectures—"The English Renaissance," "Decorative Art in America," and "The House Beautiful"—all of which pointed to beauty as the secret to a meaningful life, whether it be found in Italian art, contemporary England, or in the homes or cloaks of Colorado miners. Indeed, "illustrating in a public way" would come to mean not only lecturing but also "performing" off the stage.

Wilde's tour lasted for almost a year, during which he gave nearly 150 lectures. He traveled up and down the Eastern seaboard, through Midwestern cities like Chicago, St. Louis, and Lincoln, and on to California, spending time in San Francisco and returning east to spend memorable days in the mountains of Colorado. His lecture schedule was grueling—almost every night for weeks straight—and he often complained about the practical arrangements, writing Morse to take care of an incompetent assistant, simplify the schedule (he often crisscrossed states within a few days), or order him new clothes. He faced several disruptions, including a feud with a fellow lecturer which threatened to outlast his stay, an arrest for failure to deliver a promised lecture, a near-total swindle at the hands of a confidence man, and a few incidents of being hooted and hollered off the stage.[6] Wilde took it all in stride and emerged as a success, at least in his own representation of the event.

He was not far off. Wilde was given the treatment that had awaited other British visitors such as Harriet Martineau (before her speech on abolition) and, most memorably, Charles Dickens. As it would for all lecturers in America, Dickens's lecture tour became a standard, approached but never met, against which foreign authors self-consciously measured their success. The ever-confident Wilde couldn't help but compare himself favorably to Dickens in his letters home:

> The hall had an audience larger and more wonderful than even Dickens had. I was recalled and applauded and am now treated like the Royal Boy. I have several "Harry Tyrwhitts" as secretaries. One writes my autographs all day for my admirers, the other receives the flowers that are left really every ten minutes. A third whose hair resembles mine is obliged to send off locks of his own hair to the myriad maidens of the city, and so is rapidly becoming bald. (*Complete Letters* 126)

Dickens had been outraged by the selling of his hair during his first trip to American, but Wilde, recalling this precedent, sees it as an honor, albeit an absurd one. Notably, he had employed a hair stand-in, so it wasn't really his person that was being sold on the market. In the same letter, he quipped that "Yesterday I had to leave by private door, the mob was so great. Loving virtuous obscurity as much as I do, you can judge how much I dislike this lionizing, which is worse than that

---

[6]   The *Hartford Daily Courant* reported that Wilde had been served a notice for a "breach of contract" and would "contest the case" ("Oscar Wilde's Arrest" 3).

given to Sarah Bernhardt I hear" (*Complete Letters* 126). He even joked about his public existence, after a reporter asked him for some details of his private life, "I told him I wished I had one" ("Oscar as He Is" 87). He compared himself again to Dickens, writing to another friend, "Great success here: nothing like it since Dickens, they tell me. I am torn to bits by Society. Immense receptions, wonderful dinners, crowds wait for my carriage. I wave a gloved hand and an ivory cane and they cheer" (*Complete Letters* 127). These accounts, with their awareness of Dickens and Bernhardt, were written during his initial success in New York, and, indeed, these lectures were sold out. Some reports later claimed this was not always the case, but they were well attended.[7]

Wilde was social critic enough to understand the fickleness of the public. Sitting in Kansas awaiting his next lecture, he writes that from his window he can see a crowd gathering around a house: "It is the house of the great train-robber and murderer Jesse James, who was shot by his pal last week, and the people are relic-hunters ... The Americans are certainly great hero-worshippers, and always take their heroes from the criminal classes" (*Complete Letters* 164). Wilde perceptively identifies with Jesse James, and by doing so, acknowledges the nature of celebrity, which takes a frenzied interest in the famous, without drawing distinctions between criminals and authors, those who could shoot straight and quickly and those whose only weapon was wit. Having had his own relics sought after by the public, Wilde must have felt uneasy about the association. The shifting nature of celebrity worship was clear to him. His own reviews moved between fascination and veiled insult. One report cast his worshippers as decidedly female.[8] While many who went to see him were women, "A percentage of the men had evidently paid to see Oscar Wilde as they might have paid to see the tattooed man, feeling curiosity about the celebrity but no interest whatsoever in the subject" ("Oscar Wilde in Hartford" 2).[9] The same paper reports that he had "not been received with reverence by the press or public in Washington" ("The National Capital" 3), but "Probably Mr. Wilde's audiences have been about equally divided" ("Oscar Wilde and the Aesthetic School") about his worthiness. One mockingly announced his performance by saying, "The disciple of the beautiful will sully his classic shoes with the worldly mud and slush of our streets to-day" ("Opera House Entertainments" 2).

Perhaps surprisingly, given his penchant for performance, Wilde was not an exceptionally gifted orator. Excelling at conversation, not drama, he took elocution lessons before his departure for the United States. According to Ellmann, he told the

---

[7]   Hofer and Scharnhorst maintain his crowds lessened significantly in the West, where his lectures on "lived aesthetics" might not appeal to "rural folks scratching out a living" (3).

[8]   When he appeared in Hartford, Connecticut, one report recalled, "There probably two hundred and three hundred people in the house. Of those rather more than half were ladies" ("Oscar Wilde in Hartford").

[9]   See Mary Blanchard's "Oscar Wilde in America, 1882: Aestheticism, Women, and Modernism," in *Oscar Wilde: The Man, His Writings, and His World*, for a discussion of Wilde's appeal to women in America.

instructor, Hermann Vezin, that "'I want a natural style with a touch of affectation.' 'Well,' said Vezin, 'and haven't you got that, Oscar?'" (155). His rejection of the Dickensian dramatic model of lecturing may have come at a good time, since Americans were used to the histrionic on their stages, with lecturers imitating Dickens, and were growing suspicious of things too dramatic or "artificial." One onlooker, Helen Potter, noted that "The voice is clear, easy, and not forced … This disciple of true art speaks very deliberately, and … the closing inflection of a sentence or period is ever upward" (qtd. in Ellmann 164).

While Ellmann claims that "Wilde had lectured to them as much through rhythm and manner as through argument, heaping up cadences to make them imagine the beauty he did not define" (166), the response to his style was, overall, not effusive: One reviewer saw this "natural" voice as "monotone," complaining that the lecture "was delivered without attempt at oratory, and, with the inevitable English upward inflection, soon became monotonous" ("Boston Correspondence" 2). On a different lecturing occasion, another writer remarks that Wilde's speaking voice was "very trying to American ears … He reads monotonously with a suspicion of sing-song" ("Oscar Wilde in Hartford" 2). This reviewer was not alone; one newspaper reporter claimed Wilde always spoke in hexameter (Ellmann 158).

Wilde's public performance became most memorable not in his oratory but in visual representation and textual reproduction of his wit. Rather than embodying an idea in his voice, he would do it through the visual. Thus, his performance became less part of the repertoire, to use Diana Taylor's terms, and more part of the archive. His would be a photographic, rather than dramatic, lecture tour. Indeed, what set Wilde apart from Arnold was his attention to the visual. The now-famous poses for an American photographer captured what Wilde looked like at the time and, importantly, what he was wearing. Carte commissioned the portrait photographer Napoleon Sarony to take photographs of Wilde to be circulated during his American tour. These photos would become the most famous, even today, of the author. But photography was and is no mere medium of reality, and as Daniel A. Novak has shown in his study of the representation of Wilde's sexuality through photographs, the Sarony pictures show a man who is "at once Wilde and not Wilde—both a concrete individual and spectral type" (72). Indeed, Novak points out that for the Victorians, photographs "turned concrete individuals into anonymous abstractions" that could be easily reproduced (64). By creating a visual, transferable version of Wilde, such photographs perpetuated the duality inherent in Wilde the celebrity.[10] Indeed, his image was used for advertisers far beyond his own desires, as Mendelssohn shows (3).

---

[10]   Novak uncovers another key event that has bearing not just on Wilde's tour but on the issues of ownership raised in the tours of Dickens and Twain. Just as they were arguing for transatlantic copyright protection for their works, Napoleon Sarony was suing a lithographic company before the Supreme Court for copyright infringement. Sarony claimed his photographs of Wilde were his creations and that he, not Wilde, owned them. He won, proving that "he, not Wilde, had authored the poses in the photographs" (Novak 79). Thus, the distance between an author and his or her public image was made official by law.

Fig. 3.1   Oscar Wilde Photographed in the United States by Napoleon Sarony.
             Source: The Library of Congress

Even if the photographs didn't exist, we would still have verbal images of Wilde's appearance on the platform. Many described his look, his pose, his manner, and, above all, his clothes. His interest in clothes was hardly limited to this period in his career (three years later, in "The Truth of Masks," he would argue that even Shakespeare had been obsessed with costumes), but in America, costume helped construct his image. He arrived for his tour in a green overcoat that reached his feet, complete with seal or otter trim around the collar and on his "Polish" round cap. For his lectures he was "dressed in a black dress coat, white vest and extremely low cut shirt, with flowing white silk cravat, black knee britches, crown stockings and slippers" ("New York News" 3). The knee-breeches, especially, would be notable to audiences everywhere. Describing his lecture entrance in the style of stage directions, Helen Potter noted several details: "Costume.—A dark purple sack coat, and knee-breeches; black hose, low shoes with bright buckles … hair long, and parted in the middle, or all combed over. Enter with the cavalier cloak over the shoulder" (qtd. in Ellmann 164). It was read, at least by one reporter, as "the aesthetic costume" ("Our New York Letter" 17).

Wilde earned this attention by planning his costume in detail. He went to a "costumier" rather than a tailor once in America. His letter to Morse from St. Louis requesting more clothes preserves the assiduousness with which he faced the question:

> Will you kindly go to a good costumier (theatrical) for me and get them to make (you will not mention my name) two coats, to wear at matinées and perhaps in the evening. They should be beautiful; tight velvet doublet, with large flowered sleeves and little ruffs of cambric coming up from under collar. I send you design and measurements … Any good costumier would know what I want—sort of Francis I dress: only knee-breeches instead of long hose. Also get me two pair of grey silk stockings to suit my grey mouse-coloured velvet. The sleeves are to be flowered—if not velvet then plush—stamped with large pattern. They will excite a great sensation. I leave the matter to you. They were dreadfully disappointed at Cincinnati at my not wearing knee-breeches. (*Complete Letters* 141)

His later quip, "Strange that a pair of silk stockings should so upset a nation" (qtd. in Ellmann 164), was disingenuous.[11] It is clear he meant to make a visual statement. Indeed, his warning to conceal his identity from the costumier seems aimed at protecting the "sensation" the new clothes would cause at the moment of revelation.

His attempts at concealment failed, it seems, when the "costumier" in question spoke to the press, resulting in snide accounts: One writer commented in an article entitled "Oscar Wilde's New Clothes" that "he intends to grapple with the great

---

[11]   He didn't completely succeed in being thought shocking. As one reviewer wrote, "His dress was not in outré taste. The low collar and shirt front presenting an expanse of linen, with their accompaniment of studs and necktie are not very much more extreme than have been seen here at evening parties" ("Boston Correspondence" 2).

clothes-question in deadly earnest. He has planned and furnished the drawings to a New York artist in toggery for two costumes not only 'utterly utter,' but lovely and exhilarating beyond all modern comparison" (6). Wilde would grapple with the question not only behind the scenes but also on the stage. By design and as a function of the press, clothes would make the lecturer.

His costuming approach was appropriate for lectures on Aestheticism, especially his second, "Decorative Art in America." In it, Wilde makes the claim that Americans must find beauty in their everyday lives: "what your people need is not so much high imaginative art, but that which hallows the vessels of everyday use" (4). Americans suffer from "bad wall-papers, horribly designed, and coloured carpets, and that old offender, the horse-hair sofa, whose stolid look of indifference is so depressing" (5). Echoing the Arts and Crafts Movement in England, his was a democratized Aestheticism.

One way to produce a change, of course, was through dress. Wilde spends some time discussing clothes as a potential expression of art: "There would be more joy in life if we should accustom ourselves to use all the beautiful colours we can in fashioning our own clothes" ("Decorative Art" 6). Men are particularly in need of an aesthetic makeover. He tells his audiences that, throughout his travels, "The only well-dressed men that I saw ... were the Western miners. Their wide-brimmed hats, which shaded their faces from the sun and protected them from the rain, and the cloak, which is by far the most beautiful piece of drapery ever invented, may be dwelt on with admiration ... They wore only what was comfortable and therefore beautiful" (8). Wilde's commendation of the miner's "comfortable" clothes is an example of his sometime interest in the rustic and the natural. It must have stood in obvious contrast, however, to the visual statement he made on the stage, with buckled shoes, silk stockings, and knee breeches. Comments like this on the miners called more attention to his own dramatic dress.

Wilde's sartorial exhibitionism would be rewarded by imitation, or reproduction. It is prescient, then, that like other proponents of Aestheticism, Wilde explicitly decried art that was mechanically reproduced. Even in his short lecture on "Decorative Art in America" he complained about "machine-made furniture" (5) and lamented that, "In these days, when we have suffered so dreadfully from the incursions of the milliner, we hear ladies boast that they do not wear a dress more than once" (7–8). The problem with quick turnover and reproduction is that they do away with tradition. He goes on to say that "In the old days, when the dresses were decorated with the beautiful designs and worked with exquisite embroidery, ladies rather took a pride in bringing out the garment and wearing it many times and handing it down to their daughters" (7–8). What is wanting is both originality and permanence: "When I was at Leadville," he writes, "and reflected that all the shining silver I saw coming from the mines would be made into ugly dollars, it made me sad. It should be made into something more permanent" (13). In Wilde's formulation, mechanical reproduction is part of the larger system of trade where marketplace value trumps all other concerns, including cultural permanence or aesthetic value.

Still, it is precisely its propensity to encourage imitation or reproduction that distinguished Wilde's public personality during his lecture tour was. This fact also derives in part from Wilde's cultivation of (and reliance on) costume on the platform and in photographs. Dickens and Twain both embraced the theatrical element of lecturing, utilizing the tools of the actor as they enlisted body, voice, and drama to take full advantage of ephemeral, live performance. But the most successful playwright among this group of transatlantic lecturers was oddly anti-dramatic. Unlike the two more dramatic literary lecturers, Wilde did not exploit his voice or body movements in his performances. We've already heard about his monotone: His physical movements were also less than histrionic: "His only gestures last evening were resting his left hand on his hip, twisting his handkerchief nervously with both hands, and shifting his weight from one leg to another" ("Oscar Wilde in Hartford" 2). And yet, unlike Arnold and Henry James, who would be accused of simply reading essays, Wilde did use visual performance—he just did it with his clothes, holding poses in various attitudes to produce the full effect. His performance seems closer to *tableau vivant* than theater.

These tableaux were easily copied. The most notable example occurred during his lecture at Harvard. The front rows were filled with students dressed in Wilde-like apparel, there to mock rather than listen. The papers picked up on the plan and Wilde was tipped off. Some time into his lecture, he added, "I see certain young men, who are no doubt sincere, but I can assure them that they are no more than caricatures. As I look around me, I am impelled for the first time to breathe a fervent prayer, 'Save me from my disciples'" (qtd. in Ellmann 182). He didn't need to be "saved" from his disciples this time. Papers were embarrassed by the students' rowdiness, claiming Wilde as the winner in the contest, pointing out that the students "had the tables turned on them by the tact of the lecturer before the evening was over" ("Boston Correspondence" 2). At a similar event in Rochester, NY, students were rowdier, trying to drown out their lecturer with hoots and hollers. Halfway through the lecture, as part of a plan, an older, African-American man in formal dress and one white kid glove (such as Wilde sometimes wore) danced his way down the center of the aisle. Such imitations, in spite of their mockery, could quickly become dangerously disrespectful. One paper worried that Yale students were planning something similar and hoped that Yale would "let Princeton and Harvard bear off the palm for rowdyism and boorishness" ("The Yale Boys and Oscar Wilde" 2). A less threatening occurrence came in Denver in April of 1882, when the humorist Eugene Field drove around the town during Wilde's visit in an open carriage, dressed like Wilde, holding a lily (Wilde's signature flower) and gazing at a book. When Wilde heard of the episode, he reportedly said, "What a splendid advertisement for my lecture" (qtd. in Ellmann 191). Indeed, Ellmann claims that, throughout his career, "Wilde found ways to act and speak in full knowledge that they could and would be mocked. To be derided so was part of his plan. Notoriety is fame's wicked twin: Wilde was prepared to court the one in the hope that the other would favor him too" (136–7).

Wilde's reaction demonstrates an understanding of the fluidity of public personality. For all his careful craftsmanship of an authorial persona, he recognized that his personality could be authored by multiple forces. By the time he came to America, the source for his own persona was even in question—how much was him and how much was the already-developing caricature of him in *Patience* and in the Du Marier cartoons? He might be the originator of a role or style, but in America it could be immediately appropriated by his audience and the literary marketplace—in the form of students who mocked him, humorists who imitated him, or caricatures that produced their own parallel appearances. His use of costume provided a shorthand for Aestheticism: a version of the movement that could be extracted from his personality and made into something transferable. The photographs he had taken in New York, posing variously (and famously), act in the same way. The substance of his lectures seems to fade in comparison with the visual image of the aesthete, bedecked in knee-breeches and silk stockings. And this static image, not the live performance, is what Wilde was known for. Even accounts of the lectures themselves tend to minimize the "live" theater aspect of the lectures and focus on the clothes and the poses.

Wilde's costume does work similar to his epigrams. Wilde famously said to a customs official upon arrival in America, "I have nothing to declare, except my genius," and it was this sort of quip—not his lecture ideas—that circulated during his tour (and continues to today). It is a rhetorical strategy Amanda Anderson has taken up as the most pointed example of Wilde's belief in aesthetic distance. The epigram "seems always to pull away from the text, and from the context of the action, announcing itself as quotable, transferable, and indifferent" (Anderson 148). Wilde's epigrams "float intertextually among his works" (Anderson 148), suggesting their ability to be "transferred" easily. Anderson critiques the epigram as a form of distance that separates it from any meaningful or ethical value; she recuperates Wilde's "melodramatic" moments as self-critiques of aesthetic distance gone too far. Her analysis of the epigram is important to the lecture tour experience in that it suggests ways in which aesthetic distance can facilitate distance between the author and his public personality in the literary marketplace. Indeed, most critics see a duality in Wilde, made up of the cynical and the idealistic (in Gagnier's terms) or the proponent of aesthetic distance and moral value (in Anderson's), and the lecture tours were a moment when both sides seem to be enacted in the public sphere. His earnest, idealistic lectures were complicated by his emphasis on static poses, costumes, and one-liners, easily "quoted" or transferred into epigrammatic or caricatured versions of "Oscar Wilde."[12] The result? Another two Oscar Wildes, one that lectured in person, an embodied, contextualized self, and one that existed on a market plane—sampled, borrowed, altered, and appropriated. This last one survived, surprisingly intact, through to our own day.

---

[12] This appropriation continued after his death, as Novak writes in "Performing the 'Wilde West.'" The continued popularity of the "Wilde West" shows, in which writers imagined sometimes-erotic meetings between hetero-cowboys and the effeminate Wilde, further evidences Wilde's persona's marketplace flexibility.

"The Cruelest Hoax of All": Arnold and Celebrity Identity Theft

Oscar Wilde's tour demonstrated the way an author, despite appearing in person, could inspire reproduction of his public persona—while the tour was still going on. A few years after Wilde's visit, Matthew Arnold would see a similar "reproduction" after he'd left the United States in early 1884.[13] On April 7, 1884, *The Chicago Tribune* printed the following letter written by a recent visitor to that city:

> That which most impressed me during my stay in Chicago, as well as in other American cities of the larger sort which I visited, was a certain assumption of culture, which, upon close observation, I found to be very superficially varnished over a very solid basis of Philistinism ... I heard so much of the language of culture in the higher classes of Chicago society that I was almost prepared to admit that I had been unjustly prejudiced in the statements which I have made from time to time concerning America: but if the discourse to which I listened on the morning of which I speak stands in any way as an expression of the Chicago ideal of culture, that ideal is, I regret to say, a low one ... There was something quite pathetic to me in the thought that this discourse, with its dreary waste of unctuous commonplace, its diluted rhetoric, and its judgements, many of them so ludicrously misconceived, should be to such an audience as I saw about me, the embodiment of cultured thought, and from time to time I could not help thinking that Philistinism in its frank English expression was a less unpleasant sight than was afforded by the thinly-disguised Philistinism which was here imposing on itself and making pretenses of culture. ("Matthew Arnold: England's Incomparable Egotist" 9)

Philistines? Culture? The author could only be one person, and indeed the account was signed "Mr. Arnold." The cultured people of Chicago were outraged. Just months before, they had hosted Arnold as he made his way across the United States giving lectures. His apparent ingratitude prompted *The Chicago Tribune* to invite public outrage, subheading the letter "England's Incomparable Egotist Gives His Account of Chicago Society" and subsequently seeking interviews with those who had befriended Arnold during his stay. One such interviewee, a Professor Swing, who had hosted Arnold at the Chicago Literary Club, responded to Arnold's comments with what became a characteristic defense. Swing observed that "the trouble with Arnold is that he was disappointed. He had probably calculated on making $25,000 during his trip. On the contrary, he left for home with about $6,000." Professor Swing goes on to say that "Arnold, although 'a man of sweetness and light,' sours very easily, and after being slighted in Chicago, as he thought, had no good opinion of the public" ("Matthew Arnold: A Series of Replies to His Genial Criticisms of the People of Chicago" 3).

---

[13]   Portions of this section are drawn from "The Uses of Distinction: Matthew Arnold and American Literary Realism," in *American Literary Realism*. Copyright 2004 by the Board of Trustees of the University of Illinois. Used with permission of the University of Illinois Press.

The public—and not just in Chicago—responded with defensive explanations for their local papers. The following appeared in *The New York Daily Tribune*:

> It was unlucky for everyone that Matthew Arnold came to America at all. He had many admirers on this side of the water before his advent. Very few Americans like him now ... He had been a social disappointment, and many times a vexation that strained the limits of courteous toleration. He returned with $6,000 of the Philistines' money in his pockets. From that point of view it is not surprising perhaps that he regards us with dislike, and Chicago with the most dislike, because in this city he made no money at all. (qtd. in Lawrence 77)

The use of Arnold's terminology to deride his character continued in other responses: "Had he not been gratuitously entertained while here, had not his expenses been paid for him, his lecture profits would hardly have paid the board bills of the apostle of sweetness and light, his family, and the dog" (qtd. in Lawrence 77).

In fact, these passionate defenses were misdirected. The headline of the April 8 evening edition of *The Chicago Daily News*, the *Tribune*'s local rival, announced, "The Tribune Hoaxed!" Arnold had not written the letter at all. Frederick William Gookin describes the incident in his 1926 history, *The Chicago Literary Club*:

> The hoax which was perpetrated in April, after Mr. Arnold had returned to England, was conceived and in large part executed by one of our members who is still on the resident list. It was a brilliant performance cleverly designed to trip up The Chicago Tribune, which, for some time previously, had been suspected by journalists on the staff of The Chicago Daily News of appropriating without acknowledgment special dispatches printed in the earliest edition of the New York Tribune. What purported to be an article contributed by Mr. Arnold to The Pall Mall Gazette was concocted by our member who displayed much ingenuity in imitating the eminent English author's style ... It was arranged by the conspirators that this should be printed in just one copy of the earliest edition of The New York Tribune on Sunday, April 6, 1884, and that this copy should get into the hands of the New York representative of The Chicago Tribune. Naturally he lost no time in telegraphing such a choice morsel to this city, and it appeared in the next morning's paper ... (81–5)

Ostensibly, the "cruelest hoax of all," as *The Chicago Daily News* labeled it, entrapped *The Chicago Tribune* in an editorial theft, but the use of Arnold's name and ideas in this journalistic imbroglio requires a closer examination, especially as it drew from his recent lecture tour. The hoax letter clearly mocked Arnold's speech, his ideas, and his arrogance. The Arnold impersonator, for example, distinguished the assumption of "true" culture from Chicago's mere "pretense of culture." Arnold's "assumption of the Messiahship," as Lawrence has termed it, which had angered the public throughout his visit, was parodied as well (79). The designation of the people of Chicago as "Philistines," besides implying all the characteristics Arnold had spent his career delineating, satirized his polemical use of catch phrases to articulate his arguments. He had quickly become a caricature which could be appropriated and reused.

The hoax, which I'll return to later in the chapter, culminated a trying lecture tour. In 1883, Arnold commenced his lecture tour of the United States that went as far west as St. Louis and included Canada. Almost everywhere he went, he was met with strained politeness, partly because of an essay, "A Word about America," published before his arrival, and partly because of his performance on the lecture circuit. In "A Word about America," Arnold had written, "that which in England we call the middle class is in America virtually the nation" (85). Yet he described that English middle class as having "a defective type of religion, a narrow range of intellect and knowledge, a stunted sense of beauty, a low standard of manners" (85). This utter unconcern for winning over the audience continued in "Civilization in the United States" written after his return in 1888, in which he attacked American newspapers and the American "funnyman," an implied reference to Mark Twain, as the chief opponents of his cherished "distinction."

Arnold would end up being bewildered by American hostility, especially since he regarded his criticism as friendly. As he wrote in "A Word," "I have long accustomed myself to regard the people of the United States as just the same people with ourselves, as simply the English on the other side of the Atlantic" (71). As the public's reaction showed, this attitude did not acknowledge the American desire for a separate national identity. But Arnold felt he had earned the right to criticize: "when one has confessed the belief that the social system of one's own country is so far from being perfect ... one has earned the right, perhaps, to speak with candor of the social systems of other countries" (74). He even goes so far as to remind his readers that he is "not attacking" America but merely "holding a friendly conversation with American lovers of humane life" (93). This is the voice of the Arnoldian "alien"—the voice of disinterestedness, especially as regards nationality, one of the ideas an Arnoldian critic holds at a distance in his quest for culture. Arnold clearly underestimated how much he was seen in America as an alien of another kind. He encountered defensive responses even from the literary elite before he entered the country. More often than not, that is, Americans took him up on precisely the sort of national dispute he wanted to avoid.

In the years preceding his visit, Arnold had enjoyed only a qualified respect from writers and readers of magazines such as *Atlantic Monthly* and *Lippincott's*. His essays about British society as well as "A Word about America," written before his visit, offended the press at all levels. John Henry Raleigh argues that two elements in American culture prevented his friendly welcome: "the drive towards an indigenous culture and the conservative voice of religion" (54). In fact, the editorials and letters appearing before 1884 vary in their willingness to adopt an Arnoldian standard of judgment for American literature and culture. Americans were, unsurprisingly, more receptive to his relentless criticism of his native country. An essay in *Atlantic Monthly* of 1879 urged, "let us follow Mr. Arnold attentively in the charges which he brings against his own compatriots ... trying to suppress as far as may be a certain ignoble satisfaction we all have in hearing Englishmen berated" ("Recent Literature" 675). At other moments, however, Arnold's hierarchical system is questioned. One author wrote, "Matthew Arnold has said much of Sweetness and Light, but less of another essential element of culture—strength" (Hartstone 675). Similarly, Arnold's vision of a few alien apostles of culture (one of whom was himself) bringing the aforementioned sweetness and light to the public is countered by one writer who argued that "the effect of such individuals upon the quality of the mass has never been appreciable" ("Recent Literature" 677).

Once Arnold appeared in person, criticism grew harsher. He offended everywhere he went.[14] John P. Long characterizes Arnold's uncomfortable experience in Chicago, which was "half-frontier, half cultured" (34) and, hence, "suspicious of things British" (41). Magazines had begun to question whether a negation of "sweetness and light" was a thing to be lamented. Claiming strength, democracy, and equality as more important cultural values, the literary magazines anticipated William Dean Howells in his 1888 declaration that Americans would do well to be without Arnoldian "distinction."[15]

Both E.P. Lawrence and Long blame this chilly reception partly on Arnold's remark in one of his lectures that Emerson was not a "genius." Arnold's lecture "Emerson" is an affectionate but critical look at an American cultural hero. Arnold deeply respected the man and his work, calling Emerson's prose the most important of the nineteenth century. Though the lecture reveals a deep sense of debt, it also makes claims about what Emerson was *not*: *not* a great philosopher, *not* a great poet. Choosing to deliver this lecture first in the East soon after Emerson's death, where Emerson was particularly revered, was a characteristic failure on Arnold's part to judge his audience. Yet his measured assessment shows his own stubborn faith in the need for self-criticism, for distance even from cultural heroes. His respect for Emerson was all the more reason to approach his work critically, to his mind. To some extent, Emerson becomes a stand-in for his own position of cultural authority, down to the habit of summing up their views aphoristically. Consider his remarks on a classic Emersonian phrase "trust thyself": "With Maxims like these, we surely, it may be said, run some risk of being made too well satisfied with our own actual self and state, however crude and imperfect they may be. 'Trust thyself?' It may be said that the common American or Englishman is more than enough disposed already to trust himself" ("Emerson" 186). Arnold challenged his own tendency in one direction—in other words, his admiration for Emerson—and put it under critical scrutiny.

---

[14] E.P. Lawrence has painstakingly documented the souring of the American press on Arnold, in dailies and periodicals.

[15] Howells agrees with Arnold that there is little distinction in America, but celebrates the fact that instead, Americans have "common beauty, common grandeur, or the beauty and grandeur in which the quality of solidarity so prevails that neither distinguishes itself to the disadvantage of anything else" (66).

The reaction in the American press was a mix of aesthetic arguments and patriotic defensiveness. *The Literary World*, commenting on Arnold's judgment of Emerson, asked "What Matthew Arnoldese is this? Did we not say that Arnold has no faith? He is forever pulling down. And the present is only a new instance of an iconoclastic habit which is his second nature" (Matthew Arnold's Visit" 446). Such accounts cast him as an enemy of American democracy, guardian of the elite past. *The Nation* questioned his aesthetic judgment: "The critical telescope he brought over with him is of insignificant power to take an observation of Emerson, and … it is owing to the weakness of the glass" (500). James Russell Lowell offered another critique of Arnold's elite taste, noting, "I think that Matthew Arnold … is apt to think the superfine as good as the fine, or even better than that" (qtd. in Lawrence 70).

Arnold delivered two other lectures during his tour: "Literature and Science" and "Numbers." While "Emerson" demonstrates Arnold's identification with Americans and his commitment to critical distance, the other lectures more explicitly advocate the function of culture. "Literature and Science," written before his tour was planned and delivered in England prior to his arrival in America, defends the study of literature against the inroads scientific study was making in nineteenth-century culture. In this lecture, Arnold goes so far as to claim that the desire for literature was universal: "our hairy ancestor carried in his nature, also, a necessity for Greek" (135). This lecture reiterates many of the basic claims of *Culture and Anarchy* and "The Function of Criticism at the Present Time." Arnold argues that Americans, too, need a "criticism of life, that knowledge of ourselves and the world, which constitutes culture" (84) and "To know the best that has been thought and said by the modern nations" (89). The two statements encapsulate Arnold's push toward cosmopolitanism—elsewhere in the essay he remarks that the *world* should inform American minds—and the "disinterestedness" that is needed for individuals to evaluate their culture, state, and self.

"Numbers," his third lecture, offers insight into his relationship to lecturing, suggesting that every culture depended upon a minority— the "remnant"—to humanize and civilize it. In America, because the population is numerous, the remnant will be too, he argues, giving the American remnant a better chance of shaping general culture. In spite of a hint of sarcasm, Arnold sees promise in numbers: "The vast scale of things here, the extent of your country, your numbers, the rapidity of your increase, strike the imagination, and are common topic for admiring remark" (5). Before he allows the listening Americans to bask in their potential, however, he points out that "If we are to enjoy the benefit, I said, of the comfortable doctrine of the remnant, we must be capable of receiving also, and of holding fast, the hard doctrine of the unsoundness of the majority, and of the certainty that the unsoundness of the majority, if it is not withstood and remedied, must be their ruin" (56). He challenges his audience to serve not just the nation but also culture through disinterested thought.

"Numbers," like the other lectures, restates a common theme in Arnold's work. As Anderson has pointed out, Arnold's thinking always maintained a tension between abstract, universal principles and embodied, subjective enactment. On the one hand, he imagines that "numbers" could be cosmopolitan enough to rise above mere patriotism; such men "save States" (Arnold 32). Meanwhile, those identified directly with national institutions, such as politicians, "are making believe, plausibly and noisily, with their American institutions, British Constitution, and civilizing mission of France" (31). Still, as Anderson points out, Arnold was deeply invested in the practical sphere. Thus, while faith in objectivity and an intellectual "best self" is part of his thinking,

> there is another line of thinking in Arnold's work, one that raises up temperament, stance, and character as the site where fact and value might be reconciled, or where the promises of modernity might best be glimpsed. The emphasis here is on the successful subjective enactment or embodiment of forms of universality, as distinguished from other moments where he seems to valorize impersonal or objective standards. (Anderson 97)

The route to achieving objective criticism or disinterestedness, then, is through the individual; more than that, it is through the individual's self in all its forms: through practical action, through personal "temperament," "stance," manner, and, I would add, through the body. Part of Arnold's subjective credentials comes from his belief in the necessity for the individual to make culture known throughout the world. His is missionary work undertaken on the individual level.

Thus, Arnold carves a space between a world in which universal, objective truths are accessible to cultured individuals and a more subjective, aesthetic one in which an individual's subjective character and artistic experience are the essential medium of truth. There is value outside the individual, but the way toward it is through subjective enactment. When he tells American audiences that "having in mind things true, things elevated, things pure, things amiable, things of good report; having these in mind, studying and loving these, is what saves States," he is encapsulating this tension ("Numbers" 32). His message was reproduced in parallel fashion in his lecture tour, which was a concentrated site not just of individual embodiment and authorial discourse but also of marketplace ideals and audience-author relations.

To begin with, Arnold insisted on objective standards of value, yet he did so in a format that emphasized his subjective and, Americans imagined, biased stance. His message was that a few detached intellectuals could point the way toward culture. But how could he promote critical distance to an audience so interested in the very human and situated messenger? Arnold wanted the people to hear the cultural steward; the press reported on his accent, monocle, and muttonchops. As an author speaking, he was enacting his own principles, urging audience members to seek a disinterested, objective vision of their own country. The nature of live performance made this a difficult argument to make. Audiences saw him as extremely "interested," peculiar rather than universal, individual rather than representative: as a body, as an Englishman, and as a businessman. His first principles were questioned.

Though Arnold may have desired what we might think of as theoretical embodiment, the literal embodiment necessitated by a lecture tour left him exposed and uncertain. Reporters from daily papers focused on his personal attributes rather than his words. The primary complaint was that Arnold's elocution in the larger halls was so poor that people couldn't hear his words. As a result, Arnold's manager insisted he take lessons from an elocutionist, which he did, to great effect. Newspapers recounted the way he looked and expressed disappointment that he was not more "refined." Americans seemed to see him more as a philistine merchant than an apostle of culture. As with many lecturing authors, the manner, not the matter, became important in accounts of his lectures.

The focus on personality and appearance was debilitating in two major ways. First, it challenged Arnold's ideal of the author as a disinterested and, by implication, disembodied voice. Second, it challenged his ability to escape Englishness. National identity could be recognized in a myriad of small ways, from accent, to clothes, to facial hair, to manner. The result was that the American public could never see Arnold as a universal embodiment of culture, but only as an Englishman. With his audience constantly drawing attention to his person— sometimes during lectures when people shouted for him to speak up—the complex arguments for being a cultural alien faded.

While these aspects of lecturing challenged his claim of objectivity, the second part of his message—the individual's responsibility to enact that objectivity—was also questioned. The "distance" created by the role of celebrity subverted culture's values: in the marketplace, individuals became public personalities, divorced from ethics or value, and economically interested. Thus, while the tour was designed to enact his principles, it may have inhibited his sense of authorship. His letters from America reveal his discomfort with celebrity. He delayed writing "Emerson" until he'd had a chance to see Emerson's grave and birthplace, but he found writing on tour nearly impossible, in part because of time restraints thrust upon him as a celebrity and tourist. His frustration with the composition of "Emerson" arose from the incompatibility between the private exercise of writing and the public exercise of being a visiting, lecturing author. In one letter, Arnold knew what he wanted the lecture to be but asked, "how and when am I to write it? The blaring publicity of this place is beyond all that I had any idea of" (*Letters* 221). Public exposure of the kind that came with being a visiting lecturer made writing nearly impossible.

Still, the publicity of celebrity intrigued him. It is evident that in the beginning of his tour, Arnold regarded the newspapers as a mediating institution between himself and popular audiences. He wrote to his daughter from New York, "I am told the tickets are selling well, and all the literary and newspaper class are for me; but I cannot believe that I shall have the *gros public*" (*Letters* 261). In the same letter he promised to send her a newspaper clipping that eagerly anticipates his lectures. It was perhaps the practical man in Arnold who responded in this way. He wrote his sister that "my managers are anxious I should not refuse to see people, the press people above all, as the newspapers can do much for the success of the lectures" (*Letters* 267). As late as November, two weeks after beginning his tour in New York and Boston, he boasted that his term "remnant" from his lecture "Numbers" "is going the round of the United States" (*Letters* 269). However, publicity grew more and more annoying. Even as early as the letter to his sister quoted above, he noted that "I have seen no American yet ... who does not seem to desire constant publicity" (*Letters* 267). Arnold might have appreciated the boost to his lecture turnout aided by publicity in the papers, but he remained uneasy about its excess. He later wrote to his daughter that "they are an excellent people, but their press seems to me at the present an awful symptom" (*Letters* 271).

As his lecture on Emerson offended Bostonians, and his remarks on the need for a "remnant" offended good democrats everywhere, Arnold became a spectacle of English snobbery. The "lecture tour resulted in a weakening of his reputation here and served to strengthen Americans in the belief that all Englishmen were snobs" (Lawrence 63). And he was aware of it. He wrote that the newspapers "report all one's goings and sayings ... it is perfectly astounding but there is no real depth in it" (*Letters* 267). As the reporting turned more superficial (and negative), Arnold became aware of being on display. By January he wrote a friend that "the papers get more and more amusing as we get west. A Detroit newspaper compared me, as I stopped now and then to look at my manuscript on a music stool, to an 'elderly bird pecking at grapes on a trellis'—that is the style of the thing" (*Letters* 296). In these responses, Arnold reveals unexpected humility and even a sense of humor: "we have had a week of good houses (I consider myself as an actor, for my managers take me about with theatrical tickets, at reduced rates, over the railways, and the tickets have *Matthew Arnold Troupe* printed on them)" (*Letters* 295). He may have supported cultural hierarchy, but he remained willing to participate in mass spectacle. Still, the venture was not a financially successful one. He had hoped to make more money than he did.

The "blaring publicity" and concern over ticket sales made Arnold aware that a lecturing author had to be part of a performance-based literary marketplace, whether he wished to be or not. Not only that, but the version of himself he saw reflected in the press, the "Matthew Arnold Troupe," felt removed and simplified. The "troupe" designation seems to anticipate Mark Twain's incorporation of the author later in the century, a move which served to separate an author's private and public selves even more. His well-considered, if oft-repeated, phrases sounded like sound bites; the epigram, as Wilde found, helped reproduce a public personality. Arnold's sound bites were not, however, witty and were never meant to be taken out of context. His complex approach to critical distance—that tension between the universal and the self—was ignored; the press found the scandal of his criticism easier to reproduce. Both sides of his subtle critical formulations were challenged by the experience: the gesture toward the universal rang hollow when delivered by an embodied speaker, and the emphasis on the subjective responsibility of the individual was too complex to become part of a "persona." Rather than inspiring cultural change in America, Arnold must have been annoyed to find he'd inspired little more than a caricature. The hoax that followed his visit betrayed the only kind of "distance" that could exist in a celebrity marketplace: that of an author from his public persona.

The newspaper hoax revealed, after he had left, the authorial public personality moving beyond its source. Now Arnold's "image" was being produced not only by the author, the lecture tour, and the press but also by an "imposter" author. The hoax treated his name as public property, to be manipulated or stolen. It is also important to note that Arnold's name and phrases were used in the first place to catch another "theft." Competition—cultural and economic—between newspapers was nothing new, but the fact that they used a staunch critic of marketplace ethics in their competition is ironic. So is the fact that the public was victimized by falling for the hoax, which became clear in some people's passionate defense of Chicago following the hoax letter, when Americans lashed out at "Arnold," in response, and then were embarrassed after the truth came out. As the hoax was revealed, such people's desire to attain Arnoldian culture was censured as much as their alleged failure to do so. Those who so quickly responded with harsh criticism of Arnold appeared culturally naïve once the hoax was exposed. The editors of *The Chicago Tribune* may have been the immediate targets, but those who so publicly fell for the hoax joined Arnold in becoming collateral victims. Again, so passionate a debate about Arnold didn't even involve the principle actor in the drama. Indeed, he heard of it much later.

This two-pronged satirical hoax—mocking Arnold and those who were too quick to attack him—was replayed in the weeks following as literary magazines voiced their own responses. The editors of *The Nation* and *Harper's Weekly* were hardly defenders of Arnold's name, having disparaged his theories before and during his visit. However, the use of Arnold as bait in a marketplace hoax impressed these editors as a breach of taste. Moreover, the literary magazines chastised readers for their failure to recognize a weak imitation of Arnold's style, implying that an intimate familiarity with Arnoldian thinking was prerequisite to an appropriate rejection of it. His hierarchical vision of culture was clearly unacceptable to the literary magazines, yet the editors of these periodicals expected readers to be familiar enough with Arnold's writing to recognize the letter as a fraud. In this way, they adapted an Arnoldian framework of taste and familiarity with high art, even as they rejected an Arnoldian system that excluded the common as a valid focus for literary study.

The Nation referred to it as a "cruel joke" (307), *The Critic* as a "clumsy joke." Indeed, clumsiness seems to have been the real offense. It should have been apparent (these journalists insisted) that Arnold's style was vastly different from the "feeble prose" of the hoax, which *The Critic* deemed "commonplace" (one of the criticisms made by the pseudo-Arnold). Gookin, the historian of the affair who had delighted in the "ingenuity" of the parody, quotes another member of the club who admitted that "critical examination would reveal many flaws in it" (86). *The Critic* also predicted "it will fail to amuse even those who take it for a bit of harmless fooling" (174). *The Nation*, writing just a day after the hoax was exposed, wondered "whether the winnings of the game justify such a breach of good taste" (307). In these early responses from literary magazines, the editors defined "good taste" as a delicate negotiation of elite and vulgar impulses, as an ability to laugh at both Arnold and his attackers.

Editors adapted an Arnoldian standard of taste by criticizing those who didn't know their Arnold well enough to recognize a fraud. These targets of ridicule, professed intellectual members of Chicago society, became Arnoldian Philistines in the pages of *The Nation* and *The Critic*. For *The Nation*, the ill-advised reaction of Professor Swing, one of those who lashed out against "Arnold" before the truth was exposed, signaled a failure of aesthetic discernment: "The essay was a fair caricature of Mr. Matthew Arnold's ideas but its style was so widely different from his that no one familiar with his writings could have been deceived by it" (307). *The Nation* argued that readers "ought to have been able to detect the fraud at a glance, by the style. Professor Swing, in particular, seems to us to need a little ripening" (307). For literary magazines and others interested in claiming superior discernment, a "ripe" reader must be able to employ "critical examination," a method of discernment reminiscent of Arnold's imperative of "seeing the object as in itself it really is." The literary periodicals insisted on a firm knowledge of Arnold, publicly mocking those who apparently had less, even as they rejected Arnold himself.

Similarly, Henry James, reading the fraud letter in London, demonstrated his comfort with Arnoldian language. In a letter to his brother William, James writes,

> You enclose an extract from a newspaper purporting to be an article of Matt. Arnold's about Chicago society, and seem to believe it is his! It doesn't, I must confess, appear to me even a good hoax—full of phrases ("intelligent gentleman," "cultured people," "owner of a large grocery-business," etc.) which he is incapable of using. Nor would he talk about "Chicago-society." It seems to me poor as a parody. (*Henry James Letters* 3:39–40).

James goes on to express surprise "that this writer should have appeared to you to catch the tone in which a London man of M.A.'s stamp would express himself" (*Henry James Letters* 3:40). Like the magazines (although without knowing for certain that it was a hoax), James is amused by William's failure to recognize that such "commonplace" expressions of Arnoldian elitism could not have come from Arnold himself. His casual reference to "the tone in which a London man of M.A.'s stamp would express himself" distances himself from Arnold's pompous idiom even as he asserts a familiarity with Arnoldese.

The hoax exposed the flattening nature of the public persona, as this man of letters became a mere gathering of phrases and attitudes. It also confirmed Arnold's ideas about the problems with Philistinism. He mentions the hoax in his essay "Civilization in the United States," seeming somewhat bewildered: "It was a poor hoax, but many people were taken in and were excusably angry ... I of course instantly telegraphed back that I had not written a syllable of it. Then a Chicago paper is sent to me; and what I have the pleasure of reading, as a result of my contradiction, is this: 'Arnold denies; Mr. Medill [my old friend] refuses to accept Arnold's disclaimer; says Arnold is a cur'" (180). In this essay, written the last year of his life, Arnold has not forgotten *his* old nemesis, the Philistine press. He writes, "if one were searching for the best means to efface and kill in a whole nation the discipline of respect, the feeling for what is elevated, one could not do better than take the American newspaper" (177). There was no love lost between the perceived enemies of culture and its foremost advocate.

This episode of authorial identity theft was only a more extreme example of the fate of public "personalities" in the literary marketplace. The lecture tour might have brought the real man to the United States, and enabled Arnold to enact his own principles of embodied disinterestedness. However, the fact that the hoax occurred directly after his departure illustrates how public personality would only partly be authored by a lecturer appearing in person. The press continued to appropriate and disseminate versions of Arnold, destabilizing through multiple representations who Matthew Arnold was and what he meant in a transatlantic context.

Arnold and Wilde, though appearing in person, as others had done before them, saw themselves remade, their public personalities reshaped by these detachable, transferable elements of their identities: the epigram, the catch phrases that Matthew Arnold used (only without the wit that made Wilde so likable), the photographs and caricatures that appeared in the press, the lectures themselves. Indeed, the lectures were competing against many other forms of representation. "Live performances" had begun in part as an answer to a growing culture of mass reproduction. The experience of Wilde and Arnold show that ultimately lectures could feed, rather than mitigate, this culture. Arnold would fail to realize how important events like the hoax would be to his cultural influence. He saw it only as another example of the scurrilous press; he might have recognized it as also a poor rewriting of his message to the United States. Contrastingly, Wilde's cultivation of a persona that could be easily mocked and circulated was a way to anticipate and oversee his reproduction in American culture. Lecturing, a form of representation in which Wilde seemed only partially interested, certainly aided celebrity culture. Yet there were already signs that lecturing operated on too small and intimate a scale. Live performance was limited to a few thousand a night, at most. Photographs (like later media such as radio performances or television) were not so limited. In performing a personality that could be mechanically reproduced, Wilde was actually looking past the next great writer to appear on the American stage: Henry James.

Chapter 4
The Voice of the Master:
Henry James and the
Paradox of Performance

By the time Henry James returned to the United States in 1904 after a more than 20-year absence, the transatlantic lecture tour and visiting author were such a commonplace occurrence in American culture that the reaction in the press could only be historically comparative. Writing in *Putnam's Monthly*, H.G. Dwight suggested that

> There was neither firing of cannon nor ringing of bells on the late summer day of 1904 when a certain passenger stepped from his steamer at New York. Youths did not unharness his horses and drag him triumphantly between gala brown-stone fronts. Virgins did not bestrew the asphalt with rose, nor herald his progress with welcoming hymns … On the contrary, there was little in the event to bring it to the eye of the man in the street. (164)

Because there had been so many notable visits in the near past against which James's arrival had to be viewed, accounts, like this one, were seemingly more interested in what *did not* happen: James *was not* feted, James *was not* given a hero's welcome, James *was not* noticed. Wilmer Cave France, writing for *The Bookman*, makes a similar comparative analysis, claiming that "Mr. James has not come among us—if one may use a phrase so intimate—with the manners and intentions of certain other novelists from across the water," adding rather snidely that "nor has he been greeted as we greeted Dickens in the breezier eighteen-forties, with a brass band. He has come to take a look at us" (71). Dickens still set the standard for visiting authors in America, despite the passage of 40 years since his last visit, and his well-known lionization had become a point of reference. Though it was James's first real time out on the lecture circuit, he came noticeably late in the history of transatlantic lecture tours.

Perhaps it is because of this belatedness that his lecture tour has received less critical attention than other episodes and themes during this period of his career, such as his observations of America and subsequent account of them in *The American Scene* and the authorial performance that produced the New York Editions of his works (both of which followed his lecture tour). Even during his own time, *The Bookman* claimed that "He has, indeed, a lecture in his pocket, but rather as though it were part of his luggage than as a motive of the enterprise" (France 71). Like this writer, critics have tended to see James's lecture as unimportant, "part of his luggage" and of little interest. The lecture experience has been seen as anomalous, since James never really lectured before or after his American engagements.[1]

In fact, the lecture tour fits neatly into the narrative of James's authorship which has emerged in the last 20 years, one that takes issue with the image of the Master as an artist happy to remain apart from the popular marketplace. We now have a picture of James that suggests he was much more ambivalent in his attitudes regarding public appeal. This work has been incredibly influential in reshaping James's image, most notably in Michael Anesko's *Friction with the Market* from the mid-1980s and David McWhirter's *Henry James's New York Edition: The Construction of Authorship* from the mid-1990s.[2] Still, such critical attention has tended to focus on the rhetorical performance in the Prefaces, *The American Scene*, and James's financial concerns at the time; as a result, James as a lecturing performer has remained somewhat unexamined. Refreshingly, Heather O'Donnell has done a detailed study of the text of his two lectures, perceptively marking the shift between the first, "The Lesson of Balzac," a predictable admonition of American literary taste that focused on critical interest in authors' lives instead of their work, and his second, "The Question of Our Speech," an indictment of American speech patterns reflecting James's growing alienation from mass audiences. "The Lesson of Balzac" was educative, even hopeful, according to O'Donnell, while "In 'The Question of Our Speech,' James identifies with the English language itself, a language displaced and alienated in the American landscape" (141). O'Donnell gives the two lectures a serious reading and offers important textual analysis. Still, it is easier to see James as the bewildered, passive, literary luddite who could not, or would not, adapt to American popular culture if we don't also see him as an embodied performer. In keeping with this book's approach, the text must be weighed with and at times against the performance scenario in which James was engaged.[3]

---

[1]   James did read once, to a Boston women's Saturday Moring Club in Boston, during his trip to America in the 1880s, but rather as a local favor than a full engagement.

[2]   As McWhirter points out, the problem with the image of an elitist James "is that it purports to be a definitive, fixed image of an author always skeptical of the static, whose restless mind's most characteristic movement is an immanent one that conceives the way out as the way through. A cramped aura of sanctity has grown around what might be called James's cultural presence" (26).

[3]   As used throughout this book, "scenario" takes account of the lecture scene as a whole—including the text, the space in which it was performed, as well as the gestures, manner, and accent (especially important in transatlantic performance) of the lecturer. The term comes from Diana Taylor's *The Archive and the Repertoire: Performing Cultural Memory in the Americas*. She adds, "By shifting focus from written to embodied culture, from the discursive to the performatic, we need to shift our methodologies. Instead of focusing on patterns of cultural expression in terms of texts and narratives, we might think about them as scenarios that do not reduce gestures and embodied practices to narrative description. This shift necessarily alters what academic disciplines regard as appropriate canons, and might extend the traditional disciplinary boundaries to include practices previously outside their purview" (16–17).

Considering the text of James's lectures in and against his performative context yields a complicated picture. James's first lecture, "The Lesson of Balzac," was an outrageously ironic undertaking. That a famous author embarking on a series of lectures during which he would be photographed, interviewed, dissected, discussed, and imitated would give a lecture on the toxicity of celebrity culture had to have amused both James and his audience. Similarly, rather than see "The Question of Our Speech" lecture solely as a retreat away from the public, popular cultural sphere, I argue for it also being a culmination and embrace of public performance.

James's lecture experience was, in many ways, a two-act finale of the nineteenth-century transatlantic lecture tour. In fact, both of his lectures demonstrate how fundamental the lecture tour—and transatlantic performance and celebrity—had become to authorship at this time. First, like many authors before him, James performed a "posture of reticence," to use Leo Braudy's term, even as he worked the publicity surrounding his tour with the dexterity of a turn-of-the-century Bob Dylan. The text of the "The Lesson of Balzac" was only one of several characters in this particular performance. Second and likewise, even though textually "The Question of Our Speech" pushes back against the popular and toward an elitist standard, as a performance, it did anything but. Like his successful predecessors Dickens and Twain, James embraced the lecture format with true performative gusto (albeit in his reserved way). Thus, shortly before James began preparing his permanent, legendary status as the "Master" in print through the New York Edition, he was actively engaging in the ephemeral, embodied experience of the public performer, subjecting his image to other discursive forms of representation in the chaos of newspaper and magazine coverage that followed. Finally, James's transatlantic identity, which he announced with the pronoun "our" in "The Question of Our Speech," exposed the fault line in the transatlantic relationship. Over all, the disconnect between James's spoken word and the performance scenario, including the audience response, reflect how text and performance were so often at odds with each other. Even the Master, when thrust into the chaotic world of celebrity and performance, could let slip his grip on the unity of form and content.

"On the Spot"

When James undertook his American tour, it was with both enthusiasm and trepidation. As criticism of the past 20 years has shown, James wanted to visit his native land and was weighing whether the yield, either from increased interest in his written work or through the production of another book, would offset the costs. In fact, once arrived, he realized "his sense of his resources [was] distorted" (Kaplan 487).[4] A letter to his brother over a year before his trip reveals a mixed

---

[4]   Anesko has established James's income over his career. Ultimately, his lecture fees equaled $4050, which would have doubled his (albeit varying) yearly income (usually around $4,000) (Anesko 177).

and multi-layered desire to go. William, fearing his brother would be shocked and dismayed if he were to see American culture after more than 20 years of self-imposed exile, had urged James not to come. In response, James offers at least three reasons why he remains adamant about coming. The first is a sense of age and a desire for experience sooner rather than later; writing from Lamb House in England, he reminds William that if he doesn't go to America, "I should settle down to a mere mean oscillation from here to London and from London here—with nothing (to speak of) left, more, to happen to me in life in the way of (the poetry of) motion" (*Correspondence* 238). Second, he specifically wants to see his home. He's been absent so long he can refer to "My native land, which time, absence and change have, in a funny sort of way, made almost as romantic to me as 'Europe,' in dreams or in my earlier time here, used to be" (*Correspondence* 238). Despite William's warnings of its decidedly unromantic development, James believes it will bring him a sense of fulfillment and reconnection with a now-strange past. Third, and most relevant here, he anticipates a complex payout as well. As he tells William,

> the actual bristling (as fearfully bristling as you like) U.S.A. have the merit and the precious property that they meet and fit into my ("creative") preoccupations; and that the period there which should represent the poetry of motion, the one big taste of travel not supremely missed, would carry with it also possibilities of the prose of *production* (that is of the production of prose) such as no other mere bought, paid for, skeptically and half-heartedly worried-through adventure, by land or sea, would be able to give me. (*Correspondence* 238)

Indeed, James recognizes that through "prose of production" or the "production of prose," the trip would deliver material value. James's long-standing interest in the transatlantic subject, and especially the American subject in a transatlantic context, makes this desire to travel back to his native land seem inevitable. But in expressing his intention, James is actually in keeping with many authors of the time. For so many, traveling would give rise to writing. More interesting, in the context of his forthcoming lecture tour, traveling, or engaging in the "poetry of motion," cannot be "supremely missed." In fact, there was already pressure on many authors, not just on the author most identified with the transatlantic sphere, to be present or appear in person to their transatlantic audiences.

But his uneasy relationship with American audiences—the variable in the above equation—is clearly on his mind in these letters as well. He wonders to William

> if you also are accessible to the impression of my having *any* "professional standing" là-bas big enough to be improved on. I am not thinking (I'm sure) vaguely or blindly (but recognizing direct limitations) when I take for granted some such Chance as my personal presence there *would* conduce to improve: I don't mean by its beauty or brilliancy, but simply by the benefit of my managing for once in my life not to fail to be on the spot" (*Correspondence* 238–9).

In other words, he needs some kind of popular American support even to have a visit noticed. Still, he can't resist adding the French "là-bas" almost in defiance of his stated desire for American popularity. This stepping back from the popular even in the act of approaching it is indicative of how he would approach his lecture tour in the coming year. But he is clear, here and elsewhere, that his presence is needed if he is to remain relevant. By 1905, authors who were or wished to be successful in the transatlantic market knew they needed to be "on the spot," even if briefly, in order to connect with audiences. By 1905, travel was easy enough for this to be an expected occurrence.

James and American Audiences

Despite this potential American tepidness, James wanted to be "on the spot." For James, being "on the spot" came to mean not only being in his native country but also meeting face-to-face with audiences on whose support he could not count. In a way, he had already written a version of his lecture tour 20 years prior in his 1886 novel about live speech—*The Bostonians*. The final pages of that novel produce a nightmare version (for the lecturer) of a lecture tour. As Basil Ransom and Olive Chancellor wage their great battle for ownership of Verena Tarrant, the narrator merges, at times, with Ransom in his estimation of the lecture audience as a frightening prospect. As the audience becomes impatient waiting for Verena to emerge, Ransom "had a throb of uneasiness at his private purpose of balking it of its entertainment, its victim—a glimpse of the ferocity that lurks in a disappointed mob" (416). The position of the performer—Verena, in this case—is clearly tenuous. Ransom predicts "They'll howl and thump, according to their nature ... Hear them, the senseless brutes" (430). When Olive Chancellor decides to go out in Verena's place, we anticipate an angry reaction and imagine Olive "trampled to death and torn to pieces" (432). The imagery of the animalistic, savage, devouring crowd is a blunt exhibition of what was possibly a fear of live audiences.

By his own account, James's earlier experience with theater played out more like the nightmare version he creates in *The Bostonians*. In 1905, when he ventured to lecture in America, it had been ten years since his embarrassing, nearly traumatizing, failure on the London stage. His play, *Guy Domville*, was hissed at and booed. Worse than that, however, James himself ventured onto the stage at the end of the play in answer to some marginal applause. Standing on the stage, James witnessed first-hand what could be the author's "relationship" with a live audience, and it was not reassuring. As he wrote to his brother, "All the forces of civilization in the house waged a battle of the most gallant, prolonged and sustained applause with the hoots and jeers and catcalls of the roughs, whose *roars* (like those of a cage of beasts at some infernal 'zoo') were only exacerbated (as it were) by the conflict" (*Letters* 3:508).[5] The animal imagery, associated with the "roughs" who

---

5   Leon Edel, of course, helped to construct James as an author who drew back in horror from the excesses of the marketplace because of what it did to the author. In Edel's reading, this was brought home to James during his experience bringing *Guy Domville* to

had bad taste, would resurface later in his analysis of American speech, but it also gestured back toward his earlier imaginings of mass audiences in *The Bostonians*.

Still, the image of James as an elitist with only scorn for popular audiences has been complicated in recent decades. In an effort to show James's relative interest in popular audiences, critics such as Anne T. Margolis, in *Henry James and the Problem of Audience*, and Anesko have emphasized his readiness to enter into the theater in the later nineteenth century, the period between his early success and his later phase. For Margolis, James was interested in theater because "writing for and being acted upon the stage represented a form of initiation and variety of intimate interaction which he found lacking in the triangular relationship between a novelist, his publisher, and the reading public" (57). She goes on to argue that, in the case of his theatrical adaptations, such as *Daisy Miller*, he read the applause as a stand-in for acceptance of his literary work: "It was as if James needed to feel the presence and hear the applause of the thousands who had been amused and even enlightened by the printed version of *Daisy Miller*" (Margolis 57).

The theater, then, is not just an oddity in his career, as such failed endeavors tend to be viewed by literary historians. Rather, "James's plays may indeed be literary curiosities, but his professional experiment with the theatre epitomizes the concern for fame, art, and fortune that affected the entire range of his career" (Anesko 19). Jean-Christophe Agnew agrees: "James's celebrated posture of detachment—his conjoined attitudes of icy aloofness and intense scrutiny—may have had as much to do, in the end, with the emotional and intellectual proximity he once felt to a burgeoning mass-market society as with the distance he eventually adopted" ("The Consuming Vision" 79). Likewise, Richard Salmon sees James as consistently occupied with publicity, early on with overreaching journalism, later, during his middle phase, with the institutions that encourage it, and beyond: "In his later fiction … James devised new strategies of representation in order to confront an increasingly diffuse and anonymous mass media, which threatened to render his earlier censure of biographers and journalists anachronistic" (*Henry James and the Culture of Publicity* 4). His lectures likewise reflected interest, disgust, and, above all, fascination with a live, mass audience.

The Critic of Celebrity

For decades, James was portrayed as a reticent literary celebrity. Such critical narratives emerged in no small part from James himself, who cultivated Braudy's "posture of reticence." According to Braudy, in the nineteenth century, "an increasingly fame-choked world was beginning to reach for solace and value to anonymity and neglect as tokens of true worth" (425). Perhaps no early celebrity

---

the stage. Afterward, the narrative goes, James sunk into a "melancholy," and Edel writes that "The behavior of the audience at St. James's had struck at the very heart of his self-esteem, his pride and sovereignty as an artist" and that he lived on as a result in "his private hell" (427).

has better embodied Braudy's idea: James was so concerned with the "frenzy of renown," to use another of Braudy's phrases, that beginning in Philadelphia in January 1905, he lectured about it during his American tour. Ostensibly a lecture about Balzac's literary achievements, "The Lesson of Balzac" opens with a lament on the state of literary celebrity. The diatribe—which casts several beloved novelists as mere accidents of personal celebrity rather than genuine geniuses— constitutes about one-fifth of the lecture in total. This preoccupation, and his seeming bafflement at modern American culture at the turn of the century, left an image of him as removed and alienated, shunning the marketplace and the literary celebrity that accompanied it. But, in fact, James showed a remarkable capacity for playing the celebrity novelist. And even when he didn't, the American press was glad to pick up the slack, creating a public persona for him. James's text, then, is only part of the story. In fact, this particular lecture on this particular tour might be seen as the culmination of celebrity culture in nineteenth-century transatlantic culture rather than its denouement. Transatlantic lecture tours had become so pervasive that they compelled an unnatural performer and skeptic of American celebrity culture like James to perform in front of live audiences, an ironic performance scenario that becomes clear when we place the text and argument of "The Lesson of Balzac" in the context of the celebrity that formed its background.

As a text, "The Lesson of Balzac" deals explicitly with American (and British) interest in authors' personal lives and, even worse, the American tendency to make that interest the basis of critical judgment. James criticizes the personal approach by critics in work on George Sand, the Brontë sisters, and Jane Austen; all, he argues, deserve little attention if it is based solely upon a romanticized narrative of their sad or extraordinary lives; all, it is worth adding, are women. Sand he describes as "a Personality equipped and armed, but of an artistic complexion so comparatively smooth and simple ..." that a critic doesn't have to go very far into her work ("Lesson" 59–60).[6] In other words, her "simple" work alone would not inspire the public worship that it has—her "Personality" does that.

The Brontës are in "the same lucky box" and are popular not because of their work but because of a "force independent of any one of their applied faculties—by the attendant image of their dreary, their tragic history, their loneliness and poverty of life" ("Lesson" 62–3). Indeed, they are "A case of popularity ... a beguiled infatuation, a sentimentalized vision, determined largely by the accidents and circumstances originally surrounding the manifestation of the genius" (62–3). He later refers to them as "the highwater mark of sentimental judgment" (65). James's

---

6   James invokes the term "personality" with its negative connotations, even though its meaning had various associations. We see the term emerge early in the century, when, for example, Frederick Douglass performs "personality" as a kind of democratic public self and, later, Warren and Brandeis use it to mean something more central to the self over which one should have control. Here, James uses it to dismiss authors who are all public pose with little artistic depth.

language, using "sentimental" and "beguiled" to describe the public's interest in the Brontë sisters, suggests it is the cool-headed critic who would advance into effective criticism. It is also highly gendered. Who is it that can be accused of sentimentality but women readers (or "fans"), for example? But more than an attack on the Brontës, James's critique is of the state of criticism itself, which is in "the most complete intellectual muddle ... ever achieved, on a literary question, by our wonderful public" (64). For James, it is that emotional interest in the lives of authors that does the most damage to literary criticism.

His comments were not completely disinterested. As O'Donnell points out, James had no sad or extraordinary life to romanticize, and his praise of Balzac is another way to advance appreciation of his own work: "[H]is real goal is to propound the lesson of another (similarly unappreciated) 'master'" (134). In doing so, "he urges Americans to look beyond the bestseller and advocates a critical shift which would transform his own reputation as well" (O'Donnell 136). In fact, James refers to Balzac as the "master," inviting the audience to "close up with me for an hour at the feet of the master of us all" ("Lesson" 115) and perhaps to think of him as a master as well. And like his own hoped-for legacy, the lesson of Balzac is simply that no other novelist "offers the critical spirit this opportunity for a certain intensity of educative practice" (5). It may not be sentimental or emotionally stirring, he suggests to his listeners, but it is good for you.

In addition to utilizing Sand and the Brontës, James casts Austen as a lesson in critical history, using her to discuss the ways in which authors' critical fortunes change with the times. He offers qualified praise for her work but points out, in a conventional dismissal of it, that Austen doesn't leave us curious about her "process, or the experience in her that fed it" (60). However, since she was "overlooked for thirty or forty years after her death, she really stands there for us as the prettiest possible example of that rectification of estimate, brought about by some slow clearance of stupidity, the half-century or so is capable of working round to" (61). But now, he claims, Austen is overestimated. He doesn't blame the readers (or his audience): "Responsible, rather, is the body of publishers, editors, illustrators, producers of the pleasant twaddle of magazines; who have found their 'dear,' our dear, everybody's dear, Jane so infinitely to their material purpose, so amenable to pretty reproduction in every variety of what is called tasteful, and in what seemingly proves to be saleable" (62). It is not the reader's fault, it's not even dear Jane's fault, in other words, but a literary marketplace that commodifies celebrities for profit. It was certainly not the first time James evinced concern for the way the literary marketplace worked.

In "The Lesson of Balzac," James has a genuine concern about literature not just as commodity but also as a specific consequence of such commodification. The very ease with which novels are produced—in fact, "mass produced"—irks the man who saw himself as a craftsman. He refers to the novel as being in a "bankrupt state," for a specific reason outside celebrity: "It has become an easy manufacture, showing on every side the stamp of the machine; it has become an article of commerce, produced in quantity" ("Lesson" 102). He contrasts this kind of novel with "those more precious products of the same general nature that we used to think of as belonging to the class of the hand-made" (103). His concern over how the "hand-made" novel might disappear in the face of those who have the "easy stamp" of a "machine" anticipates Walter Benjamin's iconic writing, "The Work of Art in the Age of Mechanical Reproduction." Among other things, Benjamin mourns the advent of the age of reproducible art objects that disconnect an object from tradition and from "its presence in time and space, its unique existence at the place where it happens to be" (222). Like James, Benjamin assumes that "The presence of the original is the prerequisite to the concept of authenticity" (222), investing in the concept of the "authentic" in a similar way to authors and audiences of the nineteenth century. James, of course, means his image of the machine metaphorically, that is to say that novel-writing has become rote and easy, without the finer craftsmanship that he'd seen in the past. Aside from the clear concern over "real" art vs. scurrilous art, there is also an elitist concern with novel writing being "available" to everyone, and his comments recall Hawthorne's concerns about the "scribbling women" who constituted his greatest marketplace competition and whose artistry he regarded with condescending skepticism.

Lecturing—the form in which this argument was all originally delivered—opened up a complex paradox for an author like James. On the one hand, it offered an alternative to this world of "the machine." A human body, a human performance, is ultimately original and cannot be reproduced, even by the author himself. In that sense it is "hand-made" or genuine—"the real thing," to use James's phrase. James himself could not be reproduced; the experience of hearing him speak did not have "the stamp of the machine."

On the other hand, lecturing turned the overwhelming tendency for the literary marketplace to commodify art objects from the novel to the author himself. Indeed, one source of the vulnerability involved in lecturing is the commodification of the speaker. In *The Bostonians*, Verena experiences this phenomenon, telling Ransom to buy the photographs of herself which were on sale in Boston and to "be sure and pick out a good one!" (242). Later, during Verena's lecture, Olive's sister comments that Verena looks less like a lady than "a walking advertisement" (261).[7] There is always the danger, for James, of somehow contaminating the artistic imagination by reducing it to commodification. Still, as Jonathan Freedman points out, James helped "to accomplish the commodification of 'culture' itself—to help create a sphere of autonomous high culture that could be accessed ... through the acquisition of goods whose possession would confirm the high cultural status of their consumers" (xiii). A ticket to see a Henry James lecture was just such a good; it represented acquisition of James himself. Thus, the critique in "The Lesson of Balzac" might focus on the problems of celebrity authors and market commodification of the novel, but the lecture scenario sent another message.

---

[7]   In fact, as Jennifer Wicke has argued, Verena's presentation as an advertisement is no anomaly in James's work: "Verena belongs to the long line of Jamesian American girls, but where *Portrait of a Lady* and *The Golden Bowl* obliquely relate their heroines to consumer culture, Verena's portrait is explicit" (98).

The Celebrity Critic

Like others before him, James was fascinated, if sometimes disturbed, by the close attention to his person and movements during his trip. Of course, it was ironic that James was engaged in a performance that encouraged interest in the author himself. In fact, "his American performances appealed to (and depended on) the very appetite for literary celebrity he was denouncing in 'The Lesson of Balzac'" (O'Donnell 139). Such is the fundamental irony of this particular lecture. Highly distrustful of mob audiences, highly critical of personality worship, this author undertook a series of performances that engaged with—in fact, depended on—both. To some extent he had no choice, and he knew it. If James wanted to be a voice in the international cultural and intellectual scene, he had to be "on the spot." That he undertook this most exposed, "popular" challenge during his later and most inaccessible phase in his literary career shows how powerful he still considered popular performance to be. Perhaps if the commodity advertised could be something truly educational—something better than Verena's loose, undisciplined clichés—then popular performance might be a valuable cultural force. His experience as a celebrity would challenge such hopefulness.

James went through a burst of enthusiasm after his first lecture in Philadelphia, for 500 people. In a letter to his brother William, he writes that

> my performance last night was a *complete* success, a brilliant one, an *easy* one, with no flaw save the immense and *foreseen* (this fortnight, by *me*) OVERDONE-NESS of the occasion: *5, or 6, hundred* people in a hall stuffed to suffocation, tho' very large and perfect audibility, & making for a "literary address" an inevitably rather false & "fashionable" *milieu*. But it *went* rather beautifully—& I revealed to myself a talent for lecturing. (*Correspondence* 279)

Likewise, to Mary Cadwalader Jones he writes of this first venture, "His affair at Philadelphia, a (to *him*) dazzling success; a huge concourse, five or six hundred folk, a vast hall and perfect brazen assurance and audibility" (*Letters* 4:337–8). Though he shows his excitement here, he also ironically describes himself in the third person, and later in the same letter adds parenthetically that he lectured "(for a heavy fee)." Indeed, James was sensitive to the fees issue, writing to Sarah Butler Wister, "Don't come to my horrid mercenary lecture if you can possibly help it; but if you can't help it ... come and brace yourself but (figuratively at least and sustainingly) *em*brace me!" (*Letters* 4:336–7).

Indeed, generally in his letters, James represented himself ironically and apologetically, anticipating critiques of himself as a bad lecturer, someone out for the money, and under the presumption that lecturing would naturally be looked down upon by his literary set. To Edmund Gosse, he writes he will "repeat the horrid act at Chicago, Indianapolis, St. Louis" (*Selected Letters* 215). But James clearly also evinces an interest in how much the lecturing will pay. He tells Gosse, "If I could come back here to abide I think I should really be able to abide in (relative) affluence: one can, on the spot, make so much money—or at least I might" (*Selected Letters* 215). He emphasizes the money (and his disdain for the audience) to William in St. Louis, writing that he lectured "before 300 plain gapers of the Contemporary Club ... I spouted my stuff last night 'successfully' (the cheque slipped into my hand *coram publico* & almost before I had said my last word)" (*Correspondence* 288–9).[8] About his lecture in Los Angeles to a "huge audience at a woman's club" (Kaplan 493), he writes to William's wife that "I go back to Los Angeles tomorrow, to (as I wrote you last) re-utter my (now loathly) lecture to a female culture club of 900 members (whom I make pay me through the nose)" (*Letters* 4:357). James's simultaneous discomfort and glee with being a paid performer is clear in his irony, his forced humor, and his distancing parenthesis.

One way James (and his public) conspired to keep his performances palatable was to control his audiences to keep them from being the "mobs" he distrusted in *The Bostonians*. He bragged to Edmund Gosse that his lectures were "always to private 'literary' or Ladies' Clubs—at Philadelphia to a vast multitude ... At Bryn Mawr to 700 persons—by way of a little circle" (*Selected Letters* 215). His comments regarding the audience at Bryn Mawr reveal his pride in both the number and selectivity of his audiences. He was addressing not a paying general public but members of more exclusive groups (who nevertheless paid him). He worked this theme into his lecture on Balzac. Immediately, for example, he asks listeners to divide and separate from the masses into a hierarchy of literary observers—of those who "appreciate." He appeals to "that quantity of opinion, very small at all times, but at all times infinitely precious, that is capable of giving some intelligible account of itself" ("Lesson" 56). At times an adept crowd-worker, James compliments his audience—who no doubt, having shown up for the lecture in the first place, qualify for membership in that small quantity. He opposes those whom he deems "precious" to the rest: "the biggest flock straying without shepherds ... that has ever found room for pasture." In fact, he argues, it is "as if their charge had turned, by some uncanny process, to a pack of ravening wolves" ("Lesson" 57). James reflects a similar argument made by Matthew Arnold in his lecture "Numbers," given some 20 years before to American audiences. For Arnold, it is what he calls "the remnant" who must guard the high level of critical thought (or "culture" in Arnold's terminology).

It is hardly surprising to those familiar with the image of James as a cultured elitist that he should make such an argument. Again, though, that he should do so in the form of live performances in front of audiences remains surprising or, at least, iconoclastic. There is no doubt that during his lecture tour—a tour partly about the excesses of celebrity worship—he was rather a celebrity himself. Nor could he help but soften his approach to personality worship when he found, perhaps to his surprise, that he was successful in inspiring it.

Though he never again achieved the popularity he had following the period of *Daisy Miller*'s publication, his arrival engendered a certain amount of interest in

---

8   Of the St. Louis audience, he also says his address is "too literary—too critical—for these primitive promiscuities" (*Correspondence* 289).

his writing. One New York reporter wrote that "James as a 'literary topic' seems to us more in evidence now than he has been since the era of 'Daisy Miller' and 'An International Episode'" ("Topics of the Week" 17). To the literary set, then, his lectures were of great interest. "The Lesson of Balzac" was heard by a select number of people, like the graduates of Bryn Mawr, the "League for Political Education" in NYC, or the Barnard Club, also in New York ("Lecture by Henry James" 16). His audiences, as I have said, were generally paying club members, indicating a certain level of economic and cultural prowess. They were mixed in terms of gender, though as he went on he would gain the reputation for lecturing more to women ("Henry James at the Barnard Club" 9).

James may have been aware of the great irony of increasing his celebrity quotient while lecturing about the consequences of such celebrity worship. Certainly, his lecturing style did little to encourage it, being less obviously histrionic than some of his predecessors. One of the reviewers of "Balzac" in New York did compare him to a magician with his hands, referring to him as "Standing behind a high table covered with a red cloth, like a prestidigitator behind his wonder working outfit, wearing a white tie and white waistcoat, with one hand continually in his trousers pocket" ("The Lesson of Balzac" 5). Generally, however, James's lecture was, as Robin Hoople writes, "slightly more interesting than watching paint dry" (*Inexorable Yankeehood* 191). Indeed, reviewers generally noted the fact that he did not "perform," in any dramatic sense of the word.

Indeed, his performance style in "The Lesson of Balzac" was notable for its simplicity. One newspaper notes of "The Lesson of Balzac" that "It is not surprising that a listener to Mr. Henry James 'as a lecturer' should have been struck by the absence of anything like a concession to the possibilities of the moment in the way of contemporary eulogy" (Trumbull 13). Another writer, Olivia Howard Dunbar, remarks that James "is not a 'lecturer' in our popular sense, and can scarcely be made one by placing him next to a high table and inviting him to speak from nine until ten o'clock in the evening" (24). Dunbar goes on to point out that "With the tricks of the orator, then, Mr. James, viewed as a platform figure, has no concern. The vulgarities or the ornaments, of emphasis, of cadence, of gesture, form no part of his expression" (24). It should be no surprise, these reviews of "Balzac" suggest, that James isn't "playing" to his audiences or attempting to entertain them with theatrical tricks. This is not to say that James didn't have an imposing public persona on the stage. One writer recorded that despite his "clerical aspect," a designation that suggests a middling performance manner, audience members who go to see him come away with the impression "of being in the presence of a man of tremendous power, even, perhaps, of greatness" (Dunbar 24).

But as with all lecturers—Dickens to Harriet Martineau to Frederick Douglass and certainly Oscar Wilde and Matthew Arnold—James's public persona was shaped by much more than his performance on the stage and what he said there. The American press, by this time well versed in the business of celebrity coverage, built its own version of "Henry James," and that version was not always flattering. James's style of writing was the primary target, with some writers taking to verse (as they had with Martineau) to voice their criticism. *The Washington Post* carried a poem in which the author surmises, "If I were Henry James, I tell you what— / I'd write a tale that hadn't any plot, / And none should know if in it aught befell, / For, being Henry James, I wouldn't tell." The author adds, "I'd work by indirection all the while, / And ladle in psychology and style, / Till every rival cried with envy frank: / 'Oh, would that I could sling the ink like Hank!'" (Martin C9).

If parodies of James the author frequented the pages of the *New York Times*, a focus on his person was no less present. In fact, as with Arnold and Wilde, this separate being—the public parody of "Henry James"—was countered by an equal interest in his very private body, habits, and movements. The observation of his smallest movements were reported by the press and began as soon as he arrived with this one-sentence article in the *Times*: "The first thing Mr. James did upon his return to America after an absence of twenty years was to go to the Post Office and ask for a 3-cent stamp" ("Mr. James Wished to Post a Letter" 8). This attention continued as James lectured on the east Coast and Midwest. He became the focus of similar attention in Los Angeles, where upon his arrival, the *Los Angeles Times* reported, under a subtitle proclaiming "Well-known Novelist, Alone, Slips Quietly into Apartments at the Van Nuys," that "He is unostentatious, is a keen observer of men and things, and spends much of his time out of doors. He retired very early last evening" ("Henry James Here" II 5). Such a report, at such a place—far away from the traditional stops for the visiting author—emphasizes again how very effectual appearing "in person" could be for the transatlantic author. The public was keen to know about the author himself as much as anything he or she said. The *Los Angeles Times* obligingly published this account of James's person:

> A man of middle age, have a face interlined with the brands of weariness and the benevolent lines of human kindness, a man of ample proportions who impresses more with his size when seated than when standing, a person whose clothes do not fit with tailorish precision, a being shrinking from ostentatious publicity, abstracted in some province of dreams—such is Henry James." ("Real Henry James, He Really Said It" 16)

The writer intermixes comments on his face, body, and clothes with interpretive comments on his character. The reporter plays the part of a Jamesian reader, turning an observant eye on the author himself.

Indeed, for the most part, the public wanted to see James, not reread his works. Newspaper reporters demanded his time to get an "inside" look at his life. The *Los Angeles Times* reported that James got a call at his hotel at 7:30 in the morning from a woman asking for an interview, to which James replied, "Why, Madam, it is impossible—I am in a semi-nude state of dress" ("Among Men of Action" II4). Such a report critiqued aggressive, intimate journalism even as it enjoyed the image of James's "semi-nude state of dress." As the above anecdote suggests, James was less than thrilled with this part of being the celebrity author. But like Bob Dylan after him, James's disdain for the press made its way into his public image. Interviews reported his disinclination to be interviewed. In Los Angeles, again, it was reported that "Mr. James objects to being interviewed," but then the interviewer adds that "he does not object to interviewing on his own account" ("Real Henry James, He Really Said It" 16). The reporter plays up James's hesitation and British turns of phrase by repeating his response: "since coming to America I've seen so many of you newspaper fellows that I feel all talked out. I have—uh—nothing at all to express to you, you know" ("Real Henry James, He Really Said It" 16). The reporter goes on to claim to have lost control of his subject, with James turning the process on its head to demand answers about the press from the reporter. Later, during a trip up to Portland, Oregon, it was reported that having felt betrayed by the publishing of his qualified censure of Westerners and the inevitable backlash to those comments, James "has retired into his shell, and refused to see any newspaper representative" (Henry James in Town for the Day").

Part of James's reticence was based on the fact that the Western portion of his trip was a chance to sightsee and relax, with less lecturing. But more broadly, it also helped to build his national reputation and public image. James assumes an "ostentatious reticence" in these moments (Braudy 450). However genuine that posture might be at times, there is no doubt that it became a part of James's continually developing public persona. Indeed, "The hankering toward performance of such nineteenth-century authors as Byron, Dickens, Tennyson, Whitman, and Mark Twain is the mirror image of the ostentatious withdrawal with which we associate Keats, Shelley, the Brontë sisters, and Emily Dickinson" (Braudy 449). In other words, an author couldn't escape performance culture. Even a turn away from it was conceived in response to it.

There is no doubt James's posture of reticence was at least partly genuine, but that attitude would simply not pass muster in the culture of celebrity and marketing into which he entered by agreeing to do a lecture tour. One journalist educated the Master on this very subject (and published his instruction), telling James that "in this country people wanted to know the jockey on the racer ... and that if they were so obliging as to buy and read your books it was only fair to humor their harmless inquisitiveness; that, moreover, it helped along your own affairs—to put it crudely, it advertised you" (qtd. in Dwight 168). Like Verena, James was being asked to be a walking, talking advertisement. And advertising his completed and soon-to-be published work (in this case, *The Golden Bowl*) and his lecture tour meant, as many authors had found, advertising himself. "The Lesson of Balzac" may have critiqued the culture of celebrity, but James's participation in it was inescapable.

"The Question of Our Speech"

"The Lesson of Balzac" was the lecture with which James arrived in 1904 and the one he intended to give over the course of his visit. It was an appropriate, unsurprising lecture from the critic and novelist. He gave it on the East Coast and all the way to St. Louis, after a brief sojourn in North Carolina and Florida. In late

March, 1905, James boarded a Pullman train and headed West for a "holiday." He devoted his free time to penning a new lecture, one he would give at the upcoming Bryn Mawr commencement.[9]

In the new lecture, James turned away from Balzac's place in a history of the novel, which, he suspected, was too "special and critical for ... Midwestern audiences" (Harris 306), and toward the question of American oral speech, "*our* speech." He might have also realized "The Lesson of Balzac" didn't take advantage of live performance. That he should choose to do a lecture on "our speech" through oral speech of his own seems inevitable in retrospect. But, oddly, his lectures have been largely treated as written essays, indistinguishable from published work on similar subjects. As an essay, "The Question of Our Speech" reads only as a complaint made by a curmudgeon who recognizes his obscurity. It certainly *is* that. However, like "The Lesson of Balzac," "The Question of Our Speech" as an orally delivered essay stands in contradiction to itself. In the text, James plaintively assesses the chaos of cultural change and its effect on language—a change that assigns him and his writing to a small group of elite cultural guardians. It imagines an essential, pure version of English that might be better safe-guarded by the constancy of print or a few faithful public defenders. But this is also an essay that only could be delivered orally if it were to make sense. For here, James *speaks* about *speech*, using the lecture platform to demonstrate both good and bad speech, placing principles of timelessness in the form of ephemeral performance. He argues for an unchanging idiom while he participates in the repertoire of spoken language, always the force behind changes in language. More than that, it is a recognition of the importance of speech—of performative, enacted culture, ephemeral and ever in need of renewal, which, he ironically hoped, could offer a model for cultural permanence.

"The Question of Our Speech" takes as its topic not what a culture's literary or written production should be but, rather, what that culture should sound like—a culture's oral performance. For James, speech is no unimportant thing. It not only echoes but articulates culture: "All life therefore comes back to the question of our speech, the medium through which we communicate with each other; for all life comes back to the question of our relations with each other" ("Question" 9–10). Culture, in the broadest sense, depends on speech. If Americans are falling away from this ideal, he counts himself as a guide to its recovery. He tells his Bryn Mawr audience, "you may, sounding the clearer notes of intercourse as only women can, become yourselves models and missionaries, perhaps a little even martyrs, of the good cause" ("Question" 51). As he stands in front of the audience modeling correct speech, it is clear, as O'Donnell has pointed out, that he saw himself as the first and foremost martyr to the cause, a "breaker of the silence" (James, "Question" 8).

---

[9]   See Marie P. Harris for a careful, detailed history of his lecture tours in an essay entitled "Henry James, Lecturer," in *American Literature* in 1951. Harris documents the timetable of his delivering and writing of his essays.

The fact that he emphasizes the *way* a thing is said rather than *what* is said marks a decided shift for James, whose previous "Balzac" lecture emphasized content generally and literary criticism specifically. This lecture returns to a more fundamental value: human interaction, the activity that makes everything else— including art and culture—possible. For an author less known for his interest in dialect, the shift to the oral seems striking. But, in fact, speech shows up as a key marker in many of his works.[10] As his novels might have forecasted, in this speech James refers to himself not as an observer but as the "auditor of life" ("Question" 33).

Knowing the difference between good and bad speech will allow his audience, he argues, to choose which speakers to imitate and which to ignore.[11] Knowledge of correct and incorrect speech is essential, James argues, because the young women in his audience hear so much of the bad every day. The indirect culprits are those who should be guardians of American culture and aren't: the educated elite. He reflects both his earlier comments in "The Lesson of Balzac," in which he charges literary critics with misleading the population, and also Matthew Arnold's 1880s lecture "Numbers," in which Arnold opposes what he calls "the comfortable doctrine of the remnant" to "the unsoundness of the majority" (56).

James points out three major threats against which educated Americans should be on their guard: newspapers, public or "common" schools, and the growing number of immigrants. Much has been made of James's horror of meeting immigrants in America from Eastern Europe and elsewhere in *The American Scene*. Indeed, a debate similar to the one over James's supposed elitism has played out over how to read James's reactions to the "aliens" he met upon his return to America. Briefly, there has been a revisionist thread led by Ross Posnock in *The Trial of Curiosity*, who has argued that in *The American Scene*, James seems open to a dissolving line of identity between himself and those "others." Posnock wants to resurrect the earlier James that "more 'sophisticated' readers ignored—the figure of baffling heterogeneity embodied in exorbitant curiosity" (146). In this reading, James sees himself as "alien" as the others about whom he writes. Similarly, Beverly Haviland's *Henry James's Last Romance* applies this reading to his interactions with Jewish immigrants, arguing that to some extent James identifies with the Jewish, cosmopolitan narrative. Likewise, Sara Blair has argued that James in *The American Scene* seeks to "document" the "deeper depths of the American character" (159) and "perform[s], as it acutely witnesses, an

---

[10]   Beyond *The Bostonians*, James uses speech as a reliable marker of status. Henrietta Stackpole, in *The Portrait of a Lady*, for example, speaks in a notably "common" way compared to the other characters. Likewise, Daisy Miller and, especially, her brother Randolph, use "ain't" and other subtle markers of the recent acquisition of upper-class status.

[11]   "Choosing" is a common Jamesian theme, in both fiction and in his directions for American cultural felicity. In *The Portrait of a Lady*, Isabel Archer tells her aunt she wants to know "the things one shouldn't do." Mrs. Touchett asks, "So as to do them?" to which Isabel answers, "So as to choose" (67).

emergent form of racial theater" (160), suggesting that, again, James sees identity as fluid. These all present a more palatable James for modern readers. But Kenneth Warren takes issue with this reading, convincing even Posnock that James engages in essentialist racial division. In contrast to James's usual perceptiveness, on his journey south, Warren argues, his "perceptions ... are all but indistinguishable from plantation romances or minstrel shows" (426).[12] Complicating this debate further, Henry B. Wonham makes the argument that James's uneasiness comes rather from a sense that "New York's immigrants are neither gross nor alien enough," making it hard to distinguish between types of people (Wonham 101–2).

James's comments on the subject in "The Question of Our Speech" are similar in their tenor to those he would make in *The American Scene* and are at times just as inscrutable. He both shudders at some of the elements of immigrant and ethnic minority culture and identifies with it. In many ways, though, the text of the lecture clearly establishes the case for James's conservatism, his sense of alienation from a changing American population. He complains that

> There are many things our now so profusely imported and, as is claimed, quickly assimilated foreign brothers and sisters may do at their ease in this country, and without asking anyone's leave ... but the thing they may best do is play, to their heart's content, with the English language, or, in other words, dump their mountain of promiscuous material into the foundations of the American. ("Question" 42–3)

Written in the flush of his visit, during his break in California, James's reactions seem less mitigated by reflection and analysis than they would be in *The American Scene*. His attitude here makes a modern reader squirm. Still, even in the midst of such a comment, James complicates it by personifying English itself as an immigrant, deserving better care, needing stewardship by the elite. The English language and its use "immigrated together, into the great raw world in which they were to be cold-shouldered and neglected together, left to run wild and lose their way together" ("Question" 37–8). It is this "lost way" and, interestingly, a lack of hospitality that James laments in America, where, unlike in European countries, there is no cultural guardian employed to protect it. He casts English transatlantic speech in America as an original ideal, now corrupted, as if language were once unchangeable. As a result, English is "our unrescued Andromeda ... disjoined from all the associations, the other pretenses, that had attended her ... that had helped to form her manners and her voice, her taste and her genius" ("Question" 39). From there, James moves to a disturbing image of this heroine left unguarded against those who would violate her:

---

[12] Posnock writes in "Henry James and the Limits of Historicism" that, despite James's nuanced approach, Warren is essentially right in his condemnation of James's racial attitudes.

> all the while we sleep the innumerable aliens are sitting up (they don't sleep!) to work their will on their new inheritance and prove to us that they are without any finer feeling or more conservative instinct of consideration for it ... than they may have on the subject of so many yards of freely figured oilcloth, from the shop, that they are preparing to lay down, for convenience, on the kitchen floor or kitchen staircase. ("Question" 45)

The unabashed gender, class, and ethnic prejudice, similar to James's repugnant response to diversity on the New York Streets in *The American Scene*, has rightly triggered critical response. But insofar as speech is concerned, James is here considering English to be an essential entity temporarily under the power of the forces of corruption. "She" is both the victim and the example of the "immigrant."

James goes on, with slightly less gusto, to indict the newspapers and common schools as being "in the forefront" of "this uncontrolled assault ... upon what we may call our linguistic position" ("Question" 40). But if newspapers and schools weren't succeeding, perhaps, as James's performance seems to suggest, lecturing could. He argues that for changes in speech patterns "to succeed it must be a collective and associated habit; for the greater the number of persons speaking well, in given conditions, the more that number will tend to increase, and the smaller the number the more that number will tend to shrink and lose itself in the desert of the common" (17). But, as Lynn Wardley has pointed out in discussing *The Bostonians*, "the problem with citing the voice as the touchstone and medium of the mutable republic resides in its own mutability. Now embodied, now disembodied, voices carry into public spaces where they are all too easily altered" (639). But to James, standing on the platform, modeling good speech in front of an audience, the lecture represents a format where good speech could be safeguarded and passed on. Like his use of the immigrant as metaphor, James's position on speech is something of a paradox: His lecture fulfills an elitist desire to form a standard culture by modeling it himself—unwittingly proving that standards are subject to the changing repertoire of public discourse.

Thus, if "The Question of Our Speech" signals James at his most conservative in its theme and its attack on a changing "loose" cultural intercourse, it is simultaneously an acknowledgment of public performance as a cultural opportunity—one with immense potential for the author, the artist, and the critic. The contradiction was one James must have been aware of, as he had investigated it in *The Bostonians* and elsewhere. Oral performance is by its very nature ephemeral and unstable. Yet James's performance seems to suggest that this ephemeral form of cultural transmission still offered one way to return to and safeguard a permanent, stable culture, to represent a form of cultural intercourse he deemed the basis for all human, intellectual, and artistic achievement. Lecturing in the United States was more than a financial opportunity: it served a mission of cultural improvement. James saw the educative potential in his performance. However, he married his educational message through the medium of oral performance, embracing the paradoxical potential of performance—the fragile stability of speech.

The Voice of the Master

At one point during the book-long debate between Verena Tarrant and Basil Ransom in *The Bostonians*, Verena asks the conservative Ransom, "Why would you ever listen to me again, when you loathe my ideas?" His response is telling for James's later career as a lecturer. Ransom answers, "I don't listen to your ideas; I listen to your voice." (326). Like Ransom, American audiences seemed to be listening to James's voice—or simply looking at him—as much as following his ideas in the "The Lesson of Balzac." Indeed, reviewers blatantly stated this fact. As Dunbar recorded, "The Lesson of Balzac" "served as an excuse whereby the most distinguished novelist [in] America ... may be stared at without rudeness" (24). Like Ransom listening to Verena, this audience had a "legitimate curiosity, this hearing the voice and seeing the face of a man of genius" (Dunbar 24). Even more pointed is Dunbar's claim that the audience absorbed little of the lecture itself: "it is doubtful if the most receptive hearer took away more than half of it. As a lecturer, Mr. James is an event" (25). As with most lecturers, James himself, not his critical ideas, becomes the central fact in this account; "the persons who have attended the various deliveries of this 'lecture' ... were impelled by a hunger to apprehend the lecturer's personality" (Dunbar 24). The claim reflects what many previous lecturers had experienced, yet it also helps illuminate James's shift in lecture subject.

"The Question of Our Speech" attempts to solve this problem of audience preoccupation with authorial "personality." What if the voice is all that is listened to? If the audience only wanted to "see" and "hear" the great novelist (rather than engage with his argument), "The Question of Our Speech" allowed them to do so with a better chance of engaging, if unconsciously, with his point. In other words, this particular lecture is so performance based, is so dramatic in its core, that voice (or form) and content become one. This merging of content and format seems to be one way in which James solves the problem of "personality worship" among critics. In "The Lesson of Balzac," he criticizes such superficial interest while playing to it himself. With "The Question of Our Speech" in the second half of his tour, he takes the problem for granted: audiences will focus on his performing body, but by using his performing body as an instrument, he will create a space for critical education.

To that end, "The Question of Our Speech," is specific on the subject of good and bad speech. That James imitates both is apparent even from his later, published version of the lecture. What he argues for again and again is that English speakers should maintain "a tone-standard" (12). He proposes a "sensibility to tone, the state of recognizing, and responding to, certain vocal sounds as tone, and recognizing and reacting from certain others as negations of tone: negations the more offensive in proportion as they have most enjoyed impunity" (17). As in his critical writing, James imagines a divide between an acknowledgement of standards of pronunciation and a popular ignorance of a "tone-standard." He urges speakers to stick to the "human side of vocal sound," and not follow the trend which keeps it "as little distinct as possible from the grunting the squealing, the barking or the roaring of animals" ("Question" 16), a statement that recalls the animalistic description of the mob in *The Bostonians* and implies a deeply racist opinion of immigrants (whom he deemed responsible for changing American speech for the worse).

The period of James's lectures precedes his work on the Prefaces for the New York Editions by many months. These essays seem to suggest more than they explain, so it is doubly notable, then, that in "The Question of Our Speech" he is so very concrete about what he wants.[13] Rather than concluding with his desire for a "tone-standard," James explains in minute detail what that means, mostly by discussing the misuse of consonant and vowel sounds. He is distressed to point out that spoken American English is "destitute of any approach to an emission of the consonant. It becomes thus a mere helpless slobber of disconnected vowel noises—the weakest and cheapest attempt at human expression" ("Question" 26). Again, he suggests that Americans sometimes can approach the "slobber" of animals, and do so by leaving out consonants. Even with the simple word "Yes" this is a problem. American speakers are "rarely given to form the terminal letter of our 'Yes,' or to hear it formed. The abject 'Yeh-eh' (the ugliness of the drawl is not easy to represent) … becomes a still more questionable 'Yeh-ep'" (26–7). Some, he complains, try to add consonants to make up for their loss in other words, so they'll "talk of vanilla-r-ice-cream, of California-r-oranges, and Cuba-r-and Porto Rico … and … of 'the idea-r-of' any intimation that their performance and example in these respects may not be immaculate" (27). This "consonantal recovery of balance," adding the "r" where it doesn't belong, has "the small vulgar effect of a sort of morose grinding of the back teeth" (29). We must imagine James's performance here—enacting this illegitimate "r."

From here, he moves on to the corruption of vowels in "vowel-cutting, an art as delicate in its way as gem-cutting" ("Question" 28), and catalogs some of the worst offenses. He criticizes "the flatly –drawling group—gawd and dawg, sawft and lawft, gawne and lawst and frawst" (30) as well as "the almost total loss, among innumerable speakers, of any approach to purity in the sound of the *e* … For choice, perhaps, 'vurry,' 'Amurrica,' 'Philadulphia,' 'tullegram,' 'twuddy' (what becomes of 'twenty' here is an ineptitude truly beyond any alliteration), and the like, descend deepest into the abyss" (31). The loaded commentary—with its stark choices of "purity" or "the abyss"—shows how high the stakes were for James and with what meaning he imbued the original essential "English."

The published version of this speech makes its oral tactics clear. James, like Frederick Douglass before him, is taking advantage of the lecture platform to "perform" a style of speech and self different from his own. He is echoing, in oral performance, what he heard in his audiences, coming as close to the theatrical as he ever would in his later career. The clarity and detail with which he makes his

---

[13]   This interest in speech patterns was not new. Wharton tells us in *A Backward Glance* that James was "always an eager collector of verbal oddities" (184).

argument—complete with models of good and bad speech—marks an important shift in his use of the lecture platform as a medium different from writing. Perhaps this lecture has been long ignored because as a written text it doesn't really work. Only if we imagine an oral performance does its full impact take shape.

If we can imagine James's style of speaking through these written records, we can also glean it from comments of those who heard him. Reviewers were tepid, if sometimes openly critical of his style. We've already seen reactions to his "Balzac" lecture that focused on the fact that James avoided dramatic performance. But while this may have been true for "The Lesson of Balzac," "The Question of Our Speech" opened a new set of public performance strategies. This lecture, unlike its predecessor, had "the tricks of the orator," to use Dunbar's phrase, built into its content. Reviews of this lecture tended to focus on his message perhaps because it is so linked to the form. Having merged form (or, the "tricks of the orator") with content (his critique of American speech), James encouraged the reviewers to take him up on his argument in a way they hadn't with "Balzac." And they did, explicitly rejecting the lessons of the visiting author.

The Audience Responds

As with his Balzac lecture, audiences directed some of their criticism to his written work. *The Outlook* suggests that even though some consider James "the worst writer of English, living or dead" he still had the temerity to advocate universal imitation of his style in speech ("Mr. James and English Speech" 17). Another article asks, "is Henry James the proper authority to rebuke these hard-working gentlemen? Is he himself beyond suspicion? Are his own sentences sound in wind and limb? Do his phrases always keep on track?" The authors go on to answer, "We opine, regretfully, that they do not. Take any considerable sentence from any of his novels and examine its architecture. Isn't it wobbly with qualifying clauses and subassistant phrases?" ("Henry James on Newspaper English" 155). James's phrases may have been "wobbly," but that didn't stop some from imitating him. Indeed, as with his Balzac lecture, and as many lecturers found, the visiting author's style could be readily parodied. One critic used the recent publication of *The Golden Bowl* as a point of retaliation, composing a poem that begins, "At last our Henry James returns, / 'The Golden Bowl' has long been split, / Each introspective reader yearns / To treasure every shining bit" and ends, "O! Vulgar critic who defames / With vulgar wealth of native wit / The English of our Henry James ... Our feebler intellects it shames, / Who cannot quite its meaning hit— / The English of our Henry James" (Childs BR484). While this one used the high-flown diction of what she imagined James approved, others imitated his style more directly. A classic example appeared in the *Daily Boston Globe*. A newspaper reporter attempts to describe a local fire in James's style—taking to the extreme James's admonition of newspaper writing ("The Disciple of James Covers a Fire" 40). One critic asks, "Has Mr. James considered the possible influence of his example on the unlearned! If not, let him reflect on the full significance of this reproduction of his latest style by an unlettered reporter in a Western newspaper: 'Told All in One Sentence'" (Mr. James and English Speech" 17). James's long sentences, with all his "subassistant phrases" and wobbly construction, fueled a national conversation—just as he had hoped.

Predictably outrageous to his journalistic audience was his critique of "newspaper English." Article titles following his lecture, written by those who were experts in such English, range from the polite "Henry James Speaks Unkindly of the Press" to the more aggressive "Don't Mix the Globe and Henry James." This last article, printed in Boston, mentions a *Duluth Herald* article that quotes James as saying that "Boston is addicted to bad language." The article responds, "If this be true, we shall have to begin to believe in the amiability of mothers-in-law, the philanthropy of the plumber, the ice man and the coal man, and in the approachability of Boston Girls" ("Don't Mix the Globe and Henry James" 1). James, it seems, was single-handedly uniting the country, from Boston to Duluth, in opposition against his alien presence.

More originally, audiences also took James up on his proffered conversation about speech. Indeed, audiences had already heard, and mocked, James's slow, self-consciousness of speech in his first lecture on Balzac. Wilmer Cave France, writing in response to this first lecture, writes, "As the pleasant even voice of the lecturer uttered strings of images ... his audience almost seemed to breathe, 'O still delay, thou art so fair!' and still Mr. James delayed" (72). France goes on to describe James's voice during this early lecture, claiming that "He speaks in a monotonous, agreeable voice, paying out the carefully chosen words like the links of a chain that is obviously hand-made" (71). From this account of his monotone and oral facility with complex grammar, we can suspect that in "The Question of Our Speech" James's pronunciation was the core of his theatricality, a fact that, again, shows his marriage of the message and the medium. The immediate reaction to such a self-consciously performative speech was to mock the performance. In other words, if James thought a speech about speech would get through to his audiences, he was right.

American reviewers critiqued the language James would have everyone use. As with his lecture on Balzac, then, "Question" invited the critic to become the focus of criticism. One writer bemoans Jamesian English's "paralysis of its normal functions": "it is passing out of the possession of the 'great middle class' who use it as a means of communicating their commonplace thoughts and experiences, and falling into the hands of experts, who are making it an esoteric dialect for the use of a small body of initiates" ("Mr. James and English Speech" 16). Agreeing with James's premise, this writer takes an alternative view of the result. Even Woodrow Wilson, then President of Princeton, worried that "These gentlemen should look at home before committing themselves, and remedy their own shortcomings and their laboriously correct style of writing" (qtd. in "Henry James on 'Newspaper English'" 155). James's pushing of the "correct," the "expert," and the highly bred leads even an educated community to champion strength, the vernacular, the everyday, and the vital. But the *Boston Daily Globe* took a more lighthearted approach in reprinting an item from the *Pittsburgh Post* (another example of newspapers from disparate cities finding common ground in a common enemy) entitled, "This Will Make Hank Suffer": "Mrs. Geehaw—Hev ye read Henry James' new book, Mirandy? Mrs. Giddap—I hev not. Dew tell. Has one of them wicked James' boys writ a book?" (14). In this conversation, the writer reproduces many of James's taboo speech patterns (like turning the "a" into a "y"), even reveling in turning "Henry" into the more casual "Hank," as if to celebrate American informality.

The Transatlantic "Our"

But one critique stood out among the rest. Americans bristled at James's use of the "our" pronoun. In fact, the reaction showed, James was presumptuous if he believed he could refer to his own speech—with its particularity and mix of accents—as "our speech." Indeed, one respondent wrote, "He is good enough to call it 'our speech,' but it is really the language of Mr. James in its mischievous and perplexing confusion" (qtd. in Dwight 167–8).

This reaction should not have been surprising. After his 20-year absence, he was hardly a native son, nor was he the only or most popular international author. If he was depending on audiences to welcome him in the way they did Charles Dickens, he would be disappointed. After his departure, Dwight, writing for *The Critic*, compiled a series of representative comments which suggest that James's presence was hardly an occasion for festivities. One critic called him "A man too great to be ignored, he is yet too ignored to be great" (qtd. in Dwight 167), reflecting the begrudging respect and lack of affection the American audience maintained for James. Dwight himself can't believe that "so much comment could be expended upon a person whose cryptic utterances and incomprehensible exile so little deserved the precious boon of publicity" (Dwight 165).

Indeed, his "exile" provoked discussion over exactly what James really *was*. On the one hand, a *New York Times* article on his visit to the New York Athenaeum ("of which classic club he is a member") quotes someone from the club who says that "Though Henry James, the novelist, lives abroad, he is very faithful to America, and very proud of his fellow countrymen." The reporter goes on to report a conversation with the author: "'Mr. James, if you were not an American, what would you want to be?' 'If I were not an American,' Mr. James answered, promptly, 'I'd want to be one'" ("James's Patriotism" 119). To some, then, James was American.

While at times critics seemed to allow him dual identity—one article refers to him as "the American-English novelist" ("Real Henry James, He Really Said It" 16)—they most often seemed to see James as having abandoned his native country for another. For example, James has "become more English than many a native Londoner. Words, gestures—mode of thought, even—are British to the heart. The transformation of Mr. James has been complete. He has been transplanted, budded, and fully grafted without becoming spoiled" ("Real Henry James, He Really Said It" 16). Likewise, in an account of his one-night visit to Portland, Oregon, where he traveled after his stay in California, the *Morning Oregonian* notes that at the Portland Hotel, he "registered simply Henry James, London, by that showing he did not consider this country his home" ("Henry James in Town for the Day" 1).

It was no surprise then, that his national identity caused some critical attitudes. The Portland writer goes on to account for James's preference: "Admiring the English qualities which are most un-American ... he has finally become practically an alien" (1). The *New York Tribune* guessed that "He has looked upon [America], no doubt, with eyes which are more English than American and his prospective comments are anticipated with a curiosity that is sometimes mingled with a cheerful cynicism" ("Mr. Henry James" A6). The same defensiveness that was displayed toward Matthew Arnold seems exacerbated by James being an (unofficial) Englishman by choice.[14]

After his "Speech" lecture, in an unfortunate article placement in the *New York Tribune*, an account of James's lecture was placed under another story of attack: "Highwaymen knock woman down and wrench bag away." The article, entitled "James Attacks Papers and Schools," reported that his lecture was taken as a similarly hostile act, which the first person plural "our" in the title of "The Question of Our Speech" did nothing to alleviate. Audiences above all took issue with James's criticism of American English, using some of nineteenth-century America's most tried and true defenses against foreign critics. He became a punch line, drawn into stories with which he had nothing to do. When Harvard's President used the phrase "no frills at Harvard," a newspaper writer invoked James: "Mr. Henry James, who has expressed the opinion that Americans use very poor English, would not understand, perhaps, what the President meant ... [but] Every American, old and young, however, considers that expression couched in sinewy and expressive English and thoroughly understands it" ("No Frills" 6). American English, then, was more "sinewy," stronger, more masculine and direct, and without the affectation that Anglophiles like James possessed.[15] Another review

---

[14]   During this same trip, James's special brand of American cosmopolitanism was being played out in his meeting of the President, Theodore Roosevelt. Eyeing each other with suspicion, James saw Roosevelt as jingoistic and macho, while Roosevelt saw James as less than a model of American masculinity. Robin Hoople provides a useful investigation of the two men's actual and intellectual relationship in "Great Stone Faces: Henry James, Theodore Roosevelt, and the Quest for American Authenticity."

[15]   There was a secondary and related critique as well. As with reviews of James's writing, critics claimed the style appealed to women more than men in its effete, ineffectual way. *The New York Sun* reports that James "was cooing to female audiences in the subdued tones that mark British good breeding and kindly pointing out to them the horrors of the language they spoke" (qtd. in Dwight 167). Writing for *The Bookman*, Wilmer Cave France claims that "About ninety per cent of his hearers were women, as was to be expected" (71). Some reviewers viewed James's association more positively, seeing it as a chance to

in the *Boston Globe* declared, "You say our speech lacks breeding; we contend that power is more to be preferred than mere breeding" ("Power and Breeding" 9).

James's speech, then, set off something of a familiar debate which questioned not just his judgment of American English but also whether a nation should have any static standard at all. For James, the answer was, obviously, yes: language went beyond nation; its "purity" should be protected, even if through ever-recurring performances. An article in *Current Literature* took up the question, citing a writer from *Book News* who agreed with the premise of a "pure" language but differed from James's treatment of American English. He writes, "Taking the country as a whole, and considering all classes of Americans, I am sure there is a more even English and a higher standard of purity in the United States than in Great Britain" (qtd. in "Henry James on 'Newspaper English'" 156). American democratic education, he implies, ensured that more Americans were speaking "good" English than were the English themselves. In an article from the *London Mail* (reprinted in Washington DC), Theodore Dahle points out that James based his idea of "pure" English on a select group: "If English is to be the standard by which to indict the American tongue, may I most respectfully ask, "Whose English?" (N12). Americans, however, generally accepted James's characterization of this as a problem of nationality, even though, as Dahle perceptively points out, James was holding up an international, hegemonic standard that did not really exist. Thus James occupied a purgatorial space between British and American identities. The "our" of the "The Question of Our Speech" remained a contested and ambiguous pronoun.

The Transatlantic Hesitation

The debate about James's national identity came back to his style of performed speech. There was talk about whether it was "British" or "American" speech or, even worse, some confection that was neither British nor American but only "Jamesian"—a "vernacular of one," as O'Donnell calls it (143). This personal speaking style may have indeed been a combination of British and American accents. For example, Hamlin Garland recalled it positively as "a beautiful blend of London and new England" (256–7). Either way, it reminds us that, like all lectures, this was the embodied performance of a particular lecturer.

So, while American audiences were up in arms about James's singular speech, somewhere between American and British, it was perhaps, in fact, another aspect

---

discuss young women's decorum. One letter to the editor argues that "I am glad to see that Mr. Henry James has called attention to the slovenly and incorrect speech one hears here on every hand ... One sees many beautiful women, but when they begin to speak, their slangy, ungrammatical utterances set one's teeth on edge" ("Thinks Henry James is Right" 8). In any event, the press saw James's speech as a question of gender, as in an article entitled "College and Women" which carefully summarizes James's argument for his Bryn Maw audience.

of James's identity that alienated him from the "normal" American speech: his stammer. Edith Wharton, recalling James's long visit to her home during his American trip, offers something of a defense of James's strange intonations in her autobiography, claiming that "His slow way of speech, sometimes mistaken for affectation—or, more quaintly, for an artless form of Anglomania!—was really the partial victory over a stammer which in his boyhood had been thought incurable" (177–8). How James's boyhood stammer affected his speech in general and his lectures in particular is a point of contention. Many biographers have concurred with Wharton's account, casting the stammer as a childhood challenge by which James was deeply troubled. Of his childhood, one biographer writes, "The stutter made him cautious in speech ... Harry prepared his sentences carefully beforehand, mentally navigating their difficulties. The stutter was least troublesome when he was reading aloud or reciting passages thoroughly memorized beforehand; slowly, over the years, he learned to speak without more than occasional hesitations" (Novick 21). Kaplan describes the young Henry, likewise, as "Shy, anxious, a moderate stammerer" who "increasingly feared public exposure" (58). The stammer, according to these accounts affected his social discourse, during which James spoke "carefully and slowly, choosing his words beforehand as he always did, navigating past his stutter, so that often the rapid conversation simply flowed past him" (Novick 176).

How his stammer and style of speech played out in his later life remains a point of debate among biographers and contemporary critics.[16] Kaplan casts his lecturing style as a success "despite his lifelong fear of public speaking, the difficulty of sustaining his long sentences through his stammer, and his distinctive, unusual accent" (487). His dictating was indeed one area where he managed success over his stammer, as Novick points out: "He dictated slowly, unreeling the sentences that formed themselves in his mind, his deliberate speech occasionally interrupted by the shadow of a stutter that sometimes obstructed the flow of words" (5). Hamlin Garland recalls the hesitation, saying that James could be "intolerably hesitant of speech" (262) or "maddeningly hesitant" (258). But Garland claims that "his pauses were in no sense those of a stammerer; they were filled with an effort at finding just the precise qualifier" (258). As he aged, in his last years, he was "somewhat more vocally stammering and ponderous" (Kaplan 530), though Garland, who heard James lecture, heard little of James's hesitation in that context, saying of his address on Balzac to the Twentieth Century Club that "He read well

---

16   Critics have argued about whether his elaborate written sentence structure evolved out of his speaking style, which in turn evolved out of his stammer or whether this same sentence structure exacerbated his stammer. H. Montgomery Hyde argues that during his dictating years, using a Remington typewriter and typist to record his language, James was aware that speaking his books might encourage wordiness. However, "At the same time, he felt that the gain in expression through the use of what he laughingly called "Remingtonese" more than compensated for any loss of concision. Indeed ... he had reached a stage at which, as she put it, the click of a Remington acted as a positive spur" (Hyde 161).

from his manuscript. His voice was resonant and his utterance quite free from hesitations" (259).

Indeed, as his predilection for dictation suggests, performance or reading was one arena in which his stammer might not have bothered him. One of his typists wrote that "He dictated beautifully ... he had a melodious voice ... Typewriting for him was exactly like accompanying a singer on the piano" (qtd. in Kaplan 465). Indeed, dictation's connection to oral performance called up old associations for James, perhaps of "the vision of the stammering desk-bound writer transformed by the footlights and the applause" (Kaplan 189). As Edith Wharton writes of his reading poems aloud,

> His stammer ceased as if by magic as soon as he began to read, and his ear, so sensitive to the convolutions of an intricate prose style, never allowed him to falter over the most complex prosody but swept him forward on great rollers of sound till the full weight of his voice fell on the last cadence. (185)

One can assume, then, that James, when reading his speech, had a similarly smoothly flowing performance style. But if the stammer was imperceptible to audiences as a stammer, it still may have contributed to what they perceived as his "accent." James's speech was "other": It was other in that it sounded somewhere in between American and British speech—or totally outside of either. In other words, like Martineau, like Douglass, like Dickens and Twain and all the rest, the speaking author was quite a different thing than the writer. While James's style of speech was thought to reflect his written work (in the negative sense, to American audiences), it was more linked to the body than he or they might admit. His lecture on speech was, like all lectures, both a public performance in dialogue with his transatlantic audience and a deeply personal, embodied individual production.

Following his lengthy trip to America, James returned to England to work on the New York Editions, another kind of performance. Indeed, his original intention to excite interest in his forthcoming New York Editions was not unfulfilled. When he returned to England, he began work on the Prefaces, documents McWhirter calls both the "central performance in the construction" of James's image of the Master and a "deeply ambiguous act of self-presentation" (1). McWhirter, among others, has provided a much-needed analysis of James's successful presentation of himself as the "Henry James who has come to represent the quintessential high-modernist priest of art, the creator of an art of fiction committed to pure form ..." and looks closely at James's "real-life" conditions, mostly financial, during the preparation and promotion of the edition (2). What he found was a James deeply invested in popular success and self-conscious about creating an image that concealed this fact. The lecture tour betrays a similar dual intention: capitulating to popular expectations and the machinery of public communication while expressing alienation from them. Anne T. Margolis has noted this ambiguity:

> In his public presentation of himself during his lecture tour, James seems to have achieved almost as much success in anticipating and adapting himself to

the expectations of his American audiences as he had previously experienced in his more private interaction with the ranks of the English-speaking avant-garde. The evident pride which he took in this carefully orchestrated dose of self-advertisement was merely the flip side of the conspicuous disdain for popularity which he displayed when dealing with his ever-growing circle of disciples and admirers among the rising generation … (Margolis 183–4)

Margolis characterizes James's desire for popular success as the "flip side" of his disdain for it; but in terms of his lectures, it is more than that. In fact, the lecturing author in general—and James in particular—is always performing this paradox. Both "The Lesson of Balzac" and "The Question of Our Speech" encapsulate this ambiguity in their dual functions: They are both statements meant to position the author as an elite other and simultaneously accept public performance as an effective format and celebrity as a useful vehicle. The New York Editions include forms of rhetorical performance with similar effect, but James's entry onto the stage as a physical performer created a fuller dialogue with audiences. If James was concerned about acceptance of his books, one can only imagine the kind of anxiety—and opportunity—he felt when faced with audiences; it was the challenge of his last literary-editorial project, only come to life on the stage. The New York Editions may have been aimed at presenting a permanent, lasting image of the Master, but the lecture tour embraced a popular, ephemeral, impermanent cultural performance.

Conclusion:
Performing Authorship beyond the
Nineteenth Century

Henry James's 1904–05 trip marked the real end of the nineteenth-century lecture tour. Better than any author who traveled across the Atlantic Ocean to lecture to an audience, his experience captured the possibilities and the challenges for the in-person author at this time. The lecture tour would continue as a genre, but it would become one among many avenues for author promotion. James's venture, by no means the most successful, crystallizes those tours that had come before him.

First and foremost, James was a product of a transatlantic nineteenth century and, in many ways, its spokesperson. The transatlantic relationship passed through many incarnations—and would continue to—before and after James came on the scene and lectured in his native-turned-alien country. But for James, who was no longer really "American" and not yet "British" (as he would become officially in the last years of his life), the tour exposed how essential, even expected, it was for British and American authors to travel and be seen by their transatlantic audiences. But his experience also exposed how "transatlantic" authorship didn't necessarily mean that these identities could be merged in the minds of audiences. The same American defensiveness that had greeted Harriet Martineau as she modestly spoke out against slavery, faced Charles Dickens in his earlier trip to the nation during which he critiqued copyright law, and followed Matthew Arnold even after he had left the country was still there, in 1904–05, when James dared to criticize American culture. As I have shown, their American counterparts—Frederick Douglass, Harriet Beecher Stowe, and Mark Twain were welcomed, if at times with condescension, more consistently. As essentially transatlantic as nineteenth-century literary culture was, then, James could not elide it into one identity, a British-American elite mash-up for which the pronoun "our" in "The Question of Our Speech" would sufficiently do.

James's critique of American culture also culminated a century in which the interest of audiences and authors was one-sided. While American culture was often the subject of critique, it was still notably the subject. Douglass, Stowe, and Martineau spoke in Britain and America about American slavery; Twain spoke about his American travels and performed an American character in Britain; Arnold, Wilde, and James offered (at times unwanted) advice for American culture. Dickens alone of the lecturers in this study performed his own fictional works, though even he performed scenes from his American-themed *Martin Chuzzlewit* more often than he might otherwise have.[1] Thus, authors in the nineteenth-century international literary marketplace had to deal with the country across the pond—either because of its growing importance, in the case of America, or because there lingered a need for Britain's support in political causes or cultural development. More and more, it seemed, those authors who were to have the biggest cultural impact would accomplish it in person. Live performance in another country guaranteed relevance, though not instant fellowship.

The decades following James would bring a shift from an identifiable "visiting lecturer" to a very different kind of "expatriate." As the United States solidified its economic and military power, it would transform in the literary world from the place writers must come to remain relevant to the place from which they must escape. The American excesses of journalism and the consumer culture so disturbing to Arnold, Wilde, and James remained. In addition, American Puritanism and a sense of what Craig Monk calls "a paucity of indigenous creative activity" would drive out many of the American authors who followed them (3). Most famously, Gertrude Stein, Earnest Hemingway, and F. Scott Fitzgerald, among many others, would take up residence in Paris, Hemingway's "moveable feast," joined by British authors like Ford Maddox Ford who likewise sought the particular lifestyle Paris offered. The world was expanding, so that London and New York no longer dominated even the British and American literary scene. Paris was one center of the literati—as it had often been—but this time for English-speaking writers. In fact, destinations were more diffuse; the world was smaller. There is perhaps no fact that better forecasts this transition than Twain's following his transatlantic tour in the 1870s with a World Tour in 1896, traveling through India, New Zealand, and China, among other countries. In addition, artists sought homes, not hotels, and generally avoided James's dreaded "hotel culture."[2] These were not public visits; they were lifestyle changes. Of course, one of the reasons authors would remove themselves from their homes so easily and for much greater lengths of time was that it was so much easier to get back, so much easier to communicate with their native countries. Henry James's transatlantic existence, a centerpiece of his public person and a source of ambivalence in his own life, would, in the twentieth century, because less remarkable and less agonizing.

James's lecture experience also capped a century in which the place of the literary author was in flux. Indeed, from the smaller, interested political audiences of Douglass, Martineau, and Stowe through the theatrical successes of Twain and Dickens, to Arnold's selected numbers, the literary audiences of the nineteenth century had swelled and then contracted. James's audiences were more

---

[1]   While these are not all the transatlantic lecturers who surfaced in the nineteenth century, the trend remains the same even when considering the lectures of Emerson, Irving, Thackeray, Trollope, and others.

[2]   James wrote about the hotel culture of the United States in *The American Scene*, discussing, among other things, how hotels such as the Waldorf Astoria captured the sense of "publicity *as* the vital medium" in American culture (105).

academic, specialized, and, presumably, well educated compared to those of his predecessors, anticipating audiences of most high modernist authors. Thus, the lecture tour proves to be another ground on which the slow, deliberate transfer of the literary field from popular to "high-brow" culture, to go back to Lawrence Levine's phrase, is evident. In parallel fashion, the literary lecturer also became more specialized. The overt political speeches given by such authors as Douglass and, in their limited way, Stowe and Martineau had given way to the literary yet theatrical productions of Twain and Dickens. In turn, the culturally minded discussions of Arnold, who spoke on culture and philosophy, and Wilde, who spoke on (and modeled) Aestheticism, culminated in James, who spoke on Balzac and literary criticism, albeit before changing to speak on the more wide-ranging topic of speech. The literary author was becoming just that—literary—rather than a broad cultural force on the model of Emerson. It is no surprise that this shift coincided with the previously stated one of smaller audiences and less popular aspirations. A narrower focus meant fewer interested people, and those that were would be more educated. The speaking author, a symbolic high cultural force, thus retreated away from his or her audience, becoming more a "lecturer" in the professorial mold.

While there has certainly been a revisionist assessment of modernism's relationship to the popular (as there has been in James studies), there is no doubt that the dominant narrative of the modernist era remains that high modernists, at least, cast themselves as less accessible than their nineteenth-century counterparts. So even as many were deeply interested in working with the marketplace and reaching diverse audiences, the modernist public performance was one of detachment from such concerns.[3] This is true of their work and also their public personae. Figures like Ralph Waldo Emerson or Twain, who wore multiple hats in terms of interests, careers, and audiences, are harder to find in the early twentieth century. More likely was the author who was a literary author only. Matthew Arnold's serious undertaking as Inspector of Schools while he remained a poet and a cultural critic would be less common among serious high modernists. Instead, with rare exceptions, literary authors were a specialized group, working, of course, at times on less savory jobs to pay the bills but rarely identifying outside the "writer" milieu.[4]

The celebrity culture that had subsumed the transatlantic literary world in the late nineteenth century was already an expected frustration when James arrived. He

---

[3]   The late eighties and nineties produced essential work meant to reveal the very real interaction between authors and the popular, especially Jennifer Wicke's *Advertising Fictions: Literature Advertisement, and Social Reading* (1988), Kevin J. H. Dettmar and Stephen Watt's edited collection, *Marketing Modernisms: Self-Promotion, Canonization, Rereading* (1996), and Lawrence Rainey's *Institutions of Modernism: Literary Elites and Public Culture* (1998).

[4]   Certainly, many, most famously Hemingway, were journalists, but this position still allowed an "author" identification.

wrote about it, lectured on it, and experienced it with annoyed but understanding patience and, sometimes, gratitude. Though it seemed to have always been there, modern celebrity culture saw its rise contemporaneously with the transatlantic lecture tour. For lecturing authors, a recognizable celebrity culture began in the early to mid-nineteenth century, which could at times prove dangerous to those operating on the margins of society—as in the case of Harriet Martineau, whose life was threatened after speaking out against slavery in the United States, and Frederick Douglass, who had to navigate the Atlantic waters as skillfully as he did the legality of his appearing live, in possession of his own person. By the time of the visits of Twain and Dickens, in the late 1860s and early 1870s, celebrity worship had taken on a kind of giddiness that turned to the extremes of parody and personality worship during the 1880s, when Wilde and Arnold visited. The near-celebrity fatigue with which James was welcomed might suggest it had nearly run its course, which, of course, was not the case.

Indeed, the "posture of reticence" that James perfected made him the initiator of a similar modernist pose. Celebrity performance would change, but celebrity culture was only getting started and would be helped by a continuing increase in mass periodicals, film, TV, and Internet. Paris Hilton, famous for being famous, did not emerge unprecedented, but she was certainly helped by the technologies of her day. Some celebrities would survey the scene with continued amusement, for example Gertrude Stein, who wryly said in remembrance of her own celebrity: "In America everybody is [a celebrity] but some are more than others. I was more than others" (168). Some celebrities of the early twentieth century would look aghast at the mobs that had welcomed Dickens when he arrived in America. Indeed, Leo Braudy suggests that during this period, "success begins to wear as frightening a face as failure" (Braudy 535). Earnest Hemingway's near-obsessive fear of selling out his talent and artistry for fame and, especially, fortune, was more characteristic of the twentieth-century celebrity artist.

But so is his discomfort with himself in relation to his public image. While Charles Dickens could be annoyed and amused at seeing his name splashed all over Broadway in connection with plays he had not authored, it caused no crisis of self in him or any of the others in this study. All of these writers maintained a distance from their public selves so that there was a clear divide for them, if not for their audiences, between, say, Charles Dickens the man and Charles Dickens the public author/performer.[5] Indeed, live performances helped formalize that distance, even as they personalized the experience for readers by presenting the embodied "real" self to the audience. For those who came later and were deemed sensational "geniuses" in the public sphere, there was no escaping into the private

---

[5]   In a very specific sense, this was not true for Harriet Martineau and Frederick Douglass, who were in physical danger while they maintained public performances. Obviously, the "danger" Hemingway faced was psychological, not physical, at least with regard to his fame.

realm. The private and the public seemed to merge, often with disastrous results, according to Braudy, who casts this as an American phenomenon:

> For the American natural there is a self-destructive glory in not being detached, in not taking on the cloak of European showmanship and premeditation. Samuel Clemens could still assume another name, become Mark Twain, and strut the boards playing the role himself. But that possibility may have vanished for Jack London, Ernest Hemingway, and their descendants. Vulnerability becomes more and more their stock in trade. (538)

Braudy presents these examples, in addition to Sylvia Plath, and their eventual suicides, as symptomatic of the modernist celebrity, and while his construction highlights an extreme, it does suggest the way in which the celebrity self was perhaps better regulated in the nineteenth century, when authors were more perplexed and amused at this new machine; it had not become so pervasive as to define an author's self in any way that competed with the "real" self. Performance in the nineteenth century, both as an activity and a concept, had its benefits.

The vortex of transatlantic culture, literary hierarchies, and celebrity, crystallized by the transatlantic lecture tour, would emerge out of the turn of the century in different, sometimes continuous forms. But what of the transatlantic lecture tour? It would continue, in a limited way. One version was the academic lecturer of which T.S. Eliot is representative. Eliot, like James, was an American-born British transplant. His public return to America came in the form of his Harvard lectures in 1932–33. Eliot lectured to his classes at Harvard but also conducted lectures outside that format at various universities and to interested audiences in places as far as Berkeley and Minnesota. Similarly, W.B. Yeats would conduct five such transatlantic lecture tours in America during his career, ending with his tour in 1932–33.[6] Such tours were reminiscent of those of Arnold, Wilde, and James.

The modernist celebrity that has engendered the most critical attention, though, is perhaps the American Gertrude Stein, who came to the United States for a six-month lecture tour in 1934–35 after having established herself as an expatriate in 1903. Stein came to the United States a celebrity following the publication of *The Autobiography of Alice B. Toklas*. Outside of that work, Stein was a little-read author. Her lecture tour, for critics such as Liesl Olsen, has raised "questions about the performance of being a writer—in particular, a writer whose work the public does not wholly understand" (332). She was like James in that way. In her recent article examining Stein's conflicts with the University of Chicago over her lectures, Olsen notes how, like many of the authors in this study, "Stein's affiliations were inside and out" (333). In other words, in terms of cultural hierarchies and national identity, Stein was a figure who "navigated the middle of things, who moved freely

---

[6]   According to A. Norman Jeffares, "Yeats performed admirably on his tours, but he found them exhausting and stimulating" (253).

among different circles" (Olsen 333).[7] The negotiation between high, sometimes inaccessible, art and more popular performance would continue, though few of the modernists would embrace it as enthusiastically as Stein did.[8]

Stein's success on the lecture circuit aside, in actuality, the in-person lecture tour was a throwback to an earlier time. Authors would continue to face their audiences in person, but there were many ways for an author to reach his or her public already emerging in the early twentieth century. A live performance would no longer be necessary. Even in Stein's time, technology was interfering with the in-person relationship between author and audience. Audiences still wanted the "real" thing, to have contact with the author him or herself. But now that contact would be even more mediated than it already was. Audiences would no longer get to be in the room with the author, and authors, much to some of these authors' delight, would no longer be in the room with audiences. Many things made this possible, but most pervasively, in the first part of the century, radio.

Recent work in modernist studies has taken on the interaction between modernist authors and the emerging technology of radio, most notably in the 2009 collection *Broadcasting Modernism*. As they had done in churches and performance halls before, authors' voices were ringing out, but this time over the airwaves in Britain and the United States. T.S. Eliot famously performed broadcasts for the BBC from 1929–63, while Virginia Woolf broadcast educational pieces on the art of writing. E.M. Forster gave his radio lectures on art and culture for many years as well. Indeed, some authors "wrote *for* radio, thinking as they did so about the special requirements of the medium" (Cohen, Coyle, and Lewty 2). As many have pointed out, this disembodied version of the lecture tour helps to complicate the vision we have had of a group of high modernists separate from the public. Ironically, these authors' voices were more available to more people than any before them had been.

But radio brought its own set of concerns for authors who chose to speak out over its airwaves. Arnold, James, and others had felt defensive and sometimes defenseless against a mass audience who might not always be pleased with what they saw. For early twentieth-century authors, "the radio's power and danger was in its ability to disseminate information widely and to plant ideas in the minds of the masses" (Frattarola 449). Woolf, for example, even as she participated, feared radio's power to be used for nationalistic purposes. Few held the power to decide what was broadcast, but those listening were innumerable. Indeed, in discussing

---

[7]   It is interesting to note that Stein's trip comes exactly 100 years after Harriet Martineau's, suggesting the immense changes in opportunities afforded to women celebrity authors and how the descriptor "marginal" shifts so dramatically between meaning Martineau's living on the margins of acceptable political society to Stein's being on the margins between the elite literary domain and the popular.

[8]   Stein would later say, "I never imagined that would happen to me to be a celebrity like that but it did and when it did I liked it" (4).

T.S. Eliot's first broadcast to India as part of the We Speak to India program, Coyle calls radio a "medium indifferent to boundaries" and limits (176).

This fear of a power and dominion increased by technologies that feature a disembodied, but omnipresent, voice is perhaps best seen in Charlie Chaplin's *Modern Times*, where, in addition to the famous scene of Chaplin sliding into the gears of the great machine, there is an equal distrust of the boss's voice, which appears to be omnipresent—even in the bathroom. Chaplin's character ducks into the bathroom to sneak a cigarette and a break, when the floating head of his boss appears and shouts for him to get back to work. The disembodied head and voice suggests the head of the capitalist, industrial snake in Chaplin's critique, but it also suggests an uneasiness on the part of early twentieth-century intellectuals and artists (of which Chaplin was certainly one) toward the obscurity with which technology seemed to render relationships between people—powerful or not. The editors of *Broadcasting Modernism* put this phenomenon clearly in their discussion of radio: "… radio opened up a void. To scatter words abroad in space, either through auditory sign or lonely inscription, serves as a reminder of the absent other, as well as the dissolving of the individual into massed ranks" (Cohen, Coyle, and Lewty 3). Mass culture, to which radio technology contributed, left the individual feeling lost, alienated and alone.

Not surprisingly, this alienation registers itself in the minds of many as "a voice"—a voice separate from body, from space, from context, and from listener response. We see an early incarnation of this in Joseph Conrad's 1902 *Heart of Darkness*. Conrad's megalomaniac and frightening Kurtz emerges as only "A voice! A voice!" (77) in the darkness:

> A voice. He was very little more than a voice. And I heard—him—it—this voice—other voices—all of them were so little more than voices—and the memory of that time lingers around me, impalpable, like a dying vibration of one immense jabber, silly, atrocious, sordid, savage, or simply mean, without any kind of sense. (64)

As ever, Conrad's vision isn't just about one particular wreck of a man in Africa; as it is often read, it also signals something profound about modernity. His image of the disseminated voice—"one immense jabber"—does capture a modernist malaise and confusion about the modern world. Like Henry Adams's apocalyptic diatribe in "The Dynamo and the Virgin," in which he faces, unarmed, the deliriousness of modern technology, Conrad sees an inarticulate senselessness and, most importantly, something profoundly anti-human in the modern world. The advent of such twentieth-century technology was painful to many authors. And a voice, unconnected to body or place, seems to have been one very real source of concern.

The end of the domination of the transatlantic lecture tour, then, does signify a loss, of sorts. The figure of the author had already been multiplying out in the wake of a mass literary and journalistic market—and lecture tours seemed to be a stave against such reproduction, offering, as they did, the source or authenticity of all the other representations, for a fee, of course. New technologies such as radio and voice recording in general, not to mention later developing technologies, allowed this "multiplication" to intensify. They ensured more access but, from the point of view of some, less authenticity. The demand for the author, for the real thing in an age of increasing mechanical reproduction, would go on. However, authors could now come to readers via radio, TV, film, and Internet. We can hear T.S. Eliot read "Prufrock" on YouTube and see contemporary authors on *Booknotes*. J.K. Rowling—a kind of modern day Dickens in terms of popularity—does come to the United States to do the occasional commencement address, but the fact is, she doesn't have to; a webcast from her home in Britain would also be an option.

But it wouldn't be the same, of course. The live audience—sometimes a stimulant, sometimes a thing to be feared—affected these authors in their performances, the lectures they chose to give, and their authorial personae. Audiences could shout "speak up," laugh harder at one joke than another, or behave in disruptive ways, all of which performing authors took note and to which they responded. And it went the other way as well. As many of my sources show, seeing a live celebrity author in person was a culturally and, sometimes, personally important event. Not only did newspapers report on these performances but individuals wrote about them in books of their own (Dickens was especially good at inspiring these), in letters, and in journals. Audience members in the nineteenth century knew they were witnessing a singular event: as live performance, it could never be repeated, no matter how many readings an author conducted. It would be the last era when the live performance of authorship was the *only* way for a reader, fan, or curious member of the public to see and hear a celebrated author.

Works Cited

Adams, Amanda. "Performing Ownership: Dickens, Twain, and Copyright on the Transatlantic Stage." *American Literary Realism* 43 (Spring 2011): 223–41.

———. "'Recognized by My Trumpet': Celebrity and/as Disability in Harriet Martineau's Transatlantic Tour." *Symbiosis: A Journal of Anglo-American Literary Relations* 14.1 (April 2010): 1–16.

———. "The Uses of Distinction: Matthew Arnold and American Literary Realism." *American Literary Realism* 37 (Fall 2004): 37–49.

Adams, Henry. "The Dynamo and the Virgin." *The Education of Henry Adams.* Ed. Jean Gooder. New York: Penguin Books, 1995. 360–70.

Agnew, Jean-Christophe. "The Consuming Vision of Henry James." *The Culture of Consumption: Critical Essays in American History, 1880–1980.* Ed. Richard Wightman Fox and T.J. Jackson Lears. New York: Pantheon Books, 1983. 65–100.

———. *Worlds Apart: The Market and the Theater in Anglo-American Thought, 1550–1750.* Cambridge: Cambridge University Press, 1986.

"Among Men of Action." *Los Angeles Times* 29 March 1905: II4. *Proquest.* Web. 15 Oct. 2006.

Anderson, Amanda. *Powers of Distance: Cosmopolitanism and the Cultivation of Detachment.* Princeton: Princeton University Press, 2001.

Andrews, Malcolm. "The 'Set' for Charles Dickens's Public Readings." *Dickens Quarterly* 21.4 (2004): 211–24.

Anesko, Michael. *'Friction with the Market': Henry James and the Profession of Authorship.* New York: Oxford University Press, 1986.

Arnold, Matthew. "Civilization in the United States." *Civilization in the United States: First and Last Impressions of America.* Freeport, New York: Books for Libraries Press, 1972. 157–92.

———. "Emerson." *Discourses in America.* New York: Macmillan, 1924. 138–207.

———. *Letters of Matthew Arnold.* Ed. George W.E. Russell. Vol. 2. New York: Macmillan and Co., 1895.

———. "Literature and Science." *Discourses in America.* New York: Macmillan, 1924. 72–137.

———. "Numbers." *Discourses in America.* New York: Macmillan, 1924. 1–71.

———. "A Word about America." *Civilization in the United States: First and Last Impressions of America.* Freeport, New York: Books for Libraries Press, 1972. 69–108.

Augst, Thomas. *The Clerk's Tale: Young Men and Moral Life in Nineteenth-Century America.* Chicago: University of Chicago Press, 2003.

————. "Frederick Douglass: Between Speech and Print." *Professing Rhetoric: Selected Papers from the 2000 Rhetoric Society of America Conference.* Ed. Frederick J. Antczak, Cinda Coggins, and Geoffrey D. Klinger. Mahwah, NJ: Lawrence Erlbaum Associates, 2002. 53–61.

————. Introduction. *Institutions of Reading: The Social Life of Libraries in the United States.* Ed. Thomas Augst and Kenneth Carpenter. Amherst: University of Massachusetts Press, 2007.

Baetzhold, Howard. *Mark Twain and John Bull: The British Connection.* Bloomington: Indiana University Press, 1970.

Baxter, Terry. *Frederick Douglass's Curious Audiences: Ethos in the Age of the Consumable Subject.* Studies in Major Literary Authors. Ed. William E. Cain. New York: Routledge, 2004.

Beecher, Charles. *Harriet Beecher Stowe in Europe: The Journal of Charles Beecher.* Ed. Joseph S Van Why and Earl French. Hartford, CT: The Stowe-Day Foundation, 1986.

————. Introduction. *Sunny Memories of Foreign Lands.* By Harriet Beecher Stowe. Vol. 1. New York: Cosimo: 2006. xi–lxv.

Bell, Alexander Melville. *Visible Speech in Twelve Lessons.* Washington, DC: The Volta Bureau, 1899.

Bell, Michael Davitt. *The Problem of American Realism.* Chicago: University of Chicago Press, 1993.

Benjamin, Walter. "The Work of Art in the Age of Mechanical Reproduction." *Illuminations.* Ed. Hannah Arendt. Trans. Harry Zohn. New York: Harcourt, Brace & World, 1968. 219–53.

Bentley, Nancy. *Frantic Panoramas: American Literature and Mass Culture, 1870–1920.* Philadelphia: University of Pennsylvania Press, 2009.

Bisla, Sundeep. "The Return of the Author: Privacy Publication, the Mystery Novel, and *The Moonstone.*" *Boundary 2: An International Journal of Literature and Culture* 29:1 (2002): 177–222.

"Black Slavery Abroad and White Slavery at Home." *Reynold's Newspaper* 15 May 1853: issue 144. *19ᵗʰ Century British Library Newspapers.* Web. Oct. 15 2009.

Blair, Sara. *Henry James and the Writing of Race and Nation.* Cambridge: Cambridge University Press, 1996.

Blanchard, Mary. "Oscar Wilde in America, 1882: Aestheticism, Women, and Modernism." *Oscar Wilde: The Man, His Writings, and His World.* Ams Studies in the Nineteenth Century. Ed. Robert N. Keane. New York: Ams, 2003.

Bode, Carl. *The American Lyceum: Town Meeting of the Mind.* New York: Oxford University Press, 1956.

Bohrer, Susan. 'Harriet Martineau: Gender, Disability, and Liability. *Nineteenth-Century Contexts* 25 (2003): 2 –37.

"Boston Correspondence." *Hartford Daily Courant* 4 Feb. 1882: 2. *Proquest.* Web. 15 Oct. 2006.

Bradbury, Malcolm. *Dangerous Pilgrimages: Transatlantic Mythologies and the Novel*. New York: Viking, 1995.

Braudy, Leo. *The Frenzy of Renown: Fame and Its History*. New York: Vintage, 1986.

Brougham, Henry. *Practical Observations upon the Education of the People: Addressed to the Working Classes and Their Employers*. London: Longman, 1825.

Buell, Lawrence. "American Literary Emergence as a Postcolonial Phenomenon." *American Literary History* 4.3 (1992): 411–42.

———. *Emerson*. Cambridge, MA: Belknap Press, 2003.

Bush, Ronald. "'As if You Were Hearing from Mr. Fletcher or Mr. Tourneur in 1633': T.S. Eliot's 1933 Harvard Lecture Notes for English 26 ('Introduction to Contemporary Literature')." *ANQ: A Quarterly Journal of Short Articles, Notes, and Reviews* 11.3 (Summer 1998): 11–20.

Canning, Charlotte. *The Most American Thing in America: Circuit Chautauqua as Performance*. Studies in Theater History and Culture. Iowa City: University of Iowa Press, 2005.

Chapman, Maria Weston. "Foreign Life—Western." *Harriet Martineau's Autobiography and Memorials of Harriet Martineau*. Ed. Maria Weston Chapman. Boston: James R. Osgood & Co., 1877. 2 vols. Vol. 2. n.p. *The Online Library of Liberty*. Web. 6 June 2012.

"Charles Dickens." *New York Daily News* 10 Jan. 1868: 4. *Proquest*. Web. 15 Oct. 2006.

"Charles Dickens: His Second Reading." *New York Daily News* 11 Dec. 1867: 4. *Proquest*. Web. 15 Oct. 2006.

Childs, Mary Arnold. "Ballade of Henry James." *New York Times* 22 July 05: BR484. *Proquest*. Web. 15 Oct. 2006.

Clark, Gregory, and S. Michael Halloran, eds. *Oratory Culture in Nineteenth-Century America*. Carbondale: University of Southern Illinois Press, 1993.

Claybaugh, Amanda. Introduction. *Uncle Tom's Cabin*. By Harriet Beecher Stowe. New York: Barnes and Noble Classics, 2005. xiii–xxxviii.

———. *The Novel of Purpose: Literature and Social Reform in the Anglo-American World*. Ithaca: Cornell University Press, 2006.

———. "Toward a New Transatlanticism: Dickens in the United States." *Victorian Studies: Interdisciplinary Journal of Social, Political, and Cultural Studies* 48 (2006): 439–60.

Cohen, Debra Rae, Michael Coyle, and Jane Lewty. "Introduction: Signing On." *Broadcasting Modernism*. Ed. Debra Rae Cohen, Michael Coyle, and Jane Lewty. Gainesville: University Press of Florida, 2009.

"College and Women." *New York Tribune* 11 June 1905: C4. *Proquest*. Web. 15 Oct. 2006.

Conrad, Joseph. *Heart of Darkness*. 2nd ed. Ed. Ross C. Murfin. Case Studies in Contemporary Criticism. Boston: Bedford Books, 1996.

Coombe, Rosemary J. *The Cultural Life of Intellectual Properties: Authorship, Appropriation, and the Law.* Durham, NC: Duke University Press, 1998.

Coyle, Michael. "'We Speak to India': T.S. Eliot's Wartime Broadcasts and the Frontiers of Culture." *Broadcasting Modernism.* Ed. Cohen, Coyle, and Lewty. 176–95.

Critic (12 Apr. 1884): 174.

Croker, John Wilson. "Miss Martineau's *Morals and Manners.*" *Quarterly Review* 63 (1839): 61–72.

———. Review of *Illustrations of Political Economy. Quarterly Review* 49 (1833) 136–53.

Dahle, Theodore. "American English Is Not So Bad, After All." *Washington Post* 16 July 1905: N12. *Proquest.* Web. 15 Oct. 2006.

David, Deirdre. *Intellectual Women and Victorian Patriarchy: Harriet Martineau, Elizabeth Barrett Browning, George Eliot.* Ithaca: Cornell University Press, 1987.

Dettmar, Kevin J.H., and Stephen Watt, eds. *Marketing Modernisms: Self-Promotion, Canonization, Rereading.* Ann Arbor: University of Michigan Press, 1996.

Dickens, Charles. *American Notes.* London: Penguin, 2000.

———. *A Christmas Carol: A Facsimile Edition of the Autograph Manuscript in the Pierpont Morgan Library.* New York: The Library, 1993.

———. *A Christmas Carol: The Public Reading Version. A Facsimile of the Author's Prompt-Copy.* New York: New York Public Library, 1971.

———. *The Speeches of Charles Dickens: A Complete Edition.* Ed. K.J. Fielding. Atlantic Highlands, NJ: Humanities Press International, 1988.

———. *Letters of Charles Dickens.* Pilgrim Edition. Ed. Madeline House, Graham Storey, and Kathleen Tillotson. 12 vols. Oxford: Clarendon Press, 1974.

———. *Martin Chuzzlewit.* London: Everyman's Library, 1994.

———. *Mrs. Gamp: A Facsimile of the Author's Prompt Copy.* New York: New York Public Library, 1965.

"The Disciple of James Covers a Fire." *Daily Boston Globe* 18 June 1905: 40. *Proquest.* Web. 15 Oct. 2006.

Dolby, George. *Charles Dickens as I Knew Him: The Story of the Reading Tours in Great Britain and America (1866–1970).* London: Everett & Co., 1912.

"Don't Mix the Globe and Henry James." *Boston Daily Globe,* 13 June 1905: 1. *Proquest.* Web. 15 Oct. 2006.

Douglass, Frederick. *My Bondage and My Freedom.* 1855. Ed. John Stauffer. New York: Modern Library, 2003.

———. *The Frederick Douglass Papers.* Ed. John W. Blassingame et al. Vol. 1. New Haven: Yale University Press, 1979-.

———. *Narrative of the Life of Frederick Douglass.* Ed. William L. Andrews and William S. McFeely. New York: Norton, 1997.

Dunbar, Olivia Howard. "Henry James as a Lecturer." *Critic* 47 (July 1905): 24–5.

Dwight, H.G. "Henry James—'In His Own Country.'" *Putnam's Monthly* 2.2 (1907): 164–70.

Easley, Alexis. *Literary Celebrity, Gender, and Victorian Authorship, 1850–1914.* Newark: University of Delaware Press, 2011.

———. "Victorian Women Writers and the Periodical Press: The Case of Harriet Martineau. *Nineteenth-Century Prose* 24 (1997): 39–50.

Edel, Leon. *Henry James: A Life.* New York: Harper & Row, 1985.

Ellison, Robert H. *The Victorian Pulpit: Spoken and Written Sermons in Nineteenth-Century Britain.* Selinsgrove: Susquehanna University Press, 1998.

Ellmann, Richard. *Oscar Wilde.* New York: Knopf, 1988.

Emerson, Ralph Waldo. *Nature: Emerson's Poetry and Prose.* Ed. Joel Porte and Saundra Morris. New York: Norton, 2001. 27–55.

Fatout, Paul. *Mark Twain on the Lecture Circuit.* Bloomington: Indiana University Press, 1960.

Ferguson, Susan L. "Dickens's Public Readings and the Victorian Author." *SEL: Studies in English Literature, 1500–1900* 41 (2001): 729–49.

Field, Kate. *Pen Photographs of Charles Dickens's Readings: Taken from Life.* Troy, NY: Whitston Publishing, 1998.

Foster, Shirley. "The Construction of Self in *Sunny Memories.*" *Transatlantic Stowe: Harriet Beecher Stowe in European Culture.* Ed. Denise Kohn, Sarah Meer, and Emily B. Todd. Iowa City: University of Iowa Press, 2006. 149–66.

Foucault, Michel. "What is an Author?" *The Foucault Reader.* Ed. Paul Rabinow. New York: Pantheon Books, 1984. 101–20.

Foulkes, Richard. *Church and Stage in Victorian England.* Cambridge: Cambridge University Press, 1997.

France, Wilmer Cave. "Mr. Henry James as a Lecturer." *The Bookman* 21 (Mar. 1905): 71.

Frattarola, Angela. "The Modernist 'Microphone Play': Listening in the Dark to the BBC." *Modern Drama* 52:4 (Winter 2009): 449–68.

Freedman, Jonathan. *Professions of Taste: Henry James, British Aestheticism, and Commodity Culture.* Stanford: Stanford University Press, 1990.

Fuller, Margaret. "Entertainments of Past Winter." *The Dial* (July 1842).

Gagnier, Regina. *Idylls of the Marketplace: Oscar Wilde and the Victorian Public.* Stanford, CA: Stanford University Press, 1986.

Garland, Hamlin. *Companions on the Trail.* New York: Macmillan, 1931.

Garrison, William Lloyd. *Letters of William Lloyd Garrison.* Ed. Walter M. Merrill. Cambridge, MA: Belknap Press, 1971–1981.

Gibian, Peter. *Oliver Wendell Holmes and the Culture of Conversation.* Cambridge Studies in American Literature and Culture. Cambridge: Cambridge University Press, 2009. Print.

Giles, Paul. *Atlantic Republic: The American Tradition in English Literature.* Oxford: Oxford University Press, 2006.

———. *Virtual Americas: Transnational Fictions and the Transatlantic Imaginary.* Durham, NC: Duke University Press, 2002.

Gilroy, Paul. *The Black Atlantic: Modernity and Double Consciousness.* Cambridge, MA: Harvard University Press, 1993.

Glass, Loren. *Authors Inc.: Literary Celebrity in the Modern United States, 1880–1980*. New York: New York University Press, 2004.

Gookin, Frederick William. *The Chicago Literary Club: A History of Its First Fifty Years*. Chicago: privately printed, 1926.

Gustafson, Sandra M. *Eloquence is Power: Oratory and Performance in Early America*. Chapel Hill: University of North Carolina Press, 2000.

Hale, Sarah. *The Lecturess: Or, a Woman's Sphere*. Boston: Whipple and Damrell, 1839.

"Harriet Beecher Stowe." *Liverpool Mercury etc* 15 April 1853: Issue 2493. *19th Century British Library Newspapers*. Web. Oct. 15 2009.

Harris, Marie P. "Henry James, Lecturer." *American Literature* 23 (Nov. 1951): 302–14.

Hartshone, H. "American Culture." *Lippincott's Magazine* (June 1868): 645–6.

Haviland, Beverly. *Henry James's Last Romance: Making Sense of the Past and the American Scene*. New York: Cambridge University Press, 1997.

Hedrick, Joan. *Harriet Beecher Stowe: A Life*. Oxford: Oxford University Press, 1995.

"Henry James at the Barnard Club" *New York Times* 19 May 1905: 9. *Proquest*. Web. 15 Oct. 2006.

"Henry James Here." *Los Angeles Times* 25 March 1905: II 5. *Proquest*. Web. 15 Oct. 2006.

"Henry James in Town for the Day." *The Morning Oregonian* 18 Apr. 1905. *Proquest*. Web. 15 Oct. 2006.

"Henry James on 'Newspaper English.'" *Current Literature* 39 (Aug. 1905): 155–6. *Proquest*. Web. 15 Oct. 2006.

"Henry James Speaks Unkindly of the Press." *The Hartford Courant* 9 June 1905: 1. *Proquest*. Web. 15 Oct. 2006.

Higginson, Thomas Wentworth. "The American Lecture-System." *Macmillan's Magazine* 18 (May 1868): 48–56.

Hofer, Mathew, and Gary Scharnhorst. Introduction. *Oscar Wilde in America: The Interviews*. Urbana: University of Illinois Press, 2010. 1–9.

Holland, Josiah. "The Popular Lecture." *Atlantic Monthly* 15 (March 1865): 365.

Honan, Park. *Matthew Arnold: A Life*. Cambridge, MA: Harvard University Press, 1983.

Hoople, Robin. "Great Stone Faces: Henry James, Theodore Roosevelt, and the Quest for American Authenticity." *Canadian Review of American Studies* 36.3 (2006): 345–62.

———. *Inexorable Yankeehood: Henry James Rediscovers America, 1904–1905*. Ed. Isobel Waters. Lewisburg, PA: Bucknell University Press, 2009.

Hovet, Ted, Jr. "Harriet Martineau's Exceptional American Narratives: Harriet Beecher Stowe, John Brown, and the 'Redemption of Your National Soul.'" *American Studies* 48.1 (2007): 63–76.

Howells, William Dean. "Criticism and Fiction." *"Criticism and Fiction" and Other Essays*. Ed. Clara Marburg Kirk and Rudolf Kirk. New York: New York University Press, 1965.

Hyde, H. Montgomery. *Henry James at Home*. New York: Farrar, Straus and Giroux, 1969.

Ives, Maura. "Introduction: Women Writers and the Artifacts of Celebrity." *Women Writers and the Artifacts of Celebrity in the Long Nineteenth Century*. Ed. Ann R. Hawkins and Maura Ives. Burlington, VT: Ashgate, 2012. 1–12.

"James Attacks Papers and Schools." *New York Tribune* 9 June 1905: 1. *Proquest*. Web. 15 Oct. 2006.

James, Henry. *The American Scene*. Bloomington: Indiana University Press, 1968.

———. *The Bostonians*. 1886. Ed. Charles R. Anderson. London: Penguin Books, 1984.

———. *The Complete Notebooks of Henry James*. Ed. Leon Edel and Lyall H. Powers. New York: Oxford University Press, 1987.

———. *The Correspondence of William James: William and Henry, 1897–1910*. Charlottesville: University of Virginia Press, 2004. Vol. 3 of *The Correspondence of William James*. Ed. Ignas K. Skrupskelis and Elizabeth M. Berkeley. 12 vols. 1992–2004.

———. *Henry James Letters*. Ed. Leon Edel. 4 vols. Cambridge, MA: Harvard University Press, 1974–1984.

———. "The Lesson of Balzac." *The Question of Our Speech, The Lesson of Balzac: Two Lectures*. Boston: Houghton, Mifflin and Company, 1905. 55–116.

———. "The Question of Our Speech." *The Question of Our Speech, The Lesson of Balzac: Two Lectures*. Boston: Houghton, Mifflin and Company, 1905. 3–52.

———. *The Portrait of a Lady*. 2nd ed. Norton Critical Edition. Ed. Robert D. Bamberg. New York, Norton, 1995.

———. *Selected Letters of Henry James to Edmund Gosse, 1882–1915*. Ed. Rayburn S. Moore. Baton Rouge: Louisiana State Press, 1988.

"James's Patriotism." *Los Angeles Times* 22 July 1905: 11 9. *Proquest*. Web. 15 Oct. 2006.

Jeffares, A. Norman. *W.B. Yeats: A New Biography*. London: Continuum, 1988.

Jordon, John D. Introduction. *Mrs. Gamp: A Facsimile of the Author's Prompt Copy*. By Charles Dickens. New York: New York Public Library, 1965.

Joseph, Gerard. "Construing the Inimitable's Silence: Pecksniff's Grammar School and International Copyright. *Dickens Studies Annual* 22 (1993): 121–35.

Kahane, Claire. *Passions of the Voice: Hysteria, Narrative, and the Figure of the Speaking Woman, 1850–1915*. Baltimore: Johns Hopkins University Press, 1995.

Kaplan, Amy. *The Social Construction of American Realism*. Chicago: University of Chicago Press, 1988.

Kaplan, Fred. *Henry James: The Imagination of Genius: A Biography*. Baltimore: Johns Hopkins University Press, 1992.

Kent, Charles. *Charles Dickens as a Reader*. Philadelphia: J.B. Lippincott & Co., 1872.

Knoper, Randall. *Acting Naturally: Mark Twain in the Culture of Performance*. Berkeley: University of California Press, 1995.

Lawrence, E.P. "An Apostle's Progress: Matthew Arnold in America." *Philological Quarterly* (Jan. 1931): 62–79.

"Lecture by Henry James." *New York Tribune* 26 May 1905: 16. *Proquest*. Web. 15 Oct. 2006.

"Lectures and Lecturers." *Puntman's Monthly Magazine of American Literature, Science, and Art* 9.51 (Mar 1857): 317.

"The Lesson of Balzac." *The New York Times* 1 June 1905: 5. *Proquest*. Web. 15 Oct. 2006.

Levander, Caroline Field. *Voices of the Nation: Women and Public Speech in Nineteenth- Century American Literature and Culture*. Cambridge Studies in American Literature and Culture. Cambridge: Cambridge University Press, 1998.

Levine, Lawrence W. *Highbrow/Lowbrow: The Emergence of Cultural History in America*. Cambridge, MA: Harvard University Press, 1988.

"Lines: On Miss Martineau." *Southern Literary Messenger (1834–1845)* Feb 1835: 1, 6. *APS online*. 319. Web. 15 Oct. 2006.

Logan, Deborah Anna. *The Hour and the Woman: Harriet Martineau's 'Somewhat Remarkable' Life*. DeKalb: Northern Illinois University Press, 2002.

Long, John P. "Matthew Arnold Visits Chicago." *University of Toronto Quarterly* 24.1 (1954): 34–45.

Lorch, Fred. "Mark Twain's Lecture from *Roughing It*." *American Literature* 22.3 (1950): 290–307.

———. *The Trouble Begins at Eight: Mark Twain's Lecture Tours*. Ames: Iowa State University Press, 1968.

Lueck, Beth L. "'A Little Private Conversation … in Her Boudoir': Stowe's Appearance at Stafford House in 1853." In *Transatlantic Women: Essays on Nineteenth-Century American Women Writers and Great Britain*. Ed. Beth L. Lueck, Brigitte Bailey, and Lucinda L. Damon-Bach. Lebanon: University of New Hampshire Press, 2012. 89–103.

Madsen, Annelise K. "Dressing the Part: Mark Twain's White Suit, Copyright Reform, and the Camera." *The Journal of American Culture* 32.1 (2009): 53–71.

Margolis, Anne T. *Henry James and the Problem of Audience: An International Act*. Studies in Modern Literature. Ed. A. Walton Litz. Ann Arbor, MI: UMI Research Press, 1985.

"Mark Twain." *Spectator* 18 Oct. 1873: 1302–3.

Marshall, P. David. *Celebrity and Power: Fame in Contemporary Culture*. Minneapolis: University of Minnesota Press, 1997.

Martin, E.S. "If I Were Henry James." *Washington Post* 18 Dec. 1904: C9. *Proquest*. Web. 15 Oct. 2006.

Martineau, Harriet. *Harriet Martineau's Autobiography*. 2 vols. London: Virago, 1983.

———. *Illustrations of Political Economy*. London: Charles Fox, Paternoster Row, 1834.

————. "London." *Daily News* 9 May 1853: 1. *19th Century British Library Newspapers*. Web. Oct. 15 2009.

————. *The Martyr Age of the United States*. 1839. *Writings on Slavery and the American Civil War*. Ed. Deborah Anna Logan. DeKalb: Northern Illinois University Press, 2002.

————. *Society in America*. 1837. Ed. Seymour Martin Lipset. New Brunswick, NJ: New Transaction Books, 1981.

Matt, Susan J. *Homesickness: An American History*. Oxford: Oxford University Press, 2011.

"Matthew Arnold: A Series of Replies to His Genial Criticisms of the People of Chicago." *Chicago Tribune* 8 Apr. 1884: 3.

"Matthew Arnold: England's Incomparable Egotist Gives a Few of His Impressions of Chicago." *Chicago Tribune* 7 Apr. 1884: 1.

"Matthew Arnold's Visit." *Literary World* 14 (15 Dec. 1883): 446.

McBride, Dwight A. *Impossible Witnesses: Truth, Abolition, and Slave Testimony*. New York: New York University Press, 2001.

McFadden, Margaret H. *Golden Cables of Sympathy: The Transatlantic Sources of Nineteenth-Century Feminism*. Lexington: University Press of Kentucky, 1999.

McFeely, William. *Frederick Douglass*. New York: Touchstone, 1991.

McGill, Meredith L. *American Literature and the Culture of Reprinting*. Philadelphia: University of Pennsylvania Press, 2003.

McKivigan, John. *Forgotten Firebrand: James Redpath and the Making of Nineteenth-Century America*. Ithaca: Cornell University Press, 2008.

McParland, Robert. *Charles Dickens's American Audience*. Lanham, MD: Lexington Books, 2010.

McWhirter, David, ed. *Henry James's New York Edition: The Construction of Authorship*. Stanford, CA: Stanford University Press, 1995.

Meckier, Jerome. *Innocent Abroad: Charles Dickens's American Engagements*. Lexington: University Press of Kentucky, 1990.

Meer, Sarah. "Competing Representations: Douglass, the Ethiopian Serenaders, and Ethnic Exhibition in London." *Liberating Sojourn: Frederick Douglass and Transatlantic Reform*. Ed. Alan J. Rice and Martin Crawford. Athens: University of Georgia Press, 1999. 141–65.

Mendelssohn, Michèle. *Henry James, Oscar Wilde, and Aesthetic Culture*. Edinburgh Studies in Transatlantic Literatures. Ed. Susan Manning and Andrew Taylor. Edinburgh: Edinburgh University Press, 2007.

"Miss Martineau." *The Liberator (1831–1865)* 19 Dec. 1835: 5, 51. *APS online*. Web. 15 Oct. 2006.

Modern Times. Dir. Charles Chaplin. Perf. Charles Chaplin and Paulette Goddard. United Artists, 1936.

Monk, Craig. *Writing the Lost Generation: Expatriate Autobiography and American Modernism*. Iowa City: University of Iowa Press, 2008.

Morgan, Simon. *A Victorian Woman's Place: Public Culture in the Nineteenth Century*. London: Tauris Academic Studies, 2007.

Moss, Sidney P. *Charles Dickens' Quarrel with America*. Troy, NY: The Whitson Publishing Company, 1984.

"Mr. Dickens's Farewell Reading." *New York Daily News* 21 Apr. 1868: 4.

"Mr. Dickens's Third Reading." *New York Daily News* 13 Dec.1867: 4.

"Mr. Henry James." *New York Tribune* 12 Feb. 1905: A6. *Proquest*. Web. 15 Oct. 2006.

"Mr. James and English Speech." *The Outlook* 5 May 1906: 16–17. *Proquest*. Web. 15 Oct. 2006.

"Mr. James Wished to Post a Letter." *New York Times* 10 Sept. 1904: 8. *Proquest*. Web. 15 Oct. 2006.

"Mrs. Beecher Stowe in Glasgow." *Manchester Times* 20 April 1853: Issue 466. *19th Century British Library Newspapers*. Web. Oct. 15 2009.

"Mrs. Beecher Stowe in Liverpool." *Glasgow Herald* 15 April 1853: Issue 5239. *19th Century British Library Newspapers*. Web. Oct. 15 2009.

"Mrs. H.B. Stowe at Stafford House." *Daily News* 9 May 1853: Issue 2173. *19th Century British Library Newspapers*. Web. Oct. 15 2009.

Myers, Janet C. *Antipodal England: Emigration and Portable Domesticity in the Victorian Imagination*. SUNY Series, Studies in the Long Nineteenth Century. Ed. Pamela K. Gilbert. Albany: State University of New York Press, 2009.

Nation (20 Dec. 1883): 500.

Nation (10 Apr.1884): 307.

"The National Capital." *Hartford Daily Courant* 23 Jan. 1882: 1. *Proquest*. Web. 15 Oct. 2006.

"New York News." *Hartford Daily Courant* 10 Jan. 1882: 3. *Proquest*. Web. 15 Oct. 2006.

"No Frills." *Boston Daily Globe* 29 June 1905: 6. *Proquest*. Web. 15 Oct. 2006.

Novak, Daniel A. "Performing the 'Wilde West': Victorian Afterlives, Sexual Performance, and the American West." *Victorian Studies* 54.3 (Spring 2002): 451–63.

———. "Sexuality in the Age of Technological Reproduction: Oscar Wilde, Photography, and Identity." *Oscar Wilde and Modern Culture: The Making of a Legend*. Ed. Joseph Bristow. Athens: Ohio University Press, 2008. 63–95.

Novick, Sheldon M. *Henry James: The Young Master*. New York: Random House, 2007.

O'Donnell, Heather. "'My Own Funny Little Lecture Boom': Henry James's American Performance. *The Henry James Review* 24 (2003): 133–45.

Olsen, Liesl. "'An Invincible Force Meets an Immovable Object: Gertrude Stein Comes to Chicago." *Modernism/Modernity* 17.2 (2010) 331–61.

"Opera House Entertainments." *Hartford Daily Courant* 16 Feb. 1882: 2. *Proquest*. Web. 15 Oct. 2006.

"Oscar As He Is." *St. Louis Republican* 26 Feb. 1882: 13. *Oscar Wilde in America: The Interviews*. Ed. Matthew Hofer and Gary Scharnhorst. Urbana: University of Illinois Press, 2010. 83–8.

"Oscar Wilde's New Clothes." *Hartford Daily Courant* 16 May 1882: 6. *Proquest*. Web. 15 Oct. 2006.

"Oscar Wilde and the Aesthetic School." *Hartford Daily Courant* 17 Jan. 1882: 1. *Proquest.* Web. 15 Oct. 2006.

"Oscar Wilde's Arrest." *Hartford Daily Courant* 16 Oct. 1882: 3. *Proquest.* Web. 15 Oct. 2006.

"Oscar Wilde in Hartford." *Hartford Daily Courant* 3 Feb. 1882: 2. *Proquest.* Web. 15 Oct. 2006.

"Our New York Letter." *Philadelphia Inquirer* 4 Jan. 1882: 7. *Oscar Wilde in America: The Interviews.* Ed. Matthew Hofer and Gary Scharnhorst. Urbana: University of Illinois Press, 2010. 17–18.

Poirier, Richard. *The Performing Self: Compositions and Decompositions in the Language of Contemporary Life.* New Brunswick: Rutgers University Press, 1992.

Posnock, Ross. "Henry James and the Limits of Historicism." *Henry James Review* 16 (1995): 273–7.

———. *The Trial of Curiosity: Henry James, William James, and the Challenge of Modernity.* Oxford: Oxford University Press, 1991.

"Power and Breeding." *Boston Daily Globe* 29 Dec. 1905: 9. *Proquest.* Web. 15 Oct. 2006.

Powers, Ron. *Mark Twain: A Life.* New York: Free Press, 2005.

Rainey, Lawrence. *Institutions of Modernism: Literary Elites and Public Culture.* New Haven: Yale University Press, 1998.

Raleigh, John Henry. *Matthew Arnold and American Culture.* Berkeley: University of California Press, 1961.

Ray, Angela G. *The Lyceum and Public Culture in the Nineteenth-Century United States.* East Lansing: Michigan State University Press, 2005.

"Real Henry James, He Really Said It." *Los Angeles Times* 26 March 1905: 16. *Proquest.* Web. 15 Oct. 2006.

"Recent Literature." *Atlantic Monthly* (Nov. 1879): 675.

Review of *Society in America. The Southern Literary Journal and Magazine of Arts (1835–1838)* Aug. 1837: 1, 6. *APS Online.* 568. Web. 15 Oct. 2006.

Roger, Helen. "Any Questions? The Gendered Dimensions of the Political." *Platform Pulpit Rhetoric.* Ed. Martin Hewitt. Leeds Centre Working Papers in Victorian Studies. Vol. 3. Leeds: Leeds Centre for Victorian Studies, 2000. 9–22.

Rose, Mark. *Authors and Owners: The Invention of Copyright.* Cambridge, MA: Harvard University Press, 1993.

Rush, James. *The Philosophy of the Human Voice.* 7th ed. Philadelphia: Grigg, 1893. Print.

Saint-Amour, Paul K. *The Copywrights: Intellectual Property and the Literary Imagination.* Ithaca: Cornell University Press, 2003.

Salmon, Richard. *Henry James and the Culture of Publicity.* Cambridge: Cambridge University Press, 1997.

———. "The Physiognomy of the Lion: Encountering Literary Celebrity in the Nineteenth Century." *Romanticism and Celebrity Culture, 1750–1850.* Ed. Tom Mole. Cambridge: Cambridge University Press, 2009. 60–78.

Schechner, Richard. "The Broad Spectrum Approach." *The Performance Studies Reader*. 2nd ed. Ed. Henry Bial. New York: Routledge, 2007. 7–9.

Scott, Donald M. "The Popular Lecture and the Creation of a Public in Mid-Nineteenth-Century America." *The Journal of American History* 66.4 (March 1980): 791–809.

———. "Print and the Public Lecture System, 1840–60." *Printing and Society in Early America*. Ed. William L. Joyce et al. Worcester: American Antiquarian Society, 1983. 278–99.

Smith, Sidonie. *A Poetics of Women's Autobiography*. Bloomington and Indianapolis: Indiana University Press, 1987.

Stein, Gertrude. *Everybody's Autobiography*. New York: Cooper Square Publishers. 1971.

Stowe, Harriet Beecher. S*unny Memories of Foreign Lands*. Vol. 1. New York: Cosimo: 2006.

———. *Uncle Tom's Cabin*. New York: Barnes and Noble Classics, 2005.

Sweeney, Fionnghuala. *Frederick Douglass and the Atlantic World*. Liverpool: Liverpool University Press, 2007.

Taylor, Andrew. *Thinking America: New England Intellectuals and the Varieties of American Identity*. Durham: University of New Hampshire Press, 2010.

Taylor, Diana. *The Archive and the Repertoire: Performing Cultural Memory in the Americas*. Durham, NC: Duke University Press, 2003.

"Thinks Henry James is Right." *New York Times* 10 June 1905: 8. *Proquest*. Web. 15 Oct. 2006.

"This Will Make Hank Suffer." *Boston Daily Globe* 5 July 1905: 14. *Proquest*. Web. 15 Oct. 2006.

Thomas, Brook. *American Literary Realism and the Failed Promise of Contract*. Berkeley: University of California Press, 1997.

Thomson, Rosemarie Garland. *Extraordinary Bodies: Figuring Physical Disability in American Culture and Literature*. New York: Columbia University Press, 1997.

"Topics of the Week." *New York Times* 10 Sept. 1904: 17. *Proquest*. Web. 15 Oct. 2006.

"The 'Tribune' Hoaxed." *Chicago Daily News* 9 Apr. 1884: 1.

Trumbull, Anne Eliot. "Literature and Art." *The Hartford Courant* 21 Aug. 1905: 13. *Proquest*. Web. 15 Oct. 2006.

Twain, Mark. *Autobiography of Mark Twain*. Ed. Harriet Elinor Smith. Vol. 1. Berkeley: University of California Press, 2010.

———. *The Innocents Abroad, or, The New Pilgrim's Progress*. New York: Signet Classic, 1980.

———. *Mark Twain in Eruption: Hitherto Unpublished Pages about Men and Events*. Ed. Bernard DeVoto. New York: Grosset & Dunlap, 1940.

———. "Our Fellow Savages in the Sandwich Islands." *Mark Twain and Hawaii*. By Walter Francis Frear. Chicago: The Lakeside Press, 1947. 431–6.

———. "Roughing It on the Silver Frontier." "Mark Twain's Lecture from *Roughing It*." By Fred Lorch. *American Literature* 22.3 (1950): 290–307.

Updike, John. "The End of Authorship." *The New York Times*. The New York Times Company, 25 June 2006 Web. 18 Aug. 2011.

Voskuil, Lynn. *Acting Naturally: Victorian Theatricality and Authenticity*. Victorian Literature and Culture Series. Ed. Jerome J. McGann. Charlottesville: University of Virginia Press, 2004.

Wallace, Irving. *The Twenty-Seventh Wife*. New York: Simon and Schuster, 1961.

Wardley, Lynn. "Woman's Voice, Democracy's Body, and *The Bostonians*." *ELH* 56 (Fall 1989): 639–65.

Warren, James Perrin. *Culture of Eloquence: Oratory and Reform in Antebellum America*. University Park: Pennsylvania State University Press, 1999.

Warren, Kenneth. "Black and White Strangers." *Documents of American Realism and Naturalism*. Ed. Donald Pizer. Carbondale: Southern Illinois University Press, 1998. 418–34.

Warren, Samuel D., and Louis D. Brandeis. "The Right to Privacy." *Harvard Law Review* 4.5 (15 Dec. 1890): 193–220.

Webster, Brenda R. *Women and Literary Celebrity in the Nineteenth Century: The Transatlantic Production of Fame and Gender*. Ashgate Series in Nineteenth-Century Transatlantic Literature. Burlington, VT: Ashgate, 2012.

Weisbuch, Robert. *Atlantic Doublecross*. Chicago: University of Chicago Press, 1986.

Welland, Dennis. *Mark Twain in England*. London: Chatto & Windus, 1978.

Welsh, Alexander. *From Copyright to Copperfield: The Identity of Dickens*. Cambridge, MA: Harvard University Press, 1987.

Wharton, Edith. *A Backward Glance*. New York: Scribner, 1964.

Wicke, Jennifer. *Advertising Fictions: Literature Advertisement, and Social Reading*. Social Foundations of Aesthetic Forms. Ser. Ed. Edward W. Said. New York: Columbia University Press, 1988.

Wilde, Oscar. *The Complete Letters of Oscar Wilde*. Ed. Merlin Holland and Rupert Hart-Davis. New York: Henry Holt and Company, 2000.

———. "The Decay of Lying." *Complete Works of Oscar Wilde*. London: Collins, 1960. 970–92.

———. "Decorative Art in America: A Lecture." 1882. *Decorative Art in America: A Lecture*. Ed. Richard Butler Glaenzer. New York: Brenano's, 1906. 3–15.

Winship, Michael. "The Transatlantic Book Trade and Anglo-American Literary Culture in the Nineteenth Century." *Reciprocal Influences: Literary Production, Distribution, and Consumption in America*. Ed. Steven Fink and Susan S. Williams. Columbus: Ohio State University Press, 1999. 98–122.

Wonham, Henry B. *Playing the Races: Ethnic Caricature and American Literary Realism*. Oxford: Oxford University Press, 2004.

Woodmansee, Martha, and Peter Jaszi, eds. *The Construction of Authorship: Textual Appropriations in Law and Literature*. Durham, NC, Duke University Press, 1994.

Wright, Tom F. Introduction. *The Cosmopolitan Lyceum: Lecture Culture and the Globe in Nineteenth-Century America*. Ed. Tom F. Wright. Amherst: University of Massachusetts Press, 2013. 1–19.

"The Yale Boys and Oscar Wilde." *Hartford Daily Courant*. 31 Jan. 1882: 2. *Proquest*. Web. 15 Oct. 2006.

Zanola Marcola, Annalisa. "Rhetoric and the Body: A Lesson from the Ancient Elocutionists." *Professing Rhetoric: Selected Papers from the 2000 Rhetoric Society of America Conference*. Ed. Frederick J. Antczak, Cinda Coggins, and Geoffrey D. Klinger. Mahway, NJ: Lawrence Erlbaum Associates: 2002. 77–85.

Index